P9-AET-028

PEACEFUL LIVING

Daily Meditations for Living With
Love, Healing, and Compassion

MARY MACKENZIE

PuddleDancer
PRESS

2240 Encinitas Blvd., Ste. D-911, Encinitas, CA 92024
email@PuddleDancer.com • www.PuddleDancer.com

For additional information:
Center for Nonviolent Communication
9301 Indian School Rd., NE, Suite 204, Albuquerque, NM 87112
Ph: 505-244-4041 • Fax: 505-247-0414 • Email: cnvc@cnvc.org • Website: www.cnvc.org

Peaceful Living: Daily Meditations for Living
With Love, Healing, and Compassion

© 2005 PuddleDancer Press
A PuddleDancer Press Book

PuddleDancer Press, Permissions Dept.
2240 Encinitas Blvd., Ste. D-911, Encinitas, CA 92024
Tel: 1-760-652-5754 Fax: 1-760-274-6400
www.NonviolentCommunication.com Email@PuddleDancer.com

Ordering Information
Please contact Independent Publishers Group, Tel: 312-337-0747;
Fax: 312-337-5985; Email: frontdesk@ipgbook.com or visit www.IPGbook.
com for other contact information and details
about ordering online

Author: Mary Mackenzie
Editing: Meadowlark Communications, Inc., www.larkonline.net
Indexer: Phyllis Linn, Indexpress
Cover and interior design: Lightbourne, Inc., www.lightbourne.com
Cover photography: www.gettyimages.com

Manufactured in the United States of America

1st printing, September 2005

10 9 8 7 6 5

ISBN: 978-1-892005-19-9

Library of Congress Cataloging-in-Publication Data

Mackenzie, Mary, 1958-
    Peaceful living : daily meditations for living with love, healing, and
compassion / by Mary Mackenzie.
        p. cm.
    Includes bibliographical references.
    ISBN: 1-892005-19-0
    ISBN: 978-1-892005-19-9 (pbk. : alk. paper)
1. Conduct of life. 2. Interpersonal communication. 3.
Nonviolence--Psychological aspects. 4. Meditations. I. Title.
    BF637.C5M323 2005
    158.1'28--dc22

                                        2005017820

To my parents
John and Muriel Mackenzie
with love.

CONTENTS

ACKNOWLEDGMENTS

My heartfelt thanks to Lorna McLeod, my writing partner, whose stability, strength, expertise, and empathy were paramount to the success of this book; and to Charlotte Babcock for the countless hours of editorial support, advice, love, and encouragement she provided that helped shape the book.

I am deeply grateful to my dear sister Barbara Katz, who helped edit this book, and whose love and support have always been a source of inspiration to me.

I am grateful to all the people who have inspired and guided my personal growth through the years, including Deb Bennett, Jamie Whelan, Sandy Reiff, Kathy Lampros, my family whom I adore, and all my lovely, sweet, and enduring friends.

I am deeply grateful to Marshall Rosenberg for creating the process of Compassionate Communication, which transformed my life, and for all the Compassionate Communication trainers who taught me how to live from a peaceful heart, including Lucy Leu, Liv Monroe, Sylvia Haskvitz, Sura Hart, Gary Baran, Wes Taylor, Joanna Mills, Jean Ryan, Jorge Rubio, Darold Milligan, Robert Gonzales, Susan Skye, Miki Kashtan, and so many more.

My acknowledgments wouldn't feel complete without expressing my sincere appreciation to Chuck McDougal for bringing Compassionate Communication to Arizona, and for his continued sponsorship.

Introduction

Everyone in the class gasped; we were stunned by our poignant realization. The Nonviolent Communication trainer had led us through a process in which we identified our greatest need, and every one of us was surprised at what we uncovered. In the next exercise, we had identified all the things we were doing to meet our greatest need. Not one of us could identify a single behavior that would help us! In fact, we were acting in ways that guaranteed failure.

I realized in that moment that I had spent my life protecting myself by building walls between myself and other people, responding to them in a defensive or aggressive manner, and not allowing their love to pass through my tough exterior. All these behaviors were strategies to meet my need for protection. However, they made it impossible for me to meet other, more pressing needs for love, nurturing, caring, community, belonging, and intimacy. Had it not been for this trainer and Nonviolent Communication, I might never have noticed how my behaviors were ensuring my unhappiness.

Nonviolent Communication is also known as Compassionate Communication; you will see these terms used interchangeably as you read through this book. It has taught me how to be present to the moment, to identify my underlying needs in situations, and to consciously choose behaviors that are in alignment with those needs. Today, I live more authentically, more directly, more lovingly, and more peacefully than I ever dreamed possible. I have transformed my relationships with family members, friends, and business colleagues to such a degree that I can no longer imagine the grief I used to feel in these relationships. I am sincerely and profoundly grateful for how living the Nonviolent Communication process has altered the course of my life toward peaceful living.

Each daily meditation in this book offers an inspiring quote, information on an aspect of Nonviolent Communication, and an action step that you can take each day to integrate these principles into your life.

My hope is that these daily meditations will help you start each day more centered and connected to yourself and your values. For those new to this process, may the daily messages reveal new tools for directing the course of your life toward your deepest values and needs. For those who are familiar with Nonviolent Communication, may the meditations help further ground you in its techniques and reinforce what you have learned. Together, may we fathom a different way of being in the world, a way that allows for everyone's needs to be valued equally.

The more each person lives in harmony with her values, the closer we are to manifesting world peace. It will not happen overnight, but each step we take, each moment that we choose not to snap at our children or the grocery clerk, each time we consider someone else's needs, world peace is closer. It is inevitable.

Peace and blessings on your journey.
—Mary Mackenzie

Feelings and Needs Lists

In Nonviolent Communication, it is essential to recognize feelings and needs. The following tables, which are drawn from Marshall B. Rosenberg's *Nonviolent Communication: A Language of Life*, will help orient you to the language of feelings and needs. If you like, you can begin to familiarize yourself with it by reviewing the tables now. It may also be helpful to refer back to them as you progress through the daily meditations in this book.

Some Basic Feelings We All Have

Feelings when needs "are" fulfilled _____

Amazed	Joyous	Comfortable
Moved	Confident	Optimistic
Eager	Proud	Energetic
Relieved	Fulfilled	Stimulated
Glad	Surprised	Hopeful
Thankful	Inspired	Touched
Intrigued	Trustful	

Feelings when needs "are not" fulfilled _____

Angry	Hopeless	Annoyed
Impatient	Confused	Irritated
Concerned	Lonely	Disappointed
Nervous	Discouraged	Overwhelmed
Distressed	Puzzled	Embarrassed
Reluctant	Frustrated	Sad
Helpless	Uncomfortable	

Some Basic Needs We All Have

Autonomy _____
- Choosing dreams/goals/values
- Choosing plans for fulfilling one's dreams, goals, values

Celebration _____
- Celebrate the creation of life and dreams fulfilled
- Celebrate losses: loved ones, dreams, etc. (mourning)

Integrity _____
- Authenticity · Creativity · Meaning · Self-worth

Interdependence _____
- Acceptance · Appreciation · Closeness · Community
- Consideration · Contribute to the enrichment of life
- Emotional Safety · Empathy
- Honesty (the empowering honesty that enables us to learn from our limitations)
- Love · Reassurance · Respect · Support · Trust
- Understanding

Physical Nurturance _____
- Air · Food · Movement, exercise
- Protection from life-threatening forms of life: viruses, bacteria, insects, predatory animals
- Rest · Sexual expression · Shelter · Touch · Water

Play _____
- Fun · Laughter

Spiritual Communion _____
- Beauty · Harmony · Inspiration · Order · Peace

Meditations for
JANUARY

JANUARY 1

If we ourselves remain angry and then sing world peace, it has little meaning. First, our individual self must learn peace. This we can practice. Then we can teach the rest of the world.
—The Dalai Lama

Setting Goals for the New Year

What do you want to focus on this year? What are your goals, hopes, and dreams? It's important to make your goals concrete and specific. Don't just say that you want to be happier; consider how you would like your life to be different. What if your goal is to support world peace by living your own life more peacefully? Consider the specific ways you will do this, such as learning Nonviolent Communication, taking a course on anger management, working a twelve-step program, or seeing a therapist. If your goal is to contribute to world peace, your actions can be very specific and concrete. Avoid focusing on what you don't want, such as conflict at work. Rather, focus on what you want, such as harmony at work. When your goals are concrete and positively worded, you can begin to manifest them. This simple process can have a profound impact on your success.

Take a few minutes today to write down your goals for the year, knowing that the goal-setting process is the first step toward manifesting your dreams.

JANUARY 2

*The Nonviolent Communication process strengthens
our ability to remain human, even under trying
conditions. It reminds us about what we already
know—how we humans were meant to relate to
one another—and assists us in living in ways
that concretely manifests this knowledge.*
—Marshall B. Rosenberg, PhD

Nonviolent Communication

Nonviolent Communication is a communication process
and a model for living that was developed by Marshall
B. Rosenberg, PhD, more than forty years ago. It is used
in thirty-five countries worldwide. The two primary
components of this process are: 1) a process for living that
values everyone's needs equally, and that values connections
with people more than being right or winning; and 2) a set
of tools that helps us do this.

Most of us have been taught a way of living that
promotes distrust and self-protection. In contrast, Nonviolent Communication teaches us that true safety lies in
our ability to openly connect with ourselves and other
people, to live authentically, and to respond to all situations
with compassion and humanity. This process promotes
peaceful living on a daily basis.

Be aware today of the times that your behaviors or
attitudes promote distrust and self-protection, rather
than compassion and humanity.

JANUARY 3

I saw my Lord with the eye of my heart, and I said:
Who art Thou? He said: Thou.
—Al-Hallaj

What Is Nonviolent Communication?

Nonviolent Communication (sometimes known as Compassionate Communication) is a way of interacting that facilitates the flow of communication needed to resolve differences peacefully. It focuses on shared human values and needs, and encourages the use of language that increases goodwill, and avoidance of language that contributes to resentment or lowered self-esteem.

Nonviolent Communication assumes that enriching life is the most satisfying motivation for doing things, rather than being motivated by fear, guilt, blame, or shame. It emphasizes taking personal responsibility for choices and improving the quality of relationships as a primary goal. It is effective even when other people involved are not familiar with the process.
—Marshall B. Rosenberg, PhD

The four components of Nonviolent Communication are:

Observations—observing a situation without moralistic judgment, or diagnosis.

Feelings—expressing to another how you feel without assigning blame.

Needs—expressing to another which of your universal needs are unmet or which you would like to have met.

Request—expressing a specific, doable request of another person in an effort to help you meet your needs.

For today, focus on making observations without moralistic judgment in at least two of your interactions.

JANUARY 4

I am not easily frightened. Not because I am brave but because I know that I am dealing with human beings, and that I must try as hard as I can to understand everything that anyone ever does.
—Etty Hillesum, Holocaust survivor

Improving Relationships as a Primary Goal

Compassionate Communication suggests that improving the quality of our relationships is a primary goal. Indeed, that connection with ourselves and other people takes a higher priority than being right, winning, making more money, or looking good to other people. If you focus on *improving the quality of your relationships* through deeper connections, you will improve the state of your life, enhance the peace and love in your life, and feel better about yourself.

I learned this through personal experience. I worked from time to time with a business colleague. Over the years, our relationship deteriorated to the point where we had no civil connections with each other. Our association was worst just as I was starting to look at how I contributed to the angst in my relationships. As a result, I started to focus more on my connections with people rather than trying to be right or to win arguments. Within a remarkably short time, my colleague was telling me how much she admired the changes

I was making and how much she enjoyed her relationship with me. We both expressed our sadness for our earlier behaviors. Today, we are close colleagues who work together in a variety of projects and easily call each other a friend.

When you shift your focus to valuing your connection with other people, you improve the quality of your life and your relationships. Everyone who crosses your path will benefit from this shift of focus. It is inevitable.

Be aware today of the times when your priority is to win or to be right rather than to connect, then shift your focus to connection with others.

JANUARY 5

Try not to become a man of success, but rather,
try to become a man of value.
—Albert Einstein

Giraffe Consciousness

In Compassionate Communication, we use giraffes as our metaphor because they have the largest heart of all land mammals (forty pounds!). They remind us to connect from the heart. They also have long necks, a metaphor for seeing far down the road. So when we say or do something, it is important for us to be conscious of the potential long-range consequences of our actions. It's about being fully present to our actions and words, knowing that each action creates a reaction. When we consciously choose to respond to life with compassion, peace, and harmony, we meet our own needs for these positive qualities.

Be aware of your own or other people's actions that demonstrate a giraffe consciousness to you.

JANUARY 6

Love is the only force capable of
transforming an enemy into a friend.
—*Martin Luther King Jr.*

The Jackal as a Teacher

In Compassionate Communication, we use the jackal as our metaphor for that part of us that is critical, judgmental, or self-righteous. We chose the jackal image because they walk low to the ground, tend to be more interested in satisfying themselves in the moment, and are less likely to consider the future ramifications of their actions. My inner jackal says things to me like: "Who do you think you are? You can't do THAT! You are too much—too intense, too demanding, too weak . . . " Can you relate to this jackal? Or maybe you have your own version.

I used to ignore my own inner jackal because I thought it was mean and uncaring. Then, after much empathy, I started to realize that it holds wisdom for me. When it tells me that I'm too intense, I believe it is trying to protect me from rejection. When it tells me, "You can't do that!," I believe it is trying to protect me from the disappointment of failure. I may not enjoy its methods, but I now know that it has my best interests at heart.

Do not think that ignoring your jackal will be healing. The more you ignore your jackal, the louder and fiercer it howls! Your jackal truly cares about your well-being. Hear it, empathize with it, learn its intentions, and create more satisfying strategies to meet your needs. This journey is filled with self-care, love, nurturing, and healing for both of you.

> Pay attention to what your inner jackal
> has to teach you today.

JANUARY 7

Speech is a mirror of the soul: as a man speaks, so is he.
—Pubilius Syrus

Tragic Expressions of Unmet Needs

Marshall B. Rosenberg, PhD, who developed the Compassionate Communication process, uses the phrase "tragic expressions of unmet needs" to illustrate how often we do things that aren't likely to meet our needs. The copy machine doesn't work, so you hit it and scream at it. I'm guessing you're frustrated because you would like ease and predictability when using it. Will hitting and screaming help you meet this need? How about the ways that you communicate with other people? For example, your husband forgets to change the oil in your car for the third week in a row, so you say: "You haven't done that yet? Do I have to do everything?" I'm guessing you're angry and confused, and want relief, support, and fairness. In another example, you may feel angry, hurt, or scared when someone yells at you on the phone, so you shut down and don't say anything. Is it possible for you to meet your needs for understanding, consideration, and respect if you don't say anything? It's not that the way you communicate is bad; it's tragic, because it won't help you meet your needs.

This simple realization was transformative for me and it helped catapult me into changing my behaviors to better meet my needs. So, the next time you feel hurt, angry, sad, or disappointed, consider the potential results of the action you're about to take. Will it help you meet your needs? If not, consider a different approach that is more likely to satisfy you.

Today, notice how often you do things that will
not help you meet your need in the situation.
Make a different choice that will.

JANUARY 8

Nobody sees a flower—really—it is so small it takes
time—we haven't time—and to see takes time,
like to have a friend takes time.
—*Georgia O'Keeffe*

Empathy, a Potent Healer

I cannot say it enough. Most of us rarely feel truly heard and understood. Empathy, the simple act of hearing someone and focusing your attention on them, can be incredibly healing. Try to listen for the feelings and needs behind someone's words. This isn't always easy, but the results are remarkable.

Here's an example. One of your kids says, "We never do what I want." That might be hard to hear if you focus on the words he uses and if you think 90 percent of your life is focused on meeting his needs. Take a deep breath and listen for what they are; I'm guessing respect, and a say in decision making. You don't have to agree with him, by the way. All you're doing is trying to understand his view of things. You could respond with, "Are you frustrated and want more say in the family's decision-making process?" That's it! Now, carry the conversation through by listening for his feelings and needs and expressing your own. The whole conversation might sound like this, "Yeah, you and Dad always get your own way." "So, you think we're only doing what we want without considering what you want?" "Yeah." "I feel sad about this because I know I spend a lot of time considering your needs, and then often neglecting my own. I guess we both want the same thing, balance and respect. You and I would both like to know that the other one values our needs too. Do you agree with that?" "Yeah, I guess." "Would you be willing to talk about what we are both hoping for tonight, and maybe brainstorm ways we can both get what we want?" "OK."

If we focus on the words, we often miss the point. Listen deeply to the needs the other person is trying to convey. Once you understand each other, you will be ready to resolve the situation.

Empathize with at least one person today.

JANUARY 9

People are disturbed not by things,
but by the view they take of them.
— *Epictetus*

Stimulus vs. Cause

Feelings are a result of met or unmet needs, not the actions of other people. Hard to believe? Consider what can happen when a dear friend punches you in the arm as a greeting. You might be happy to see him and you enjoy the punch in the arm because your needs include fun, friendship, and connection. On another day, this same friend gives you a punch on the arm. You are still happy to see him, but your arm had been injured the day before, so the punch stimulates pain. In this case, you will probably be feeling concerned because you need protection and relief from the pain. Both instances had the same stimulus—a good friend punched you in the arm—but your feelings about it changed depending on your own met or unmet needs. Therefore, while what people say or do is the stimulus, the actual cause of our feelings comes from our met or unmet needs.

Notice how your feelings are the result of
your unmet or met needs today.

JANUARY 10

The greatest deception men suffer is
from their own opinions.
— *Leonardo da Vinci*

Moralistic Judgments

Moralistic judgments imply that other people are wrong or bad because they don't act in ways that are in harmony with our values. If you see someone driving faster than you think is safe, you might say that they are a maniac driver. If someone talks slower than is fun for you, you might say that they are boring. You may also do this to yourself when you think that you're fat because you don't weigh what you'd like to, or that you're a bully if you regret something you just said. Anytime you judge someone else or yourself as bad or wrong, you are expressing a moralistic judgment.

Another way of looking at things that allows you to evaluate your circumstances without judgment is to express how something affects you. For instance, when I see someone driving faster than I think is safe, I may say or think, "When I see that person driving that fast I feel scared and I'd really like the road to be safe." Or, if I'm discouraged with my weight, I could say or think: "Ugh. I am so frustrated with my weight. Losing twenty pounds would really give me hope that this can shift." Judging the situation only creates distance and additional hurt feelings. Acknowledging our feelings and connecting those feelings to our unmet needs (safety and hope) can help us to connect with ourselves and others, and to heal.

Notice how often you make moralistic judgments of
other people and how you feel when you do this.

JANUARY 11

Do not consider painful what is good for you.
—*Euripides*

Losing Our Judgments

Have you ever noticed how one minute something can seem
so utterly painful you're sure it must be bad, then, a short
time later, the most amazing results happen, so then you
think it's good? This has happened to me countless times.

Consider the time my car died when my finances were at
an all-time low. That was bad, I thought. Then my dad called
and offered to let me use his car because he had bought a
new one. He said I could pay him for the car when my
finances improved. His car was in much better condition
than my last car and I was then glad that my car had died.

Another time, I wanted to hire someone who I thought
would be a perfect fit in my organization. She accepted the
position and then called two days later to decline. I thought
that was bad. Then, two years later, I talked to the director
of the organization she had chosen over mine. They were in
the process of firing her and they were expecting a lawsuit.
Apparently, her presence in the organization had stimulated
pain for many people and office morale was at an all-time
low. Then, I thought it was good that she hadn't accepted
my offer.

Do we have to judge these life events as good or bad? Can't we simply acknowledge when we're feeling pain or happiness, connect to our met or unmet needs, and have faith that the Universe will organize the results? Judging life's events does not support healing, connectedness, or harmony; in reality, it only adds to confusion, pain, and worry.

> Today, make a clear choice not to judge your day
> as good or bad. Instead, acknowledge the feelings
> and needs that are present, and leave the rest
> up to the Universe.

JANUARY 12

*Sometimes a slight difference in where we stand can
dramatically change how we see things.*
—*Melody Beattie*

Enemy Images

Do you harbor negative thoughts about others? Do these negative feelings affect your ability to enjoy those relationships or communicate effectively? When you foster resentment or anger toward other people, your focus is on your perceptions of the other person's foibles. Your ability to compassionately connect to them is severely limited. True healing comes when you acknowledge your unmet needs. You can achieve deeper compassion when you also acknowledge the needs that the other person is trying to meet with their behaviors. When you do this, you have a greater tendency to step out of judgment, which fosters resentment and anger, and move into understanding, which fosters compassion and connection.

> Be aware of the enemy images you harbor toward other people and begin the process of translating those images to bring relief to you.

JANUARY 13

Love is not a possession. It is the flow of God's energy.
—*Swami Chidvilasananda*

Listening Deeply

Love and compassion don't recognize right or wrong, good or bad. If you're struggling in a relationship, try not to judge it. Rather, focus on what you both want.

What is the important thing behind both people's words and actions? If someone says, "You don't care anything about me," what do you think she really wants? I'm guessing she wants to be valued and cared about. She might also want her needs to be considered. If you focus on her words, you may recall all the times you've done a caring thing for her. Or you might argue about whether you care or not. This type of argument results in more anger and contempt because it doesn't demonstrate that you've heard the other person, or that you care about them.

A more effective response could be focusing on the underlying needs you're hearing behind the words, such as:

"Sounds like you're bummed and you'd like to know that I value you. Is that right?" You might not agree with the person's statement. You don't have to. All you are doing is acknowledging her feelings. Once she feels heard, you have set the stage for a full conversation to resolve the situation.

Commit to connecting to the feelings
of at least one person today.

JANUARY 14

It does not matter how slowly you go
so long as you do not stop.
—Confucius

Valuing Everyone's Needs

A friend of mine called to tell me that her husband had left her. He had spent the last couple of years wrestling with his feelings about their marriage. He never discussed his discontent with her. In fact, she first heard of his unhappiness when he was leaving her. She was in shock and devastated.

My sadness about her situation was attached to my desire to live in a world where people value everyone's needs, not just their own, and where we value commitment and connection. It is sometimes challenging to live these values. Talking things through can be laborious and painful, but the alternative can be the end of a relationship. If you're feeling unhappy about a relationship you are in, whether it's personal or professional, consider how important this relationship is to you. Is it worth it to you to risk ending this relationship by keeping your unhappiness to yourself? Or would you like to try to work it out? Talking about it doesn't guarantee that you will like the resolution, but not talking about it guarantees continued unhappiness.

> If you are in a relationship you are not happy with, commit to talking with the other person today in an effort to connect about both your needs.

JANUARY 15

Life is short, but there is always
time enough for courtesy.
—*Ralph Waldo Emerson*

Demands vs. Requests

When you demand that someone do something, their only choice is to succumb or rebel; they either do what you asked or they don't. Sometimes, a demand can look like a request. You say, "Honey, will you please mow the lawn today?" It sounds like a request, but notice what happens if your partner says, "No, not today, I'm beat and I'd like to relax." If you don't get angry or feel judgment, it was a request. If you think: "How much rest could one person need? He is so lazy!", you've probably made a demand.

The trick to asking something as a request is valuing everyone's needs *equally*. Do you truly value your husband's need for rest, or is your own need for orderliness more important to you? When you value everyone's needs *equally*, then you are more willing to come to solutions that satisfy everyone. Here's how this might look after your husband just said he wanted to rest instead of mowing the lawn. "So, you really want your rest today. I get that, especially after the week you had." "Yeah, thanks." "I want you to get your rest, honey. I'm also worried about the yard not being mowed by the time my parents get here tomorrow. I'd really like our place to look nice for them. Do you have any ideas how you could get your rest and we could get the lawn mowed by tomorrow morning when they get here?"

In this example, the wife acknowledged the husband's need for rest and also asserted her own request that the lawn be mowed by the time her folks arrived. She is asserting her need, not the solution. They could decide to hire a neighbor to mow the lawn, or he could mow the lawn tomorrow morning, or she could mow the lawn if he agrees to pick up some other jobs in preparation for her parents' visit. It could have been difficult for her to acknowledge other options if she was adamant that he mow the lawn that day. Such a demand limits the possibilities and creates distance between people. Making a request that truly values everyone's needs *equally* opens possibilities and helps build connection.

Be aware of how you feel today when you hear someone's request as a demand. Can you think of a response other than succumbing or rebelling?

JANUARY 16

*It is the mark of an educated mind to be able
to entertain a thought without accepting it.*
—*Aristotle*

Empathy Doesn't Mean Agreement

Sometimes, people tell me that they can't empathize with someone because they don't agree with them. An example could be a teenager who tells her parents that they don't care about her. Or a friend who tells you that you were late, even though you thought you were right on time. Remember that empathy is about being present to a person's feelings and needs. It is acknowledging another's experience, not necessarily agreeing with it. If you have a different opinion than the other, empathize with her first. Then, state your feelings and needs with regard to the situation. For example, if your teenager tells you that you don't care about her, you might consider saying, "Are you feeling hurt because you want to know that I care as much about your needs as mine?" Once you've heard her out, you could say: "Wow, I'm really surprised and sad to hear this because I love you so much, and I sometimes lose myself because I'm so focused on helping you. Will you tell me what you heard just now from me?"

Remind yourself today that empathizing with someone
does not constitute agreement.

23

JANUARY 17

He that knows least commonly presumes the most.
—Thomas Fuller, MD

Observation, the First Component of Nonviolent Communication

Your five-year-old just drew on your wall with crayons and you think, "He's trying to make my life difficult because he's mad at me." Or your husband comes home later than he had agreed to for the third time this week, so you think, "He doesn't care about my feelings at all." Sound familiar? People often decide why something happened before talking with the other person. The "whys" in these examples were, "He's trying to make my life difficult because he's mad at me" and "He doesn't care about my feelings at all."

The only facts you know in these situations are that there are crayon drawings on the wall (if you saw the child drawing on the wall, you could also identify the artist), and that three times this week, your husband has come home later than you remember he agreed to. In Nonviolent Communication, this is called the observation: the facts of what you saw or heard. Think of it as a snapshot of what happened or a recording of what was said, without adding in your own judgments or reasons why you think it happened.

When you make observations, you open the possibility for deeper connection with the other person. You might say to your husband when he gets home: "You know, this is the third time this week you've come home after six, and I'm feeling confused and annoyed because I thought you agreed to be home by five thirty these nights. Was this your understanding as well?" As in all situations, there are a lot of ways that you can approach the conversation. The point is that if you broach the subject without a predetermined idea of why something happened, you have greater opportunities to connect with the other person and meet your needs.

Make a commitment today to notice exactly what was said or done, and avoid making assumptions about why things happened.

JANUARY 18

Resolve to find thyself; and to know that he
who finds himself, loses his misery.
—*Matthew Arnold*

Feelings, the Second Component of Compassionate Communication

Many of us were taught to *think* and not *feel*. We may have been taught to consider how others feel, but few of us were taught to check in with *ourselves*—to notice how *we* feel about things, such as how we feel when we're with someone, how we feel when we do something, or what we could do to feel better about something. This focus on thinking about the other has lessened our connection with self, and has contributed to our denial of self. So, when I suggest that people connect with their feelings and express them to others, they are shocked at how challenging this can be. If we are not used to expressing our feelings, we can feel vulnerable. Even simply noticing our feelings can be overwhelming if we're used to thinking about other people's reactions.

As overwhelming or threatening as it may seem in the beginning, and as vulnerable as you may feel, the rewards are worth it. You will start to expand your feelings vocabulary and begin to notice how you feel about something, even when you're not trying. Then, I predict that you will start making different decisions—decisions based on your feelings rather than what you think someone else is feeling. You may even notice that you've been doing things you don't enjoy, or spending time with people you don't enjoy. Acknowledging your own feelings could start the process for a dramatic transformation in your life.

For today, notice how you feel about things.
If you start wondering what other people are feeling,
gently turn your focus back to yourself.

JANUARY 19

There are so many kinds of voices in the world,
and none of them is without significance.
—*1 Corinthians 14:10*

Needs, the Third Component of
Compassionate Communication

In Compassionate Communication, we consider *needs* to be universal. That means that while we all have the same needs, such as for love, support, shelter, food, joy, caring, etc. (refer to the needs list in the front of the book), we choose different ways to meet our needs. For instance, I have a need for transportation and so I choose to own a car. When I travel long distances, I choose to fly, and I have also used Amtrak. The need in all these examples is transportation; my methods or strategies are a car, plane, and train. One of my sisters lived in a dangerous Seattle neighborhood once. She had a need for safety, so she befriended the gang members in her neighborhood. They could visit her and hang out in her house anytime they wanted. She never locked her door so that they had free access. This method might not work for some of us, but it fully met her need for safety.

When we start to distinguish between our universal needs and the strategies we choose to meet those needs, we can bring clarity to our relationships. Let's imagine that you and your friend are arguing over where to go on vacation. Choosing the right place is a strategy to meet your needs. But what are the needs that you are each trying to meet with this vacation? Don't assume that everyone is trying to meet the same needs as you. You might find that you are primarily interested in fun, and your friend is primarily interested in rest. Consider both your needs, and then discuss places that would accommodate them. Changing the focus of your conversations to needs can open the possibility for everyone's needs to be considered and met through a peaceful resolution.

Be aware of the difference between universal needs and the strategies you choose to meet those needs.

JANUARY 20

We should not let our fears hold us
back from pursuing our hopes.
—*John F. Kennedy*

Requests, the Fourth Component of Compassionate Communication

Over the past few days, we have looked at the first three components of Compassionate Communication: observations, feelings, and needs. The fourth component is making a *request*. This component is critical because it clarifies for you and the people in your life what it would take to meet your need. Imagine that you said to your teenage daughter, "Honey, it seems like I haven't seen you very much the last couple of weeks and I'm sad about that because I miss you and I'd like to spend more time with you." If you don't make a request, your daughter has to guess what you want. She may guess that you want to spend lots of time with her, when what you really want is a couple of hours one night this week. Or, she may assume that you are criticizing her for valuing her friends more than you. Or, she may think that no matter how much time she spends with you, it will never be enough for you. Making a request can bring clarity and relief to a conversation and greatly lessen any tension in the situation. Your request could sound like this: "Honey, it seems that I haven't seen you very much the last couple of weeks and I'm sad about that because I miss you and I'd like to spend more time with you. *Would you be willing to schedule a couple of hours that we can spend together some evening this week? We could brainstorm what we'd both enjoy doing.*" In reality, your daughter might still resist your request. However, the opportunity for mutual satisfaction is much greater when you are clear about what you want.

> Make at least one specific and doable
> request to someone today.

JANUARY 21

The situation is critical . . . but not serious.
—Sonia Choquette

Evaluations vs. Feelings

Has someone ever said to you, "I feel like you just don't care about me!" or "I feel you are not being honest" or "I feel manipulated, betrayed, judged." All of these statements reflect an evaluation that someone is having about another person. Someone who says "I feel like you don't care" may be saying this because she actually feels angry, hurt, or scared. "I feel you are not being honest" could be the result of the speaker feeling worried or confused. And I guess that when she says that she feels "manipulated, betrayed, or judged," it may mean that she actually feels sad, hurt, or angry.

It's important to be clear about your feelings because it helps you own how you feel, rather than blaming the other person for doing something you see as wrong, and expressing your feelings helps the other person know how deeply this issue affects you. In addition, stating true feelings rather than evaluation brings clarity and connection to both the speaker and the other person.

Be aware today of times when you are attempting to express a feeling, but you express a thought instead.

JANUARY 22

Do not judge and you will not be judged. For as you judge others, so you will yourselves be judged . . .
—Matthew 7:1

Understanding Our Judgments

Many of us have learned patterns of speaking that backfire. One of these is judging other people. Often, we do this to feel better about ourselves, and possibly to meet our own needs for acceptance and belonging, yet just the opposite happens. Whenever we judge someone else in any way, we create a barrier and distance between us and the other person. This occurs every time we judge another person as lazy, stupid, a bad dresser, egotistical, or uncaring. Every moralistic judgment separates us from other people and limits our ability to meet the very needs we set out to meet, such as feeling better about ourselves, acceptance, and belonging.

Instead of judging, then, notice how you feel about someone's actions, or how you feel when you see something. If you are skiing and someone cuts in front of you, rather than thinking she's a jerk or a maniac, consider that you feel scared and you'd like the slopes to be safer. This slight shift from judging other people to awareness of how their behavior affects you can make a profound difference in your ability to live peacefully.

Be aware of your moralistic judgments today, and make a conscious effort to shift from judgments to an awareness of your own feelings and needs.

JANUARY 23

Birds sing after a storm; why shouldn't people feel as free to delight in whatever remains to them?
—Rose Kennedy

Comparing Ourselves to Others

Comparisons are a form of judgment. There always seems to be someone who is better looking, more intelligent, or more enlightened than we are. Similarly, there seems to be an endless supply of people who are not as bright as we, who are worse drivers, and who are less witty. The minute we compare ourselves to other people, we are setting ourselves up for pain and discouragement. We are setting them up, too, and erecting a barrier between ourselves and them.

Try your very best to avoid comparisons. Instead, notice how you feel about other people's assets or foibles. Rather than saying that your neighbor is more beautiful than you are, consider enjoying her beauty and acknowledging that you would like to improve your own looks. Or better still, enjoy her beauty and enjoy what you think is beautiful about yourself. The more you avoid making comparisons, the more likely you are to create greater connections with others.

Be aware of the comparisons you make today.

JANUARY 24

True freedom is to share
All the chains our brothers wear,
And, with heart and hand, to be
Earnest to make others free!
—James Russell Lowell

The Three Stages of Emotional Liberation

We all go through stages of emotional maturity. In Nonviolent Communication, we identify three primary stages of emotional maturity, the last of which is emotional liberation.

Many of us start at Stage 1, which is thinking that we are responsible for other people's feelings. At this stage, we feel bad if our partners are distressed and we worry about hurting other people's feelings. We often deny our own happiness so that others will be happy.

Stage 2 is when we start to notice and grieve how much of our life has been spent denying our own happiness. Very often, people at this stage feel angry and resentful, and meeting their own needs becomes urgent. At this stage, people tend to say things like, "That's your problem; I'm not responsible for your feelings."

In Stage 3, we integrate the first two stages. We come to realize that everyone is responsible for their own feelings, but we also recognize our role if we do something that stimulates pain in another person. We also start to value the needs of *everyone*, not just the other person's need or our own. The world seems more abundant as we realize that it is possible to value everyone's needs equally. As this happens, we become able to consider everyone's feelings and needs without taking responsibility for them. We are free to be compassionate and loving to many people, even ourselves. Indeed, we have reached emotional liberation.

Take a few minutes to ponder what stage of emotional maturity you are currently in. Celebrate that stage, even if you haven't reached Stage 3. You are moving toward emotional liberation.

JANUARY 25

Hatred is a feeling, which leads
to the extinction of values.
—José Ortega y Gasset

Defusing Anger

Many of us are afraid of our anger because we haven't learned how to express it in a way that brings relief or that helps us meet our needs in the situation. Consider someone who calls people names in a rage, or hits another person, or walks off slamming the doors behind him. All of these are methods for expressing anger, but does the person ever feel relief from these actions? Such expressions of anger are tragic expressions of unmet needs because the person isn't likely to satisfy them. Consider a different approach to anger, one that helps you fully express your anger and is more likely to help you meet your needs for relief, to be heard, or to be understood.

Start with an understanding that no one else is responsible for your anger. It is most likely a result of your judgmental thoughts that someone should do something differently or better, or your expectations of other people. Even if you can't see your own judgments in the heat of anger, you start by understanding that you take full responsibility for it.

The first step in defusing anger is to stop and breathe. Don't say anything. Remind yourself that you are responsible for your anger and that blaming the other person will be counterproductive. Then start to notice the blaming, judgmental thoughts that are running through your head. Do not say these out loud; just notice them quietly. These messages could look like: "He is such a pig. All he cares about is himself. This situation is impossible . . . " Step 2 is to notice your unmet needs, such as support, love, and ease. Step 3 is expressing your feelings and unmet needs. For example, "I am so angry right now because I would really like to hope that we can find a way to work this out in a way that we both can feel good about!" Notice that the focus is on the speaker's feelings and unmet needs, not the other person's foibles. If you hope to resolve your angry feelings, you must focus on your own feelings and unmet needs. Such an expression of anger is more likely to inspire resolution.

If you feel angry today, take a moment to identify
your feelings and unmet needs before
responding to the other person.

. . . truth could never be wholly contained in words.
All of us know it: At the same moment the mouth is
speaking one thing, the heart is saying another . . .
—*Catherine Marshall*

Meeting Our Need for Honesty

I can't begin to tell you how many times I hear people accuse others of being dishonest. The search for the truth can keep people in pain for years. I used to think that I was being honest if I didn't say something untruthful, but I could decide to withhold some of the truth. Later, I began to think that withholding the truth was dishonest. Honesty is in the eye of the beholder. My needs for honesty are met when I can look people in the eye and speak my truth, or when I decide that speaking my truth will be more harmful than withholding it.

If I find myself ducking behind a display at the grocery store to avoid addressing an unresolved issue with someone, my need for honesty has not been met. If I am worried that two people might get together and compare notes about something I have said, I have not met my need for honesty. Each one of us decides whether we are living in ways that meet our need for honesty. And we each decide whether someone else's actions meet it. Try not to spend so much time seeking the truth. Instead focus more attention on whether *your need* for honesty has been met. When it is, you can live more freely.

Be aware today of whether you are
meeting your need for honesty.

JANUARY 27

The ways parents interact with their children contribute to shaping children's understanding of themselves, their parents, human nature, and the world around them. A parent who takes a toy away from a toddler who had just taken it from another child, while saying, "No grabbing," teaches both children that grabbing is OK—for those with more power. A parent who unilaterally imposes a curfew implies that a teenager can't be trusted to make thoughtful decisions about his life. Instead, in both words and actions, parents can convey two key ideas: 1. Everyone's needs matter, and 2. If we connect sufficiently, we can find strategies that will work for everyone.

—Inbal Kashtan

Communicating With Children

The empathy process of hearing another's feelings and needs works beautifully with children of all ages. Once I had two young boys, ages six and three, visiting me for a week. One time, Gary, the six-year-old, kicked the three-year-old in the stomach and started screaming at him to get out of the way. The younger boy looked stunned and confused. I was also stunned because I hadn't seen anything to indicate that Gary was becoming frustrated.

I started by empathizing with the three-year-old who was crying. "Are you scared and confused because you don't understand what just happened?" "Yeah." "And, are you feeling hurt because you'd like your brother to have a different way of telling you he's upset?" "YEAH! He's mean."

Hey, Gary, why did you do that?" "Because you were sitting on a marble and I was down to the last one!"

Then I empathized with Gary. "So, Gary, are you frustrated because your brother wasn't paying attention to the game the way you like to?" "Yeah. He's always messing things up. I wish he'd just play the game or go do something else." "So, you'd like him to make up his mind and to be as serious as you are about play time." "Yeah." Next, we worked out a solution that met both children's needs.

Such empathy offers profound learning opportunities to children, expands their feelings and needs vocabulary, and teaches them the positive results of valuing everyone's needs.

The vocabulary that you use should be modified to fit your child's age and learning ability. *Feeling* words that can easily be understood by children are: sad, glad, excited, proud, playful, mad, confused, tired, scared. *Need* words that can easily be understood by children are: safety, food, love, privacy, fun, play, choice, rest.

Be aware of opportunities to model the
empathy process with children today.

JANUARY 28

Our feelings result from how we choose to receive
what others say and do, as well as our particular
needs and expectations in that moment.
—Marshall B. Rosenberg, PhD

Feelings Are a Response to Our Met or Unmet Needs

When I worked at a university, I had four to five appointments per day. Often, when someone was late for their appointment, I felt frustrated because I wanted my schedule to be predictable. Then I noticed that sometimes I liked it when they were late because it gave me a break between appointments. Although it is sometimes easy to blame others for how we feel, the truth is *our feelings are a result of our met or unmet needs.* An example of this could be when your boyfriend tells you that you're beautiful. I'm guessing this meets your needs for acceptance and affection. How about if your boss tells you you're beautiful? For many of us, this would not meet our needs for respect and trust. In both cases, the stimulus is the same—someone telling you you're beautiful, but in each case, we are trying to meet different needs. So if you are feeling hurt, sad, angry, or disappointed, try to consider what your unmet needs are, and see if there are other ways you can get them met. Try your best not to blame other people for your feelings.

Be aware of how your needs affect your feelings today.

JANUARY 29

I think there is choice possible to us at any moment,
as long as we live . . . There is a choice,
and the rest falls away.
—Muriel Rukeyser

Liberating Ourselves From Our "Shoulds"

Do you have a long list of things you should do, or that you have to do? Do you ever catch yourself saying, "I have to go to work," or "I have to go home to let the dog out," or "I have to go home and make dinner for the family"? Every time you tell yourself that you have to do something, you disconnect yourself from the needs you're trying to get met, and you diminish the joy in your life.

Try to translate your "shoulds" and "have tos" into the need you are trying to meet. Translating "I have to go to work" into "I'm going to work because I value the income it provides my family" is more empowering. Similarly, "I'm going home to let the dog out because I want her to be comfortable" or "I'm going to go home to make a nice dinner for my family because I really want them to eat healthy" can bring more joy to tasks. Once you connect with the need you're trying to meet, you might change your mind about doing a particular activity or task. You might call your teenage neighbor and ask if she'd walk the dog. Or you may decide that your real need is rest, or completing the project you're working on, or connecting with a friend. Other times, just connecting to the need you're trying to meet by your behaviors can release you from the dreaded "shoulds."

Today, make a list of all your "shoulds." Translate at least two items on your list into your needs and then decide whether you want to do these activities.

JANUARY 30

Sometimes I forget completely
what companionship is.
—Rumi

Bringing a Dead Conversation Back to Life

Let's say you're sitting at the dinner table with your new brother-in-law who is talking and talking and talking about stuff that you simply cannot relate to and don't care a whit about. You could get up and leave the table, sit there and think what an incredible bore he is, invest some energy noticing every flaw in his physical appearance, or roll your eyes at your dad across the table.

Or you could take it upon yourself to bring life into the conversation. The best way to do that and meet your own need for connection without stimulating pain in other people is to find a way to connect to their passions, feelings, or desires. Try it! "Wow, Eric, it sounds like the history of ant migration is really fascinating to you, and something that you've been researching for a long time. Was there some kind of life-changing moment that caused you to invest so much time on this?" By doing this, you shift the topic from ant migration to Eric's personal passion for ant migration. You begin to connect with Eric. Another way of doing this could be: "Eric, it sounds like the history of ant migration is really fascinating to you. How do you think this research will directly affect or change your life?" Any time you connect to your own and other people's humanness, you bring life into the conversation. Try it. I think you'll be surprised at how effective this is.

> For today, bring at least one dead conversation
> back to life by connecting to the other
> person's feelings, passions, or desires.

JANUARY 31

Out beyond ideas of wrongdoing and right doing,
there is a field. I will meet you there.
—Rumi

Evaluating Ourselves With Compassion

Do you engage in negative self-talk? This can be a message you give yourself, such as "Well, that was stupid." Or "I know better and I did it anyway!" Or "I am so fat." Every time you criticize yourself, you cause yourself to feel shame and guilt, which promotes depression and stagnation. When you think about it, how likely are you to promote positive change if you are feeling shame?

Another way to look at your foibles is to acknowledge your needs (or values) that aren't met by your actions. You can translate "Well, that's stupid" into "I am so frustrated that I did that because it doesn't meet my needs for integrity."

"I know better and I did it anyway!" could be translated into "I am so ticked because I would like to trust myself more." And "I am so fat" can mean "When I weigh thirty pounds more than I would like, I feel sad because I want to take better care of myself."

When you translate your negative self-talk, you are more able to connect to the underlying needs you are trying to meet, rather than stimulating shame and guilt, thus providing greater opportunities for change.

> Be aware of your negative self-talk today and
> take a few moments to connect with your
> unmet needs associated with the issue.

Meditations for
FEBRUARY

FEBRUARY 1

*Mourning in Nonviolent Communication is
the process of fully connecting with the unmet
needs and feelings that are generated when
we have been less than perfect.*
—Marshall B. Rosenberg, PhD

Mourning Our Disappointments

We mourn when we acknowledge the feelings and unmet
needs associated with regret without any sense of guilt or
shame. When we do this, we can see how our behavior has
negatively affected our lives, and we become more willing
to try to do it differently next time. If on the other hand,
we tell ourselves that we are bad or wrong because of our
actions, we are likely to feel shame and guilt, which promote
depression and hopelessness. Such an approach is unlikely to
lead to positive change. The process, then, is to acknowledge
the feelings and needs that are stimulated by the behavior
we regret.

Let's say that you're trying to resolve a problem with
the phone company. You wait for ten minutes to talk to
someone. That person transfers you to someone else and
you wait five minutes for the new person. This happens
three more times. Now you have been on the phone for
thirty minutes and have had only brief conversations with
someone until they transferred you again. By the time you
speak to the "correct" person, you are less than courteous,
and your voice is angry and impatient. The person on the
other end says, "I'm only trying to help you, ma'am."

Instantly, you know something's up. Check in with yourself and ask yourself what your feelings and needs are. I guess you feel annoyed and want greater ease. You hope that the problem will be resolved with a real live human being, so connection is also a need. It's amazing how much better you'll feel once you acknowledge this. Still, you regret how you talked to the young woman who truly was just trying to help you. So you say: "I appreciate (or recognize) you're trying to help. I regret the impatience and frustration in my voice. I have been on hold for thirty minutes and transferred to four different people. I would really like this process to be easier. Do you think you can help me with my problem?"

Mourning is acknowledging our regret to ourselves. Sometimes, it can involve giving yourself time and space to deal with pain and emotion. In other times, a simple acknowledgment of our unmet need is enough. Once we have fully mourned our unmet need, we will feel relief.

Take a few moments today to acknowledge
the feelings and unmet needs associated
with one of your behaviors.

FEBRUARY 2

I have never seen a person grow or change in a
constructive direction when motivated
by guilt, shame, and/or hate.
—*William Goldberg*

Forgiving Ourselves

Every single time you say or do something, you are trying to meet a need. Here's an example. You're on the phone with a friend who has called you at breakfast time, and your cereal is getting mushier by the second. With impatience in your voice, you say: "I've got to go! Do you think you can work this out on your own?" After you hang up, you feel regret.

Forgiveness begins when we acknowledge the needs we were trying to meet in the situation. It's not about rationalizing our actions. It's more about simply connecting with what our needs were. In this example, our need might be for a certain texture or flavor in our breakfast. Or maybe it's a need related to values; we don't want to waste the food we prepared. Once we connect to these needs, it is amazing how much relief we can feel just from knowing that we were trying to meet them. Then we can acknowledge our regret for acting as we did, and consider how we could do it differently next time. In a sense, this means acknowledging both parts of ourselves—the part who was trying to meet a need and the part who took the action we regret. Offering ourselves this compassion can be an effective motivator for change. Next time, we could say: "My corn flakes are getting soggy, and I'm worried about wasting food. Would it be OK with you if I called you in a few minutes to continue this conversation?"

Today, notice that your actions are an attempt to meet
your needs. Then acknowledge any regret you
may feel about your choice of strategies
for meeting those needs.

FEBRUARY 3

She must not swing her arms as though they
were dangling ropes; she must not switch herself this
way and that; she must not shout; and she must not,
while wearing her bridal veil, smoke a cigarette.
—Emily Post

Needs and Values

Needs and values are synonymous in Nonviolent Communication. Both are universal. Emily Post's instructions were probably motivated by her values—respect, dignity, and integrity for women. I share those values, only I choose different ways to meet them, such as speaking my truth, keeping my word, and honoring my physical needs. The way we choose to live by our values often changes as we get new information and as society changes; however, the underlying values remain the same. Update your behaviors but be true to your values; they represent the core of who you are.

Be aware of the underlying values that
prompt your behaviors today.

FEBRUARY 4

See the world as yourself.
Have faith in the way things are.
Love the world as yourself;
Then you can care for all things.
—Tao Te Ching

Seeing People's Similarities

We are all one—all creatures on this planet are one. We all have the same universal needs for love, caring, nurturing, intimacy, and support. If you don't see yourself as separate, you won't be. Try to hold on to this simple principle: If you truly believe that we are all one, your language and actions will follow. For instance, if you value your needs more than your spouse's, you might try to "get" him to do something he doesn't want to do rather than consider his needs. When we act in this way, we forget our connection to other living beings, and instead we act in ways that keep us separate.

Today, act as if you believe to the depth of your being
that all people are one.

FEBRUARY 5

*For several centuries now, we have overemphasized
the intellect. It is fine in its place. It is not, however,
the most authentic way of knowing. The most
authentic comes from the heart.*
—Sonia Choquette

How to Hear Difficult Messages

Have you ever been sitting home reading or watching TV, enjoying your space and peacefulness, when your partner comes home and says something like: "Aren't the dishes done yet? I am so sick of coming home to a messy house!," then walks out of the room to take a shower? It's easy to feel shock and hurt in such situations, and then feel confused about how to handle it.

I suggest that you try empathizing with him by saying something like, "It sounds like you're really annoyed that the dishes weren't done by the time you got home because you were hoping the house would be neat." "Yes! I'm tired and frustrated, and after a hard day at work, I'd really like to come home to a clean house." "And, on top of the dishes not being done, you've really had a rough day?" "Yeah, today was truly awful." "I get how frustrating it can be at work. How about if I do the dishes while you take a shower, and then can we talk about the dishes? I'm noticing that I simply hate doing dishes and that's why they aren't done as often as you'd like. I really want to help you meet your need for orderliness, and I'd also like to meet my needs for ease and fun. Would you be willing to have this conversation after your shower?" "Sure."

Notice that the first thing she did was empathize, listening to his feelings and needs. Then, when she thought she had heard him, she asked for what she wanted, which was a conversation to discuss both their needs. He was much more willing to have this conversation once his needs were heard, and when he had more confidence that she valued both their needs.

Tempting as it is sometimes to argue with someone who expresses themselves in ways that stimulate pain in us, try to refrain. Arguing is likely to result in both of you feeling hurt and frustrated. By empathizing instead, you both stand a better chance of feeling relief and reaching a peaceful resolution.

Be aware of opportunities today to choose empathizing over arguing with someone who is angry, and notice how it affects your ability to resolve the situation.

FEBRUARY 6

You must be the change you want to see in the world.
—*Mahatma Gandhi*

Peace Starts With You

Sometimes the discord in the world feels overwhelming, and world peace seems impossible. At times like these, it can be tempting to give up. However, peace will be a reality when individuals from around the world become committed to living their own lives peacefully. Peace starts with each individual. If you are consumed with anger, resentment, and hate, you promote violence. If you are consumed with harmony, tolerance, and compassion, you promote peace. Each time you refrain from doing harm—snapping at the store clerk or yelling at your children or partner—and each time you empathize with someone, you are working toward peace. We can each do our part to create world peace by creating compassion and peace in our daily lives.

> **Be aware of how your attitudes or actions
> promote peace or discord today.**

FEBRUARY 7

Killing people is too superficial.
—*Marshall B. Rosenberg, PhD*

Expressing the Depth of Our Anger

Some people use hitting, yelling, name-calling, gossip, or other forms of abuse to express their anger. In the Compassionate Communication process, we see these expressions as ineffective, superficial ways of expressing anger. After all, what is accomplished by violence? Only retaliation. Repressing or "stuffing" our anger isn't effective either, because we tend to carry the burden of resentments with us. When our anger is not heard or resolved, we will not feel relief.

Consider learning this new way to express your anger. It is more likely to bring you relief and resolution. Anger is created when we blame or judge someone else as bad or wrong, so the first step is to relieve the other person of the responsibility for our anger. We are responsible for our own feelings. The next step is to identify our unmet needs, such as support, caring, or respect. The third step is to acknowledge our feelings, and the fourth step is to make a request, either of someone else or of ourselves.

As an example, say that you are angry with your son for shaving your cat. Remember that anger starts with a judgment. In this case, you are probably thinking your son is insensitive, cruel, and self-centered. Your response may be to yell at your son. Rarely does such an approach bring relief or resolution. Your unmet needs might be your values concerning caring for other living creatures, respect, and consideration for everyone's needs. And you probably feel annoyed, angry, hurt, and scared. When you start to uncover your unmet needs, you will feel instant relief. If your pain is deep, you may start remembering other occasions when this need wasn't met with your son or other people in your life. Each time a new memory pops into your head, acknowledge your unmet needs and feelings. When you begin to notice a sense of relief, ask yourself what you can do to get your needs met in the present. It may be enough to simply acknowledge the needs yourself. Or you might want to make a request of your son or someone else. Once you have consciously connected to your unmet needs, you are more likely to make a request that will truly meet them.

Be aware of how your anger is a result of blame or judgment of others; then connect to your unmet needs in these situations and notice if you feel relief.

❋

FEBRUARY 8

All rising to a great place is by a winding stair.
—*Francis Bacon*

Using Anger to Serve Life

Sometimes we need to empathize with a person before he can hear our anger. Consider that all anger is an expression of an unmet need. If we focus on the need, rather than the actions, we are more likely to connect compassionately with other people. For instance, if your son shaves your cat, what do you suppose his unmet need might be? Could it be attention, fun, or adventure? Rather than staying stuck in your judgments, consider empathizing with him by saying: "When I see that you shaved the cat, I feel horrified because I value consideration and respect for all living things. I'm wondering, did you do that because you wanted adventure and fun?" Work to connect with the needs your son was trying to meet through his actions. Empathizing with someone doesn't mean that you like, respect, or agree with his behavior. It only means that you are trying to understand what needs drive it. Once you have connected with his needs, he is more likely to listen to your pain around the situation and create resolutions that value everyone's needs, including the cat's!

Be aware of opportunities to empathize
with someone's anger today.

FEBRUARY 9

Act nothing in a furious passion.
It's putting to sea in a storm.
—Thomas Fuller, MD

Using Anger as a Warning

If you are feeling anger, you are experiencing an unmet need. When you recognize it as a warning signal, it can be a life-serving tool. There is no hard and fast rule that we must instantly react to our anger. Nor is there a statute of limitations on expressing it. So, rather than react to your anger immediately, take the time to examine it and to discover your unmet need embodied in the judgment that is creating the anger. When you do this, you will have a much greater opportunity to resolve the situation in ways that are satisfying to everyone involved.

See your anger as a warning signal that you have an
unmet need today and resist acting immediately.

FEBRUARY 10

Everything has beauty but not everyone sees it.
—Proverb

Beauty Is in the Eye of the Beholder

Do you have a tendency to make a judgment that something isn't beautiful when it doesn't meet your needs for beauty?

How about when your daughter comes home with her eyebrow pierced? Do you think that her piercing makes her look ugly, or do you think that eyebrow piercing doesn't meet your own needs for beauty? When your date shows up in a polyester leisure suit, do you think he looks stupid, or do you recognize that his choice of clothes doesn't meet your needs for beauty? When your friend who is thirty pounds overweight shows up in a miniskirt, do you think she looks ridiculous, or do you consider that her outfit doesn't meet your needs for beauty?

It may seem like a small distinction, but the difference between judging someone as stupid or ugly and acknowledging that your own needs for beauty aren't met can be the difference between simply acknowledging your needs and putting distance between yourself and another person. The truth is that all our judgments separate us from other people. In making them, we set up an "us and them" dynamic. When we acknowledge our needs instead, we are simply stating what's going on within ourselves and are better able to stay connected.

Be aware today of how you judge beauty,
and how that distances you from others.

FEBRUARY 11

No legacy is so rich as honesty.
—*William Shakespeare*

Specificity Is the Key

Do you sometimes feel frustrated about situations in your life, while being too embarrassed to make a specific request, or perhaps annoyed because you'd really like the other person to "just get it"? I recognize this dynamic when I hear someone say to her partner, "I want you to help out more around the house." Often when someone hears this, they say (or at least think): "What do you mean? I do a lot of stuff for the house!" Most people want to contribute positively to each other's lives. So if your needs are not being met, the other person probably doesn't know how to meet them, or how to meet yours and his simultaneously.

Consider making a clear request, such as: "I notice that I spend most of my nights and weekends doing housework, paying bills, and taking care of my car. I'm frustrated about this, and I'd enjoy more support. Would you be willing to take responsibility for paying the bills and managing both our cars?" Making a specific and doable request as soon as you perceive your need is your best hope for getting it met. It is also the best hope for meeting the other person's need to contribute to your life!

Make at least one specific, doable request of someone today as soon as you perceive your need.

FEBRUARY 12

*The longest journey you will ever take is the eighteen
inches from your head to your heart.*
—*Anonymous*

Connecting From the Heart

Do you find it easier to have an intellectual conversation
with someone than an honest, open, and heartfelt one? If so,
you're not alone. Many of us struggle with intimacy, yet
we long for it—it is our most powerful need. I worked in
higher education for fifteen years, so I understand the safety
in talking about things from an intellectual perspective. I also
truly enjoy conversations with bright, well-read people that
stretch my intelligence and outlook. Such conversations meet
my needs for learning, challenge, and mental stimulation.
Shifting my focus and connecting from the heart, expressing
my true feelings to others, even if I think they might not
like me afterward, takes courage. But it is very satisfying. I
have never experienced anything more intimate than deep
connection with another person. As I have focused on my
need for connection, I have created freedom in my life. I
no longer have to hide, pretend, or justify myself, and I am
surrounded by loving people. This freedom has opened the
floodgates to let compassion and love flow from me. It is a
blessing.

Take the opportunity to meet your need for intimacy by
being fully authentic with at least one person today.

FEBRUARY 13

The story of a love is not important—what is important is that one is capable of love. It is perhaps the only glimpse we are permitted of eternity.
—Helen Hayes

Loving as an Expansion of Self

What a relief to feel love and to give love! There was a time when I didn't think I was capable of loving someone because I was convinced that loving others meant losing myself. Or that loving someone meant that I had to hurt in some way.

Today I know that we all have a tremendous capacity to love as long as we are willing to be authentic. The minute we start to attach rules and judgments to our love, or tell ourselves that we need to do something we don't want to do, we limit our capacity to love. If we take care of our own emotional needs, our ability to give and receive love grows exponentially.

Practice expressing your love authentically
and without rules today.

FEBRUARY 14

Life is the first gift, love is the second, and understanding the third.
—Marge Piercy

Getting Our Need for Love Met

"I just want you to love me." How many of us have either heard this or said it to someone else? How would it look if your need for love was met? Would someone say the words, "I love you"? Would they buy you flowers weekly, or spend time listening to you talk about your day, or is it a combination of things? Many people might think, "Well, any of those would work for me!" What would you like most?

Some people think that as they go through life, they will miraculously meet someone who will meet their need for love. It doesn't have to be that serendipitous. If you're in a relationship right now, consider what your partner could do to meet your need for love. Also consider your partner's need. Don't ask him to suddenly be able to connect to his feelings if that is a struggle for him. Based on who he is and who you are, how could your need for love be met? Be specific. General statements, such as "I just want you to love me" or "I would like you to be more attentive and listen to me more" won't work. He may already think he is attentive. What would being attentive look like to you? And how will he know if he's been attentive enough? We all want to contribute to one another's lives. No one is happy if he thinks his partner is unhappy in the relationship. It is our responsibility to help the people in our lives meet our needs for love.

If you are not in a relationship, consider what would best meet your needs for love. You may think of many ways, but what would feel best to you? By imagining, you can create possibilities and begin the manifestation process.

For today, make a specific list of things that
would meet your needs for love.

FEBRUARY 15

Life itself is the proper binge.
—*Julia Child*

Teaching People to Love Us in Ways We Enjoy

Several years ago, when I visited my parents, my mother bought candy as a welcoming gift for me. I was trying to avoid sugar, so I often felt annoyed by this. After one of these visits, the thought came to me that she bought candy to express her love. What if I created a new way for her to express it that felt better to me?

The next time I went home, Mom offered me candy. When I said no, she looked disappointed. So I said: "You know what I could really use, Mom, is new underwear. How would you feel about buying me new underwear?" She was delighted. Her face lit up and she said: "Oh, yes. Let's go shopping right now!" She ran and got her coat and purse and we were on our way. While we were at the mall, we picked up a few things for her, we had lunch, and we talked and laughed. It turned out to be a very sweet day. Could I buy my own underwear? Yes, of course. I was thirty-five years old at the time. But my mother adores me, she wants to contribute to my life, and I really did need new underwear. At first I felt a little embarrassed having her buy my underwear, but then I saw the sheer joy in her face.

We are a gift to the people who love us. Sometimes we need to help them find ways to express their love to us. It would be such a shame if we didn't give them opportunities to meet *their need* to contribute to *our life!*

Be aware today of people who are trying to express
their love to you, and help them do this in ways
that bring pleasure to you both.

FEBRUARY 16

Anyone who's a great kisser I'm always interested in.
—Cher

The Top Five Deal Breakers in Relationships

A friend of mine tells me that everyone should become
aware of their "top five deal breakers" in relationships.
These are things a person decides she must have in order to
be happy in a relationship. Usually, I hear people identify
their top five deal breakers as strategies, such as "I want him
to enjoy gardening, to be a good cook, to have a good job,"
etc. Instead, I suggest you look at needs that you are trying
to meet, and open yourself to a variety of strategies to meet
them. Focus on what you want from a relationship rather
than how it will look. Try "I want him to meet my needs for
love, courtesy, support, fairness, consideration, abundance,
and fun." See how many more ways the Universe can meet
your needs. For instance, maybe my need for abundance
can be met by someone who is independently wealthy, so
he doesn't have to "have a good job." When you shift your
focus from strategies to needs, you may be pleasantly surprised at what the Universe brings to you.

Today, express at least five needs you would like to
meet in a current or future relationship,
aloud and in writing.

FEBRUARY 17

I propose a new way. Radical Self-Acceptance.
Simply luxuriate in where you are right now.
—Sark

Body Image

Do you look at yourself in the mirror and think: "Ugh. How
did this happen?" Do you catch yourself being hyper-vigilant
about the parts of your body you wish looked different? If
we have a poor self-image, we usually have a great need for
acceptance and belonging, and we tell ourselves that it is
unlikely we will meet these needs if we look the way we do.
Our strategy is to change our physical appearance.

Like Sark, I embrace radical self-acceptance. Every
morning while you're lathering yourself in the shower, caress
every part of your body and say aloud all of the reasons you
appreciate it. In Toltec cultures, this is called a Puja. It is a
sacred act of honoring your body. If you say it aloud, it will
begin to shift the way your brain sees your body. Remember,
the brain believes what we tell it and helps us find ways to
prove what we believe. It wants to create truth. If we teach
our brain that we don't like our looks, it will help us make
that true. When we change the way we look at ourselves, we
change our truth and we can meet our needs for acceptance

and belonging. Try this and see if you experience a shift. For me, this is a powerful morning routine, as important as my meditations.

Try honoring your body with a Puja every
morning for the next two weeks.

FEBRUARY 18

*The first problem for all of us, men and women,
is not to learn, but to unlearn.*
—*Gloria Steinem*

Returning to Our Innate Selves

We are naturally compassionate. The desire to give and receive compassion is our innate way of being. Our task now is to unlearn the years of training that have taught us to fight for what we want, to fight to be right, to fight to win. It may feel awkward at first. Feeling awkward does not mean that something is unnatural, only that it is different. We can feel that way because we have been acculturated in a society that values winning more than compassion. As you shift your own values toward compassion, it will begin to feel natural to you, and you will have an increasing sense of returning home.

Make a conscious choice to return to your innate nature
of living compassionately today.

FEBRUARY 19

I kiss the God in you that allows you
to give us what you did.
—Nafez Assailey

Expressing Appreciation

Heartfelt appreciation expresses how a person's actions have influenced our life. It is about how we receive the actions, not about judging the person. If a friend takes time off work to drive you to the doctor's office, you could say, "You're great for taking me to the doctor." Such a comment, albeit a positive one, indicates you are in the position to judge that the other person is "great." It provides little information other than that her action is appreciated.

On the other hand, you could say, "I really appreciate you taking time off work to drive me to the doctor's office because I was feeling worried about this procedure, and I feel safer and more at ease with you here." Saying this provides the other person with more information, helps her understand how she contributed to you, and deepens your connection.

There are three steps to expressing appreciation using Compassionate Communication: First, state what the other person did (taking time off work to drive you to the doctor's office). Second, express your feelings (appreciation). Third, state your needs that were met (safety, support, and ease). If you'd like someone to fully understand how their actions have affected your life, and if you'd like to deepen your connection to that person, use these steps to express your appreciation.

Use the three steps outlined above to express
appreciation to at least one person today.

FEBRUARY 20

*One can know nothing of (anything) that is worthy
to give unless one also knows how to take.*
—Havelock Ellis

Receiving Appreciation

For many of us, receiving appreciation is a struggle. We
often react either with egotism, thinking that we're superior,
or by diminishing the appreciation, saying things like, "Oh,
it wasn't a big deal." or "This? I've had it for years!" Either
way, we're not fully letting in someone's appreciation of us.

Humility is the most successful way to accept appreciation. Acknowledge that the person's life has been affected
by your actions and enjoy the feeling of warmth you have
when you contribute to a life. When someone tells me that
she enjoyed a workshop I gave, I like to say: "I appreciate you
telling me that. I'm glad to hear that your needs were met
by the workshop." I don't walk away thinking I'm a "great
speaker." I just feel the warmth of knowing I stimulated
peace in someone's life.

Accept someone's appreciation today by
acknowledging how you feel when you hear
that you have enhanced her life.

FEBRUARY 21

I believe a leaf of grass is no less than
the journeywork of the stars . . .
—Walt Whitman

We Each Contribute to Our World

I recently heard an American Indian woman talking about her tribe. She said that her community believes that every single person has a purpose and a place in supporting the whole tribe. Sometimes the purpose is apparent. Sometimes it might appear that a person's contribution is negative. In the latter case, she believes it may take several generations before the person's contribution can be felt, and it may never be attributed to them. Still, everyone contributes to the tribe's evolution.

In some circles, I've heard it said that "God doesn't make mistakes." I believe this now, and it brings me comfort. I used to think that I was a mistake, that somehow I slipped through the cracks, that I wasn't really supposed to be here. That meant that I didn't have a "place" in the Universe. When I lived from this consciousness I felt sad, hurt, confused, and hopeless because I had such a longing to belong and to be valued. Today I feel comfort knowing that I do belong and that you belong. We each provide our own brand of support toward the evolution of living beings on earth. Thank you for doing your part.

Be aware that every person on this earth, including you,
is here for a specific purpose. Enjoy the peace
you might feel when you acknowledge this.

FEBRUARY 22

The best way out is always through.
—*Robert Frost*

Empowering Ourselves Through Our Choices

Every time we do something because we think we have to, or because we think we should, we are motivating ourselves through guilt and shame. How does it feel to do this? It can feel overwhelming and restricting. Sometimes, it can actually feel like there's a heavy weight on our chest. Try a new way—discard the words "I have to" and "I should" from your vocabulary and only do things you value doing. Maybe you're thinking: "That's impossible. There are some things we just have to do!"

Consider your job. Do you go to work in the morning because you have to or because you want to? You are in your job for a reason. Do you need the money? Do you live in a small town that you love, but which offers few good-paying jobs? Or are you working so your spouse can go to school? Whatever your reason, you are working to fulfill some life-enriching purpose. Connect to that purpose and change your language to "I'm going to work because I love living in this small town" or "because I value the options afforded by the money I make here." Shifting the energy that motivates our actions can bring empowerment and joy to our lives.

Notice today when you tell yourself that you have to do something. Then consider the underlying needs you are trying to meet with the activity.

FEBRUARY 23

Global peace.
Beginning from within,
One being at a time.
Because . . . YOUR PEACE COUNTS.
Be the cause of peace happening!
—Mackenzie Jordan

Make Peace in Your Life and
Make Peace in the World

Every minute we focus on what we want, we manifest its appearance into our lives. I started my enlightenment journey eighteen years ago. At that time, I was in so much emotional pain that I couldn't even imagine that peace was possible for me, and I certainly didn't imagine that I could contribute to a peaceful world. I often found myself slipping back into old behaviors, indulging in what seemed like endless hours mourning over past behaviors and agonizing over my decisions. I often thought that I wasn't getting anywhere—for all my work, effort, and suffering, I still wasn't happy. I didn't understand then that every moment I focused on my goal of peace in my relationships and within myself, I was shifting my consciousness. Even the moments filled with regret served my bigger goal because I was at least becoming more aware of my self-destructive behaviors. Each awareness, each action, each moment produced growth.

Some of us start in so much pain that it takes us longer to achieve peace, but it is available and possible for all of us. Even more remarkable, when we bring peace to our own lives, we contribute to world peace. Think about the image of a small pebble that is dropped into a calm pond. The pebble causes ripples that reverberate to each shore. Even a small pebble makes an impact. So do you. Focus on bringing peace into your own life and your shift in consciousness will reverberate throughout the world.

Make a conscious effort to focus on what
you want most in your world today.

FEBRUARY 24

*What would make you happy? It's a simple question,
but one with profound consequences. Asking and
answering that question, then acting on it, is often
our path—a path that will lead to the next step,
a path that is in our best interest.*
—*Melody Beattie*

The Importance of Making Requests

Have you ever waited in a restaurant for a friend who finally shows up a half hour later than you agreed? When she walks in, you may say in the best Compassionate Communication you can muster: "There you are! You know, when you show up a half hour later than we agreed, I feel pretty annoyed because I have such a limited lunch hour and I'd like to know if I should go ahead and order, or just wait a few more minutes."

Notice that there is no request with this statement, only what you would like. Requests are a specific action to help you get your needs met. There are two kinds of requests.

One is for action, asking someone to do something specific such as washing the dishes within a half hour. The other is for connection, asking someone to do something that will help you connect to each other, such as asking her to reflect back what you said, or asking her to tell you how she feels about what you said. If we don't make specific requests, people are left guessing and/or wondering about what will meet our needs. Under these circumstances, our chances for getting our needs met are limited at best.

So try ending with this request: "There you are! You know, when you show up a half hour later than we agreed, I feel pretty annoyed because I have such a limited lunch hour, and I'd like to know if I should go ahead and order, or just wait a few more minutes. *Would you be willing to call me the next time you think you might be running more than ten minutes late?*" Another request might be, *"Would you help me understand why you are so late?"* Any request will help complete the communication and let the other person know exactly what you would like to happen.

Be aware of opportunities to make specific requests
today that will help you get what you want.

FEBRUARY 25

That is why whenever we make assumptions, we're asking for problems. We make an assumption, we misunderstand, we take it personally, and we end up creating a whole big drama for nothing.
—Don Miguel Ruiz

Nothing But the Facts

Observation free of judgment, evaluation, or a story about why somebody said or did something is critical to creating a connection with others and maintaining a Nonviolent Communication consciousness. There is often a large gap between what we experience and the story we make up about it.

Imagine you see someone driving down the road twenty miles over the speed limit. A common judgment I used to have was, "What a jerk!" In fact, the only information I have is that this person is driving twenty miles over the speed limit. I know nothing else about his story. His gas pedal may be stuck, he may be rushing his sick mother to the hospital, or he may just enjoy driving fast. The observation in this situation is that the person is driving twenty miles over the speed limit. When I judge the situation by calling him a name, I cloud my ability to be present to him and to see him as a human being. When I have the presence to simply observe the facts of the situation, I am less judgmental of him and more at peace with myself.

Be aware of how your judgments
cloud your observations today.

FEBRUARY 26

When we appreciate and honor the beauty of life,
we will make every effort to dwell deeply in the
present moment and protect all life.
—Thich Nhat Hahh

Differentiating Needs From Strategies

Sometimes it is hard to remember that needs are universal and strategies are specific. Strategies are the methods we use to get our needs met. When we focus on needs, our world can feel abundant with possibility. When we focus on a particular strategy, our world can feel scarce. Conflicts arise when we argue for a strategy. Resolution comes only when we value everyone's needs and seek mutually satisfying solutions. This sounds easy, but sometimes we don't have the clarity of mind to understand that there are countless strategies to meet each of our needs. Letting go of a single-minded focus on our strategy is a paradigm shift in itself.

Say you call a friend and ask her to go to a movie. She says she's tired and doesn't want to go out. Would you say thank you and hang up? Another method is to focus on both your needs. Is your need fun and connection with your friend? Is her need rest and relaxation? How could you both get your needs met in this situation? How about you pick up a movie and dinner and bring them to her house? In the meantime, she can take a bath and a short nap and put on her jammies. The evening may look different than you had originally planned, but will your needs still be met? Focus on the needs, even when you feel hurt, sad, disappointed, and vulnerable, and watch your world open with possibilities. If you are having trouble coming up with any other strategy than your first choice, be honest about this and ask for support.

Create a small list of the ways you
could meet a need today.

FEBRUARY 27

*I want to connect more than I want to be right
and more than I want to win!*
—*Mary Mackenzie*

Connection, Connection, Connection

Do you get into "right fights"? You know you're in one when you're arguing with somebody in order to be right or because you want to win. In these arguments, we are rarely trying to connect. Being right is the name of the game. Why do we do this? For many, it is an attempt to meet needs for safety, acceptance, and understanding. What we usually receive, though, is discontentment, discord, and hopelessness.

What would happen if we wanted to connect more than we wanted to be right or win arguments? This theme is actually my personal mantra. In charged conversations, it can be easy to forget our goal to connect because we are so experienced in right fights. Consider trying to center yourself in these moments by asking yourself: "What do I want? What needs do I hope to meet from winning or being right?" No matter what the situation is, try this answer, "To connect!" And ask, "Am I likely to be successful if I say what is on the tip of my tongue?" Invariably, the answer is no. By simply grounding yourself with these questions and considering other strategies you could use to meet your needs, you will be more able to empathize with the other, and to express your feelings compassionately. As a result, you will enjoy deeper, more meaningful relationships, while reducing the frequency of judgments you have of yourself and others.

Notice if you enter into a right fight today and shift your focus to connecting with the other person.

FEBRUARY 28

You never know what is enough until you
know what is more than enough.
—William Blake

Defining Enough

Do you ever find yourself working and working, but not really knowing what success would look like? Several years ago, I realized that I spent a lot of my energy striving to be the best, but because I didn't know what the best was, I never achieved my goal. There was always someone better, something else I could be learning, and something else I should be doing. It was a relentless search for an impossible goal. This focus brought enormous pain and disappointment into my life.

So I set out to discover for myself what "enough" would look like. For me, it's simply doing my best in any moment. Sometimes, if I'm tired and feeling sick, my best looks different than when I am rested and fit. If I catch myself criticizing my performance, I ask myself if I am doing my best in that moment, and if there is anything else I could do to help the situation. If the answer is that I'm already doing my best, I can relax. If there is something else I can do, I do that. It's no longer about performing to some unknown standard; it's more about showing up to the best of my ability in each situation, and being content with that. It's enough for me to simply do my best. What is enough for you? How much money is enough? How big a house is enough? Define enough. If you have more work to do to achieve it, consider what you could do right now that would head you in the direction of attaining your goal. If you have already achieved it, celebrate!

Identify one goal and one thing you can do today
to achieve that goal and do it.

FEBRUARY 29

The deepest need of man is the need to overcome his separateness, to leave the prison of his aloneness.
—Erich Fromm

Opening to Intimacy

Some time ago, I was at a gathering of two thousand people. I was feeling very sad, vulnerable, and lonely, so I chose to sit by myself in a crowd of people I didn't know. Then I heard my name blaring across the crowd. A group of my friends were calling me over to sit with them. They were screaming for me to join them over the chattering of thousands of people. I chose to stay where I was because I thought I wanted to be alone with my vulnerability.

Later, I talked with one of those friends about the situation, and she said: "I can guarantee you didn't want to be alone, Mary. You were just too uncomfortable to trust that we could love you even in your sad and vulnerable state. Do you think that to be our friend, you always have to be fun or you always have to be ready to listen to our disappointments?" What a revelation this was. I suddenly saw a pattern I have used my entire life—when I'm lonely and vulnerable, I insist on being alone. Not because that's what I want (let's face it, this solution will certainly not relieve my loneliness), but because I don't trust that my friends will love me even in my lowest moments. In reality, they would probably have helped me heal from that difficult night much sooner than I was able to alone.

Intimacy is what most people want when they feel vulnerable and sad. Do you have behavioral patterns that block intimacy? When we are feeling our most vulnerable, we often want intimacy but also tend to keep it at bay. Acknowledge your need for intimacy, and find people you can trust to love.

Notice if your behaviors block your success
in meeting your need for intimacy.

76

Meditations for
MARCH

MARCH 1

To bring forth the soul of our being, we must be in
our bodies, rooted to Earth, able to draw from the
universal source of energy.
—Diane Mariechild

Connecting to Self

Have you ever tried to engage in a conversation with someone, but had to struggle to stay present? Or have you tried to resolve a conflict with someone, but spent most of the time dealing with the chatter in your own head? In my experience, what we do in these situations is get stuck in our own chatter. When this happens, we cannot heal or resolve the issue. I spent years in anguish, and it wasn't until I learned self-empathy in the Nonviolent Communication process that I started to experience relief. At first I wondered if empathizing with myself would be a never-ending procedure. What I learned, though, was that I had years of unresolved issues to acknowledge and heal. Eventually, through consistent self-empathy, I healed enough to allow myself to be present in interactions with others. The chatter quieted. It is such a relief to be present to myself and to the people in my life. I wish everyone knew how much connecting to and healing ourselves can improve our relationships with others.

The four steps to self-empathy are:

Enjoy the jackal show—acknowledge the judgments you have in the situation.
Feelings—connect with how you feel.

Needs—connect with the universal needs that are unmet in the situation.

Request—notice whether you would like to make a request of someone else to help meet your needs.

Through self-empathy, you will be more present to yourself and to others in your life.

Take a moment to empathize with yourself today.
Notice how you feel afterward.

MARCH 2

*All you need to do to receive guidance is
to ask for it and then listen.*
—*Sanaya Roman*

Know Your Truth

Many people let others' opinions determine how they judge their own actions. Some people think it's OK to take pens from the office because "everyone does it." Or they think that it's OK to keep the extra change that the cashier gave by mistake because "it was her error, not mine." Integrity is about showing up day after day in harmony with our own values. I don't want to kick my dog even though my neighbors might think it's OK. I don't want to spank my children just because my parents spanked me. I want to decide what is in harmony with my values and act accordingly. Only then is my need for integrity met. Social norms no longer matter to me or influence me. My values guide my behaviors and choices.

What are your deepest values? Are your actions in harmony with them?

> Notice if your actions are in harmony
> with your values today.

✳

MARCH 3

Knowing is not enough; we must apply.
Willing is not enough; we must do.
—*Goethe*

Become Willing to Express Appreciation

Many of us are reluctant to express appreciation because we think that means we are brown-nosing, or because we think the other person doesn't want to hear from us. Indeed, if you use appreciation as a manipulative tool to get what you want, you are misusing it. But if someone has enriched your life in some way, I suggest you tell him about it. Your appreciation might be just the gift he needs to brighten his day.

A few years ago, I received a phone call from someone who had attended one of my trainings. She told me that she was moved to call and tell me how the training she attended had changed her life. She expressed hope and joy, which she hadn't felt for several years. We both cried on the phone: she because she was so full of love, and I because I felt such appreciation that she had gone out of her way to tell me how I had touched her life. I have yet to meet one person who doesn't want to contribute to another's life, and I have yet to meet one person who doesn't enjoy hearing how he has done so.

Express your appreciation to at least one person today.

MARCH 4

*By developing a vocabulary of feelings
that allows us to clearly and specifically name or
identify our emotions, we can connect more easily
with one another. Allowing ourselves to be vulnerable
by expressing our feelings can help resolve conflicts.*
—*Marshall B. Rosenberg, PhD*

How to Express Feelings

Expressing how we feel about something gives the other person an idea of how important it is to us. It lets them know how we feel: for instance, mildly annoyed, angry, or deeply hurt. Perhaps you think people will know this simply from your tone of voice, but feelings of hurt, anger, fear, and resentment can often sound alike. Fear and excitement have the same physiological effects on us, and are often expressed in the same body language. It is our responsibility to express ourselves fully, rather than expecting the people in our life to guess how we feel. When we are explicit, we have a much greater opportunity to get our needs met.

For today, fully express to at least one person
how you feel in a situation.

MARCH 5

*Any change in one part of your life
affects all other parts.*
—*Gloria Karpinski*

Enjoying the Jackal Show

When I am emotionally charged, my brain can begin an
internal chatter that keeps me from focusing on the situation
I'm in. Before I learned Compassionate Communication, I
tried to ignore this chatter or censor it by thinking: "Oh,
Mary, you shouldn't feel that way. Don't be so impatient.
She's not feeling well, you know." My self-censorship kept
me frustrated and agitated. Now, when I allow my inner
jackals to have voice and I listen to what they need, I can feel
calm in a few seconds. In Nonviolent Communication, this
is called *enjoying the jackal show*. In this instance, "enjoying"
refers to the kind of pleasure we get from peacefulness, calm,
or clarity rather than the kind of fun we might experience
eating an ice cream cone with a friend.

Some time ago, a sick friend asked me to take her mail to
the post office. She proceeded to tell me how to separate local
and out-of-state mail and exactly which mailbox to use for
each. I had gone through a particularly tiring day and had a
need for ease. When she started with the specific instructions,
my inner jackal started in with: "Has she noticed that I am

forty-six years old? Am I the only one who notices this? Really, I have mailed thousands of letters during my lifetime all by myself. No wonder she doesn't feel well; she spends so much time controlling every detail of her life!" My jackals can be very biting and judgmental. After hearing this for a few moments, I began to empathize with myself by thinking: "Mary, are you tired and want ease? Are you annoyed and want your friend to respect your ability to figure things out on your own?" Connecting to myself in this way only took a few seconds and helped me to become more present to the situation at hand—my friend's illness and my own need for ease. So I said to her, "You know, I'm noticing how tired I am and I'd like ease with this situation, so would you be willing to trust my ability to mail your letters without further instructions on how to do it?" She said: "Oh! Sure." Off I went to the post office, still feeling tired but less agitated.

Enjoying the jackal show is being present to what the jackals are telling you, including the underlying needs they are trying to meet. Our jackals hold wisdom and relief for us if we listen to them.

Be aware of your inner jackal chatter today and make a commitment to listen for the underlying needs they are trying to tell you about.

MARCH 6

*Just as splinters get embedded in our body, old
emotions and beliefs can act like toxins and become
embedded in us, too. Now is a time of cleansing.*
—Melody Beattie

Life-Alienating Communication

We have all learned patterns of speech that keep us separate
from other people. These patterns can look like judgments,
criticisms, and blame, and they are prevalent in our society.
In each case, the speaker separates herself from the listener
by preoccupying herself with moralistic judgments. She
categorizes others as good or bad, right or wrong. She makes
comparisons, denies responsibility for her actions and choices,
or makes demands of others, threatening them with blame
or punishment if they fail to comply. Marshall B. Rosenberg,
PhD, who developed the Nonviolent Communication
process, call these speech patterns tragic, life-alienating
expressions of unmet needs. In each case, we do things in an
attempt to meet needs, but because of our communication
technique, we rarely meet them.

Life-alienating communication may seem easy sometimes
because it's familiar, but the results are also painfully familiar.
And when we engage in it we miss opportunities to meet our
needs for caring, love, nurturing, honesty, intimacy, and many
others.

Be aware of times when you are judging others, making
comparisons, or denying responsibility for your actions.
Notice how these communication patterns affect your
connection with other people.

MARCH 7

The only way to master love, is to practice love.
—*Don Miguel Ruiz*

Every Angry Message Is a "Please"

Sometimes it is hard to remember, but every time someone speaks or acts in anger or frustration, he is saying "Please!" Consider the please when your child says, "We NEVER get to do what I want to do!" The child is saying: "Please, I want fairness and fun. I want to know that you care about my needs, too." How about when your wife says to you as you walk in the front door: "Where have you been? I've been waiting for you for an HOUR!" Perhaps underneath this statement, she is saying, "Would you please consider my needs for predictability, respect, and trust?"

OK, maybe these are too obvious. What is the "please" behind your boss's statement? "This presentation was deplorable. The computer didn't operate properly, the graphics were juvenile, and the timing didn't work. I was embarrassed to present this to the Board, and it must not happen again." Maybe she's saying "please" to higher-quality presentations and maintaining a certain image with the Board.

The next time someone expresses their disappointment, frustration, or anger toward you, take a moment to consider the "please" behind their words. When you do this, you have a much greater opportunity to resolve conflicts peacefully.

When a person's communication is difficult to hear, notice the "please" behind it. When you can hear it as "please," does it shift how you feel?

MARCH 8

We cannot defend freedom abroad
while deserting it at home.
—Edward R. Murrow

Interdependence vs. Dependence/Independence

Interdependence, in a Nonviolent Communication process, assumes that each person is autonomous. It refers to a consciousness that values everyone's needs equally, recognizes that all people have choices and are responsible for their actions, and focuses on abundance rather than scarcity. Autonomous people come together because they recognize that by doing so, they have more abundance and strength. This applies to intimate relationships, businesses, church groups—any people who come together to achieve a greater goal.

The dependence/independence paradigm assumes that either we have to be with someone else to be whole, or that we don't need other people at all. This fosters the beliefs that we are dependent on others to achieve happiness, that everyone is responsible for others' actions and feelings, and that we must focus on scarcity rather than abundance.

When we maintain an interdependent consciousness, we expand the possibilities in all our relationships.

Make a commitment to live autonomously today.
Notice where it is a challenge for you to
maintain this consciousness.

MARCH 9

Judgments, criticisms, diagnoses, and interpretations
of others are all alienated expressions of our needs.
If someone says, "You never understand me,"
they are really telling us that their need to
be understood is not being fulfilled.
—Marshall B. Rosenberg, PhD

A Focus on Needs

Imagine that your wife comes home from work and you ask her to go dancing and she says: "Oh no, not tonight, honey. I'm just beat after a long week." It sounds as if she might need rest and relaxation. Let's imagine that your needs are for fun and physical activity. Can you think of another strategy that could meet both your needs and hers for the evening? How about you work out at the club and bring home a movie and dinner afterward? Or maybe you both stay home tonight and rest, but make a date to go dancing tomorrow night. Or your partner could take a nap, and afterward you spend the evening in bed making love. There are endless ways to meet our needs. Conflict occurs when we argue over strategies, like whether to go dancing or not. When we actively value everyone's needs, we foster openness and deeper connection in our relationships.

Be aware of opportunities to focus on needs in order to resolve an issue with at least one person today.

MARCH 10

Why do you walk through the field in gloves
When the grass is soft as the breasts of doves
And shivering sweet to the touch?
—Frances Comford

Hearing a Yes Behind a Perceived Rejection

It is often easy for us to hear rejection when someone says no to us. If we focus on the rejection, we may feel hurt and fail to take the time to understand what is going on with them. However, if we focus on their feelings and needs, we are more likely to uncover what they want and what prevents them from complying with our request.

Say you asked your partner to clean out the truck to prepare for your weekend trip. He says, "No, the game is about to start and I want to watch it." You could hear this as a rejection, or you could hear the yes behind his no and say, "You've been looking forward to watching this game all week, haven't you?" He may say: "Yeah, I have. And I'd like to watch the game without having other responsibilities. I really want this time to myself." You could say: "I can really understand the need to relax. I'd like you to have this time to yourself and I'm also worried about getting everything done before our trip. After the game, would you be willing to brainstorm with me how we might get the truck cleaned?"

If we hear what the other person is saying yes to (in this case, a relaxing afternoon watching the game), rather than what he is saying no to (cleaning the truck instead of watching the game), we are more likely to succeed in getting our needs met and helping the people we love get theirs met too. This is a way of valuing the other's needs as much as our own, and can be a powerful conflict resolution tool.

> Be aware of at least one opportunity today to
> hear someone's yes behind their no.

MARCH 11

*Avoid using the word to speak against yourself or
to gossip about others. Use the power of your word
in the direction of truth and love.*
—Don Miguel Ruiz

Four Ways to Hear Any Message

How do you hear other people? In Nonviolent Communication, we see four possible ways to hear any message:

Judging or blaming others: You never think about my needs, or You're always late.

Judging or blaming ourselves: I should be more loving and caring to others, or He's right, I *am* always late.

Empathizing with ourselves: I feel sad and hurt because I'd like her to understand where I'm coming from. When I show up later than I agreed to, I feel sad and disappointed because I want my friends to trust me.

Empathizing with others: Are you disappointed because you'd like to know that I value your needs as much as mine? Are you angry and wanting some reassurance that I'll show up when I say I will?

In every interaction, we have a choice of responding in one of these four ways. The goal is to make a conscious choice about our response. The more present we are to ourselves and our needs, the more likely we are to see our choices.

Notice the choices you have when you receive someone's communication today.

MARCH 12

A theme may seem to have been put aside, but it keeps returning—the same thing modulated, somewhat changed in form.
—Muriel Rukeyser

Defining Needs

In Compassionate Communication, we define needs as resources that life requires to sustain itself. Our physical well-being depends on our needs for air, water, food, rest, and shelter. Our psychological and emotional well-being relies on support, love, nurturing, honesty, and care. All human beings have the same needs. Regardless of our race, spiritual upbringing, how we live, or where we live, we all have the same needs to sustain our lives. The difference is in the strategies we use to meet those needs. We all have a need for play, but we have different strategies to meet it. I like to ride horses, hike, and go to movies to meet my need for play. Other people might enjoy extreme sports, knitting, or scuba diving. The need is the same in all cases—play. The strategy is what we do to meet that need.

Needs are universal; everyone has the same ones. Strategies are specific; we all choose unique ways to meet our needs. The more we can separate the need from the strategy, the more likely we are to resolve conflicts with ease.

Be aware of the differences between
your needs and strategies today.

MARCH 13

*With every choice you make, be conscious
of what need it serves.*
—Marshall B. Rosenberg, PhD

Saying Thank You Without Judgment

In Compassionate Communication, we believe that everything a person says or does is either a "please" or a "thank you." In our culture, saying "thank you" usually involves an expression of appreciation in the form of a judgment or evaluation. Remember, judgments and evaluations can create disconnection or tension in our relationships. This is true whether we judge someone as good or bad. Say your son mowed the lawn and you said, "Son, you're great." In this statement, you express appreciation by judging him as great. A way of expressing appreciation that is clearer and connects you to him is to tell him how his actions enriched your life. This could sound like, "Son, when you mowed the lawn as you promised, I felt such relief and appreciation because I really value follow-through and trust."

When you hear "thank you" today, notice how your actions have enriched the person's life. When you become aware of it, do you feel it differently?

MARCH 14

*I'm no longer afraid of storms, for I am
learning how to sail my own ship.*
—Louisa May Alcott

Achieving Safety

I spent most of my life looking for my personal safety in other people. With this attitude, I spent a great deal of time determining whether someone was safe or not, judging other people as abusive, and blaming other people when I felt hurt or disappointed. The result was that I felt afraid because I depended on others to keep me safe, and I didn't feel empowered to manage my own life. Nonviolent Communication teaches that safety is not something that other people can provide. I can best meet my needs for safety when I gain trust in my ability to take care of myself. In this model, safety can come from such tools as learning ways to meet my own needs, speaking up when I am unhappy or worried, and trusting my own instincts. When I trust myself, I am empowered to stop looking to others for my safety.

Be aware of how you look to other people
to meet your need for safety.

MARCH 15

Check with your body. It knows almost instantly
if the connection is a good one.
—Sark

Empathy vs. Sympathy

When we sympathize, we relate an aspect of someone's story to ourselves, such as when we say: "Oh, I know just how you feel. Last week he did the same thing to me." Another example is: "It's going to be OK. You'll see. I've been through this. Next week you'll feel much better about it!" When we empathize, we reflect the feelings and needs of the other, saying something like "So, you're really worried and want resolution soon?" or "Are you shocked and seeking clarity about why this happened?" Both methods have their value, but in a Nonviolent Communication process, we prefer empathy because it helps people connect more deeply to their own and other's pain, and helps resolve issues with clarity and ease. Empathy is a profound healing technique.

Be aware of when you are giving someone sympathy
rather than empathizing today.

MARCH 16

Every thought is new when an author expresses
it in a manner peculiar to himself.
—Marquis de Vauvenargues

Idiomatic vs. Formal Compassionate Communication

Do you sometimes feel awkward when you use the four components of Compassionate Communication (observation, feeling, need, request)? The four components are a tool to help people interact with others in a connected and compassionate manner. Formal use of the language is very valuable for people just learning the Compassionate Communication process. However, the true foundation of Compassionate Communication is to maintain a consciousness that values everyone's needs. If you can truly maintain that consciousness without using the formality of the four components, go for it! For example, formal use of the four components might be: "When you make applesauce with sugar, and I'm allergic to sugar, I feel frustrated and confused, because I value my health. Would you be willing to make another batch for me that doesn't have sugar?" Idiomatic Compassionate Communication could sound like this: "Your applesauce has sugar in it? Oh, I'm really bummed cause I was excited about having some, but I get sick when I eat sugar. How would you feel about making a small batch without sugar for me?" Both methods mentioned an observation, feeling, need, and request. To some, the second method would sound more fitting for everyday conversation. Both of them, however, are honest and connecting.

Be aware of when you are using idiomatic or formal
Compassionate Communication today.

94

It is tempting to sleepwalk through life.
To tell half-truths, listen halfway, be half-asleep,
drive with half attention . . . Wake Up!
—Sark

Honesty Is the Key

Do you sometimes struggle with honesty? Do you ever have something you'd like to say to someone, but worry about how she will receive it? In Nonviolent Communication, we see expressing honesty as a gift of our authenticity, and an opportunity for others to support us in getting our needs met. When we are honest with others, we give our relationships an opportunity to flourish and deepen. When we are not honest, we tend to create resentments and judgments, which bring discord and emotional distance to relationships. The four components to expressing ourselves honestly are:

Observation: expressing the facts of what happened.
Feeling: expressing how we felt about it.
Need: clarifying our needs that were met or unmet.
Request: making a specific and doable request.

Notice and act on opportunities to be honest
and authentic with someone today.

MARCH 18

To practice nonviolence, first of all we must
learn to deal peacefully with ourselves.
—*Thich Nhat Hanh*

Making Demands

When we ask something of a person and there will be negative repercussions if she doesn't comply with our wish, we are actually making a demand. When we do this, she has only two possible responses: to rebel or to submit. Hard to believe? Consider what happens when you tell your sixteen-year-old daughter that she can't go out with her friends tonight. She can submit by doing as you say, or she can rebel by either sneaking out of the house to be with her friends or arguing with you. How about if you told your partner that you just have to have sex at least twice a week? Again, she can submit by giving you what you want, or she can rebel by withholding. Rarely does either party experience satisfaction when someone submits to them, or rebels against them. You may get what you want, but she may be negative or disgruntled. If your partner increases her sex activity because she's worried you'll be upset, she will likely participate with less creativity and enjoyment. This dynamic limits both people's chance for enjoyment. Neither submission nor rebellion is a win for anyone. Demands limit the possible responses, and deaden the opportunity for joyful participation. You will have more success in getting your needs met by considering everyone's needs and coming to mutually satisfying resolutions.

Notice when a request you make today is actually a demand. Is there a way you can change it into a request?

MARCH 19

Tell me who admires you and loves you,
and I will tell you who you are.
—*Charles Augustin Sainte-Beauve*

Overcoming Insecurity in Friendships

Do you ever wonder why a person you enjoy spending time with is attracted to you? Do you wonder if he really likes you? Many of us don't know the impact we have on other people. Sometimes, with close friends and family, it is clear to us why people value having us in their lives. And, sometimes it's just not. Wonder no more. Now is the time to take action. Consider asking a question using all four components of Compassionate Communication:

Observation: "Sometimes when we're together
Feeling: I feel a little awkward and I'm telling myself that you probably have much more important things to do.
Need: I like the intimacy that I experience when I spend time with you.
Request: Would you be willing to tell me what needs of yours are met by spending time with me?"

Such a question can bring deeper connection as both of you voice the needs that are met by your friendship. It can also be such a relief to know what's going on with the other person, rather than wondering about it.

Ask at least one friend how being your friend enhances her life today.

MARCH 20

Love is, above all, the gift of oneself.
—Jean Anouilh

Asking for Acceptance

A friend of mine recently told her spouse that she wanted him to accept a particular aspect of her personality that he has struggled with. If he accepts it, it doesn't mean that he has to agree with it or enjoy it. Nor does it prevent him from taking care of himself if her behavior stimulates pain in him. It simply means that he accepts that her behavior is a part of her totality, and decides he can live with it. Who among us could honestly love every single aspect of our partner's personality and every single behavior? What an onerous task that would be. But many of us can appreciate our partner's whole being and the many ways that he contributes to our life. This is acceptance.

Notice an aspect of one person's personality today that you don't usually enjoy. Then decide whether you are willing to accept it as part of the whole person.

MARCH 21

Let him that would move the world,
first move himself.
—Socrates

Being the Change We Seek

I spent much of my life wanting more intimacy, joy, and connectedness, and I wanted other people to provide them for me. At one time in my life, I was frustrated because in staff meetings the participants weren't connecting with one another as much as I wanted them to. This didn't meet my needs for integrity because Compassionate Communication had taught me how to create deep connections. I felt a great deal of pain around this issue for months. Then, one morning I woke up with a message running through my head: *"Mary, if you want deeper connections, then connect! Don't expect other people to do it for you."* I started to argue with myself. "Oh, I couldn't do that. I'm embarrassed. What if no one else wants to connect? What if . . . " *"What was it you wanted again?"* "I want to be more connected with the staff in our meetings." Finally I got it. I wasn't willing to connect with them but I wanted them to connect with me! I had set up a difficult situation for my colleagues and myself. So, with a great deal of fear, I attended the next staff meeting with an intention of connecting. I did this for the next three staff meetings in a row. Two participants mentioned how much they appreciated my behavior, and how much it helped everyone shift their attitude about staff meetings!

Is there something you would like more of in your life right now? Try not to look to other people to provide the kind of experiences you want. Can you think of a way that you can be the change you seek? Be those experiences yourself, and then watch the miracle of transformation happen.

Make a conscious effort today to respond to
the people in your life the way you would
want them to respond to you.

MARCH 22

All that we are arises with our thoughts.
With our thoughts, we make our world.
—Buddha

Change Your Thoughts to Change Your World

If you want to live more compassionately, begin to notice the thoughts you have about yourself or other people. If you find yourself judging or criticizing, work on shifting your attitude.

Several years ago, I became aware of my judgmental thoughts about others and made a commitment to shift them. Over the years, several people had told me that I was too stern and gruff. For a long time, I thought it was their problem until I realized that I simply didn't have meaningful relationships, and that my behavior turned people off. Then I focused primarily on my judgments of others. Every time I had a judgmental thought about someone, I translated it into my feelings and needs. I would translate a thought such as, "Could you be any slower?" into thinking, "I'm feeling frustrated because I'd really like to get to the movie on time." I made a translation every time I caught myself judging someone. Then I started translating negative messages I thought about myself every time I noticed them. Four months later, I started feeling different, and people started to say that I seemed softer and more joyful. It was amazing. Change your thoughts and you change your life.

Just for today, try to notice when you have judgmental
thoughts about yourself or other people. Then try to
translate those thoughts into your feelings and needs.

MARCH 23

*Look forward to the power of love replacing the
love of power. Then we will know peace.*
—*William Gladstone*

Love Trumps Everything

You'd really like the dishes to be done right after dinner, so you try to force your teenage son to do them each night. Or, maybe you'd like your employees to arrive at work promptly at eight in the morning, so you create punishments if they don't comply. You think you have some power because of your position as parent or supervisor, and you might even think you're wiser than the others. But how much fun is it, really, to try to force people to do what you want? How much fun is it, really, to wield power over other people? Take a few minutes to connect with other people about why they don't want to do the dishes right after dinner tonight, or why they struggle to come in at eight in the morning, and then create solutions that meet both your needs. It is a loving thing to do. It's loving because you are taking the time to consider their needs rather than just focusing on getting what you want. Such a basic shift in consciousness can make a profound difference in your relationships, both personal and professional. Love trumps everything.

Create an opportunity to connect with other people's needs when determining a solution to an issue. Notice how you feel afterward.

MARCH 24

What loneliness is more lonely than distrust?
—*George Eliot*

Meeting Our Need for Trust

I once dated someone whose stories changed frequently. He always had an explanation if I asked him about them. Other times, he told me things that I simply didn't believe. Still, I questioned my own reality throughout the year we dated. I didn't focus on whether *my needs for trust were being met.* I focused on *whether he was telling the truth.* In a sense, I tried to meet my needs for trust by listening to someone else's reality. I learned a valuable lesson in this relationship. It doesn't matter what the truth is. What matters is whether my need for trust is met. I don't have to blame other people and think of them as liars. I only have to focus on whether my needs are met. If they aren't, I make specific requests to meet my needs, while also respecting the other person's needs. This shift in focus has dramatically improved my relationships.

Be aware today of times when your need for trust is not met and what you can request when it isn't.

MARCH 25

Freedom is the supreme good—freedom
from self-imposed limitation.
—Elbert Hubbard

Safe Experimentation

Do you ever find yourself trying for perfection, and then feeling discouraged at your progress? Harrumph! Let's make a pact for today that we won't even try for perfection. It isn't possible, anyway, and expecting it limits our ability to feel joy. So let's just set it aside. Instead of perfection, let's try safe experimentation: Acknowledge that whenever we try a new behavior, it's bound to take us a few times before we get it right.

Let's use learning empathy as an example. Empathy is listening for the feelings and needs of another person. Pick just one person today to empathize with. It could be your boss, colleague, friend, child, partner, or mother. Anyone will do—even the cashier at the grocery store. If that person expresses some discomfort, sadness, hurt, or any emotion, simply say back their feelings and needs. Here's an example. When getting your car fixed, you ask the owner how things are going. He says: "Really well, actually. I hate to complain about business, but man, we are so busy it's hard to keep up." Any idea what his feelings and needs might be? How about trying this: "Kind of a double bind, huh? On the one hand you're glad for the extra work, but on the other you're kind of overwhelmed?" "Yeah, exactly." Bingo. You've just empathized with your car mechanic. Then, notice how you feel afterward, and how you think the other person might feel.

Remember, we're not looking for perfection. We're looking for safe experimentation.

Try empathizing with one person today and
then notice how you feel afterward.

MARCH 26

Rejection is divine intervention.
—Author unknown

Accepting Outcomes

Have you ever wanted something that you didn't get? At first you might have felt disappointed and hurt, maybe even discouraged, and told yourself that you had been rejected. But then something you liked even better came along and suddenly you were relieved that the first thing hadn't happened. Phew, another close call! Let's use this as a model to view rejection another way. Years ago someone told me that "rejection is divine intervention." This was a revelation to me. Imagine seeing all rejection this way. And why not? If we believe that everything happens for a reason and every person is here for a reason, why not also believe that a sacred power is working on our behalf even when we don't get what we think we want? Our job is to do our footwork every day, which means that we do whatever we can to create peace and joy in our world. The Universe will take care of the rest. What a relief!

If you experience rejection today, remind yourself that rejection is divine intervention and notice how this changes the way you feel.

MARCH 27

Never let yesterday use up today.
—R.H. Nelson

Staying in the Present

How often do you worry about the future or fret about the past? Usually if we are in anguish, it's because we're not in the present. Let's say you're worrying about how to pay your rent. Is it due today? If not, you're worrying about the future. Is there anything you can do today to help you pay the rent when it's due? If so, do it. If not, does it help the situation for you to worry about it? Or say that you feel sad about what you said to your mom last night. Is there anything you can do about it now? If so, do it. If not, does it help you to fret about it? When you notice that you're worrying or fretting, look to see if there is anything you can do in the present moment to rectify the situation. If there is, take action. If there isn't, stop worrying. Stay in the present.

Remind yourself a few times throughout your day
to focus on the present moment.

MARCH 28

. . . Words are a form of action, capable of influencing change. Their articulation represents a complete, lived experience.
—*Ingrid Bengis*

The Timing of Making a Request

It is important to keep a few things in mind when we make a request of someone. The request should be specific. If it seems vague to you, it will probably be vague to the other person. A request should also be doable. If you want something that you don't think a person can do, consider asking someone else, or consider something else this person could do to help you meet your need.

One of the most important aspects of a request is that it be expressed immediately after you have stated your observation, feeling, and need with regard to a particular situation. Let's say that you are picking up your wool sweater from the dry cleaner. Your sweater arrived as a size twelve but now it is a size two, so you say to the manager, "When I see the new size of my sweater I feel annoyed because I would like to trust that your employees will take care of my belongings." You expressed the observation, feeling, and need, but not a request. As a result the manager is likely to feel defensive and worried and might start to explain what happened, defend his employees, or respond in any number of other ways. Essentially he has to guess what you want from him. If you had ended your statement with a specific request, such as reimbursement for the cost of the sweater, he would know exactly what you wanted. He could choose to pay you the amount you requested, or the two of you could negotiate a final settlement. When we express a request immediately after we state our observation, feeling, and need, we bring clarity to the situation and lessen the potential for defensiveness or argument. Without a swift request, the other person is left guessing what we want.

Notice opportunities to make a swift and specific
request today and how this helps clarify the
situation for you both.

MARCH 29

The best mind-altering drug is truth.
—Lily Tomlin
(. . . and that's the truth, plplplpp.)
—Edith Ann

Getting Unstuck by Speaking Our Truth

Have you ever found yourself in a situation where you couldn't think of anything to say that would contribute to a resolution? When in fact, the only thing that came to mind was something you knew you would regret later? In times like these, many people will simply shut down. They won't say anything. I was leading a group recently when two of the participants had an angry exchange. After her initial attempt to express her feelings, one of the women shut down. I guessed her feelings and needs and asked her to let us know what was going on with her. She just continued to say that she was fine and she didn't have anything else to say. The next week, we talked about it again in the group. She said that she couldn't think of anything to say that she wouldn't regret later. She called this being "tongue-tied." I call it shutting down. Getting past distrust by stating our truth and listening to the other's truth takes courage. Shutting down will not solve the problem; it will never help us meet our needs. Commit yourself to speak your truth even if you can't say it the way you would like. The more you do this, the more skilled you will become at speaking up for yourself. As in all things, learning to speak up is a process that offers exciting rewards.

Commit to speaking your truth today.

MARCH 30

Tell the truth faster. Have a good life.
—Mackenzie Jordan

Speaking Up Is an Expression of Love

Before I learned Compassionate Communication, I would procrastinate over things. I would think: "Oh, it's not really *that* bad. I can get over this." I'd stew about it for a few days, weeks, or even months. Then I would blow up out of frustration. A blowup meant that I might yell at the other person or simply cut them out of my life. All because I couldn't find the right moment to express my feelings, or because I was worried about how the other person would receive the information. This process was completely unproductive and painful for all concerned. I created a mountain out of a molehill by not speaking up right away. Now I know that talking about something when it's not a big deal ensures that in most cases it won't become one. Do I sometimes worry that my honesty may stimulate pain in the other person? Absolutely. But I also know that if I don't speak up, I will generate much more pain. Speaking up for myself meets my needs for love and respect. When I'm honest with the people in my life, I demonstrate my love and respect for them. I show that I value the relationship and I want our connection to continue.

For today, speak up the minute you start to feel
annoyed, hurt, disappointed, or angry to demonstrate
your love for yourself and the other person.

MARCH 31

Handle them carefully for words have
more power than atom bombs.
—Pearl Strachan

Communicating Our Deepest Desires

If you are not happy in your relationships or in your life, the chances are good that your communication patterns are part of the problem. I have noticed that we often try to protect ourselves rather than ask for what we really want. Suppose someone sends you and several other people an email that "invites you to respond." You choose not to because you're busy or not in the mood to continue the conversation. The other person feels hurt and disappointed because what he really wanted was to hear from everyone. He "invited people to respond" because he was embarrassed to ask for what he really wanted, which was for everyone to respond. He tried to protect himself but failed to meet his own needs. Now he secretly feels resentment toward you and the other people who didn't respond. You start to notice that there is some tension between the two of you. Maybe you ask him about it and he says, "Nothing's wrong." Situations like this happen every day. When we become more willing to speak honestly about what we want, all our relationships will improve.

Be aware today of times when you
are tempted to protect yourself rather than
ask for what you truly want.

Meditations for
APRIL

APRIL 1

*Love is the recognition of Oneness, of knowing
yourself as other. The Oneness is love.*
—Eckhart Tolle

Acknowledging Other People's Reality

Can you hold onto your reality while simultaneously acknowledging someone else's reality? What I mean is, can you have an argument with your partner and speak up for your view of things, while also acknowledging his view? This ability is the ultimate goal. It eliminates right and wrong, good and bad. It demonstrates a willingness to accept that people may view things differently from us, and that we value their needs as much as our own.

Imagine you come home from work and your partner says: "You never come home on time. I am really getting tired of waiting for you." You have noticed that you were late the last two nights, but don't agree that you "never" come home on time or even that you are late most times. You can start by empathizing with him, "Are you angry because you want to trust that I'll come home when I say I will?" "Yes! Not that I'll get that, but that's what I want." "So, not only are you angry, you also feel hopeless that you will be able to trust that I'll keep my agreements with you?" "Yes. I feel hopeless." When you notice that he starts using fewer words, or when he starts to lower his voice, you can guess that he has been heard.

Now it is your turn to express yourself. "I hear that you are angry and want reassurance that I'll come home when we agreed. I want that too. I'm also frustrated because I have worked hard over the last year to change my habit of being late. This week has been especially stressful and I have been late three times because our project at work is wrapping up and I have struggled to complete it. So, when you say that I'm never on time, I feel worried and would like your understanding of how this week has been unique. Do you agree that I have been on time most nights over the last year?" Notice that a specific request is made for information about whether the other person agrees. "Well, I guess that's true. I think I got triggered because you were late so often this week and I began to worry that you were starting your old pattern again." You could empathize with him again: "Yeah, I can see how you might feel worried that a pattern was starting again. I feel regret that I didn't anticipate how much overtime I would work this week so that I could warn you."

When I think I have to win arguments or be right, my life feels scarce and limited. Imagine how it would feel to live in this consciousness, a space that is big enough to hold your own and other people's realities with love. When I live from this place, my life feels abundant and full.

For today, try to overcome your desire to be right
and win; replace it with a desire to understand
and connect with other people.

APRIL 2

There is no greater invitation to love than loving first.
—St. Augustine

Taking the First Step

Sometimes I hear people say things like, "Why does it always have to be me who takes the first step?" It can feel overwhelming when we put effort into something but other people don't participate as much as we'd like. I see this most often in couples and colleagues. One person in the relationship will begin to work on her issues. Then, as she gains clarity, she wants the other person to jump in with a similar amount of enthusiasm. When that doesn't happen, she might start to feel frustrated and place judgments on the other person, thinking or saying that the other person isn't as caring as she is. This type of circular thinking may be a trap that will keep her from meeting her needs. Consider this: Why did she start working on her issues? Possibly to better meet her needs for love and connection.

The best way for all of us to meet our needs for love and connection is simply to love and to connect. If we trap ourselves into believing that we must rely on others to provide this for us, we may often be disappointed and frustrated. You will be less likely to feel disappointment in other people if you remind yourself that when you do personal growth work, including changing your behaviors, it is to meet your own needs.

> For today, be aware of the needs you hope to
> meet by pursuing your personal growth.

APRIL 3

*She was so bankrupt, she couldn't
even afford a negative thought.*
—Sheryl Jai

When We Need Empathy the Most

Is your emotional bank account low, or maybe even empty? I try to keep my emotional bank account balanced. That is, I try not to give more than I receive, because if I'm bankrupt, I have little to give anyone, and I am more likely to say and do things I regret. This doesn't mean a quid pro quo in relationships. I don't have to get the same amount as I give to each person. I just have to keep my overall account in balance. Sometimes I might give a great deal of energy and time to a friend in need. If I feel drained afterward, I call another friend whose love and support might help balance my account. It is my responsibility to keep my account balanced; other people are not responsible for knowing when it's low.

One day not long ago I was distraught about a development in my life. I was upset enough that I was having a hard time staying present and focused. I knew I had a client coming in two hours for a session. I value my work and the contribution I make to others' lives, and I wanted to make sure that I was present, but my emotional bank account was low. So I called a friend and we talked for fifteen minutes. All she did was hear me out and empathize with me by restating my feelings and needs. I still had the painful issue in my life, but now I had a different perspective on it and I didn't feel lonely. In the end, my bank account was filled, just by being heard and loved. My client arrived in a great deal of pain, and I loved how soft and tender I could be with her because I was acutely aware of how painful life can feel, and how healing love can be.

On a scale of one to ten, how is your emotional bank account? If it's lower than you like, consider what you can do right now to bring it closer to balance. Everyone in your life, and most especially you, will benefit from this.

Be aware of your emotional bank account's balance. If it is low, do one thing today to help balance it.

APRIL 4

I can still remember my mother clutching her heart,
threatening to have a heart attack and die,
and blaming it on me.
—*Anonymous*

Motivation Through Joy

Can you relate to this quote? I spent much of my life trying to avoid the guilty feelings I had when I didn't meet other people's expectations. As a result, I developed resentments toward many people, including myself, and I was filled with rage. Either I succumbed to others' expectations or I rebelled against them. But I spent little time trying to notice what I liked, loved, and wanted. I was motivated by guilt, shame, and worry.

Then at the age of twenty-five, I had a dream to own and run a horse farm. I decided to go to college to pursue it. I wasn't certain I could succeed; I had been raised in the city and I knew nothing about horses. Still, I was convinced this was my new career, and I drove seventy-five miles each way twice a week for three years to earn a degree in Practical Horse Management. I worked my tail off without resentment or anger because it was something I wanted to do; I was motivated by joy. In the end, I decided that kind of work wasn't for me, but I had become so excited about college that I went on for bachelor's and master's degrees. When all this started, many people in my life raised an eyebrow. After all, why would I want to own a horse ranch when I didn't know anything about horses? But when they saw how committed and excited I was about it, they supported me. Really, how can you not support someone who is filled with joy?

> Be aware today of the times when you are
> motivated by joy and how you feel.

APRIL 5

It is not enough to do good.
One must do it in the right way.
—*John Morley*

The Value of Just Being

Every single being in the Universe is here for a reason. Even me. Even you. I used to think that my value came in what I *did*, rather than who *I am*. As a result I spent much of my life trying to prove my worth to myself and other people. That meant that I was competitive and I frequently won awards and achieved respected positions, but rarely did I receive them without a cost to someone else. Even just driving to the store became a competition, as I darted in and out of lanes of traffic to achieve the most efficient and direct path to the store. I also looked for validation and recognition from other people, to the point that it often became a demand. If you didn't think I was the best employee on the team, I lost interest in working with you. I strove to be the best in all aspects of my life, and when I fell short, I felt disappointed and resentful.

One day I caught myself pondering my ambition to be the best and I asked myself this question: "Well, what would the best look like? What would be enough for you?" I realized that "best" meant better than everyone else. It wasn't about being *my best*, but rather about *surpassing other people*. That meant other people were setting the bar that I strove to surpass. It was not at all connected to my values and integrity. I felt sad about this and I mourned it for a while. Eventually, though, I was able to clarify my goals. Now I enjoy challenging myself and I enjoy doing the best that I can. I value everyone's needs equally, so achieving something at someone else's expense is no longer a victory. I spend much more time *connecting* than *doing*. I am productive and I accomplish things, but I do this while meeting my own values for connection and compassion for everyone involved. Connect your goals to your values and you will experience joy. What are your values? If you're trying to achieve something, how will you know that you've been successful?

Make a list of your goals today and then
match them to your values.

APRIL 6

Recovery is about more than walking away.
Sometimes it means learning to stay and deal.
It's about building and maintaining
relationships that work.
—Melody Beattie

Commitment

Do you ever give up on disagreements by walking away, either temporarily or permanently? Do you ever simply not engage in a conflict because you're certain the situation cannot be resolved? Sometimes, taking a break from conflict is a good thing because it gives the people involved a chance to calm themselves. Deciding not to engage can be a good choice. Many times, though, people give up too soon, which decreases the possibility for resolution. This speaks to their level of commitment. How committed are they to valuing one another's needs? How committed are they to finding resolution? If we start a disagreement based on the consciousness that we want to get our own way or that the other person doesn't care, we diminish the opportunity for success before we've even opened our mouth. Commitment is about living from our values even when it's uncomfortable and tiring. It is a choice.

I once heard a speaker say that he had finally met his soul mate. He asked the audience if they knew how he knew that. They said no, but leaned forward in their seats because they were certain he was going to tell them something important. He said, "I know she's my soul partner because I say she is." He committed himself to her. Consequently, when he and his wife argue, they focus on resolution because they are committed to staying in the relationship. This small shift in attitude has dramatically deepened their relationship. Meet any disagreement with clarity about your commitment and with the goal of a resolution that values everyone involved. Who are you committed to? Does he or she know it?

> Be aware today of whom you are committed to;
> when you interact with them, be conscious
> of your commitment.

APRIL 7

*Doubt and mistrust are the mere panic of timid
imagination, which the steadfast heart will conquer,
and the large mind transcend.*
—Helen Keller

Balance as a State of Being

I used to think that balance was something that could be achieved through action, such as adjusting my work schedule to spend more time with friends and family, or to feel more rested. I often used to say that I needed more balance, and then I would state the actions I could take to achieve it. Achieving balance, then, required an increase or decrease in a particular kind of activity. Now I see balance as a spiritual practice and a state of being. While writing this book, I have expended a great deal of energy to create something that won't be published for a year. This has reduced the time I've had available to conduct trainings and classes, and I haven't yet created my class schedule for the next six months. As a result, I have thought that I need to do a better job of balancing present and future work. At the very least, I've thought I need to create my class schedule to attain balance.

Then I started to ponder what my life will look like during the next six months and I noticed that I have already scheduled much of that time; it just looks different than it has in the past. There is ample time for both trainings and writing. My work life will look different than it used to, but it has balanced itself with ease. Achieving balance, then, is about listening to my inner voice and recognizing my life as balanced, rather than acting out of habit. In this regard, balance is a spiritual practice and a state of being. You could even call it a connection to self.

If you want more balance in your life, look objectively at what you are doing. Is it possible that you are doing exactly what you want to do, or exactly what your higher power asks you to do? If so, have faith that you are in balance. If not, consider what action you would like to take.

If you are feeling out of balance today, discern whether you need to change your actions or your perspective.

APRIL 8

We have been doing the wrong things for the right reasons.
—*Melody Beattie*

121

Getting Your Needs Met

I once heard a parable about a woman who went to the hardware store every day and asked for a gallon of milk. Every day the clerk would tell her that she was in a hardware store that didn't carry milk and suggest she try the grocery store down the street. As time went on, she returned angrier and more determined to get her milk at the hardware store. She tried yelling louder, demanded to speak with the manager, and argued the facts of her situation and why milk was so important for her physical health. She tried putting her request in writing, got it notarized, and even had a friend come and talk for her. Each day she imagined a different reason for her predicament: if she just stated her case clearly enough, if she was smarter, if she was a man, or maybe if she weren't so selfish, they would sell her milk. The employees of the hardware store dreaded her visits. They simply couldn't understand why she wouldn't go to the grocery store.

Do you ever feel like the lady buying the milk? Do you ever find yourself going back to the same person for tenderness only to find it is simply not available, then thinking that there must be something wrong with *you?* This feels awful, so eventually you get mad at the other person—over and over again! It's amazing how much pain we put ourselves through.

Each of us can change our relationships by simply looking at our own behaviors. We can ask for what we want, but if we repeatedly don't get it from a particular person, it is our responsibility to find a new way to get it. No single person can meet all our needs. We don't honor our relationships when we insist that people who are unavailable or unwilling to support us meet our needs.

The next time you find yourself wanting to yell at someone for not meeting one of your needs, consider whether this person has ever met it. Then consider whether you can meet it elsewhere.

If you have an unmet need, consider the people you
ask for help, and decide if you would like to
ask someone else instead.

APRIL 9

Now that this growth and expansion has started,
I am unable to stop it. I feel no boundaries within
myself, no walls, no fears. Nothing holds me back
from adventure. I feel mobile, fluid . . .
—Anaïs Nin

Meeting Our Need for Creativity

I used to think that I wasn't creative because I didn't draw or paint in ways that I enjoyed. Today I notice that I meet my need for creativity in a number of ways. When I write something that I enjoy, when I figure something out that has been challenging, or when I decorate my home, I am creative. Webster defines creative as "resulting from original thought." Anytime you create something new in your life, you can fulfill your need for creativity. Celebrate your creativity today!

Be aware today of the many ways that your actions
meet your need for creativity.

APRIL 10

No man can be happy without a friend,
nor be sure of his friend till he is unhappy.
—*Thomas Fuller, MD*

Letting People Support Us

Some time ago I was in a serious car accident. I spent three nights in the Intensive Care Unit. When I got out of the hospital, I needed someone to stay with me for a few weeks because my brain wasn't working properly and I couldn't be trusted to make sound decisions.

Through this experience I learned that I live in a barn-raising community. My friends and one of my brothers supported me. They stayed with me, brought me food, and reminded me endlessly of the things I needed to know but couldn't remember. They remembered who I was when I couldn't. I didn't ask for this support; I didn't even know I needed it, but it kept coming for weeks and months. The thing that amazed me the most was how much love was in their giving and how much it brought our community together.

This kind of story happens all around the world. The truth is that we all love to contribute to others' lives. We love to offer support because it meets our own needs for contribution, love, caring, and making a difference. We are naturally giving people. Don't you love to help others in dire need? Is it hard for you to imagine that someone would love to offer you the same support? I suggest we all just admit that we love to support other people, and that we ourselves would like support. Don't be selfish. Let other people receive the same joy when they contribute to you as you feel when you contribute to them.

For today, admit that you love to support other people, and that you would like support yourself. Let at least one person contribute to your life today.

APRIL 11

A man who is master of himself can end a sorrow
as easily as he can invent a pleasure.
—Oscar Wilde

Acting in Accordance With Our Values

We're not perfect. Sometimes we say and do things we regret later. I used to feel somewhat justified when I snapped at a grocery clerk, or if I cut someone off in traffic. After all, they didn't know me, right? Now I know that every action we take has an impact. The nature of the impact may not be obvious to us, but that doesn't diminish its presence. Have you ever gone home and complained about another driver or a grocery clerk or a customer? The next time you are tempted to snap at someone or cut in front of another driver, consider whether you'd like to be their story that evening. Consider whether this is the kind of contribution you'd like to make to their life. Act as though you recognize and believe that your every action has an effect on other people's lives.

Be aware today of how your every action
has an impact on other people.

APRIL 12

*I have discovered that we may be in some
degree whatever character we choose. Besides,
practice forms a man to anything.*
—James Boswell

Practice, Practice, Practice

Sometimes I hear people say things like: "I didn't use Nonviolent Communication this week. Everything was going so smoothly, I didn't have to." I suggest a different approach. Consider practicing the Nonviolent Communication process every day, especially when you are happy, for two reasons: First, it is easier to practice Nonviolent Communication in situations that are not emotionally charged. This will give you valuable practice to help you maintain a compassionate consciousness when circumstances are charged. And second, if you practice Nonviolent Communication when you are happy, chances are better that you will be able to stay in that consciousness for a longer period of time. Nonviolent Communication is more than a tool for communicating. It is a way of being in which we value other people's needs as much as our own. If you don't have anything difficult to say to someone, say something enjoyable! Try, "You know when you crawl into bed before me and warm the bed, I feel such appreciation because it meets my needs for nurturing and care." Such a consciousness is bound to enhance your ability to enjoy your relationships.

Commit to living the Nonviolent Communication
process today, whether you are happy or sad.

APRIL 13

Destruction is the first step in conscious change.
The old dies so that the new might be born.
—*Gloria Karpinski*

Finding Ways to Meet Our Needs

Many people pressure their friends and partners to meet all of their needs. But it is important to remember that *there are countless ways to meet any need.* When we limit the options available to us, we limit our opportunities. Often, when we are angry with another person, we want them to hear us. But they may not be willing or able to hear us. Still, we keep going back to them and receiving the same response. We won't meet our need, though, because it doesn't occur to us to ask elsewhere.

If you find yourself in a situation like this, consider going to another person who is more likely to hear you. You may be surprised how healing this can be. When we are open to all the possibilities available to us, we become more successful at meeting our needs and living happier lives.

For today, think of three new strategies
to meet one of your needs.

APRIL 14

*The place to improve the world is first in
one's own heart and head and hands,
and then work outward from there.*
—*Robert M. Pirsig*

Keeping the Focus on Ourselves

Sometimes it takes three hours of empathy to prepare for a one-hour meeting. We all have times when we anticipate that a meeting or conversation might be challenging. I used to prepare for these moments by telling myself, "Buck up—you'll get through it." This attitude succeeded in keeping distance between me and other people. It did not succeed in allowing me to truly connect with other people or create solutions that satisfied all concerned. Now, instead of bucking up, I connect more deeply to myself and the needs I am trying to meet in the situation. I do this either through self-empathy—connecting to my own feelings and needs—or by asking a friend to give me empathy so I can receive support in connecting to them. This simple act can make an enormous difference in preparing for challenging conversations. I find that no matter how other people show up for these conversations, it is important for me to feel good about how I show up. When I am connected and open, there is a better chance that the conversation will come to a mutually satisfying conclusion. When I'm not, we all have less opportunity for success. My focus needs to be on me and my values. The next time you prepare for a challenging conversation, look at your own feelings and needs first. Then attend the meeting open to creating results that work for everyone.

Take a moment today to connect to your
feelings and needs before entering a
meeting that may be challenging.

APRIL 15

Gratitude is the most exquisite form of courtesy.
—Jacques Maritain

Experiencing Gratitude

Do you ever think you're taking life just a little too seriously?
Many of us work hard trying to improve our outlook, our
ability to communicate, and our lives. Sometimes we work so
hard, we forget to *enjoy* life. So let's make a pact to enjoy our
day. This doesn't mean we pretend that our life is enjoyable
when it's not, or that we deny our feelings in any way. It only
means that we focus on what works well, rather than what
doesn't. For example, your house payments might be higher
than you can easily afford, but you can appreciate the fact that
you have a house. Similarly, your spouse may be out of town
and you may miss him. You can also feel appreciation that
you have a spouse whom you enjoy. We can acknowledge
our sadness, disappointment, or worry without making it the
focal point of our day. By simply acknowledging the good
in our life, we immediately shift our focus. I make a mental
gratitude list every night before going to sleep. My goal is
to come up with eight items per night. Sometimes all I can
muster is gratitude for indoor plumbing or my sheets. But
even just acknowledging to myself how grateful I am for these

items can ease some of life's pressures and remind me of the parts of my life I enjoy.

Today, focus on what you enjoy in your life.

※

APRIL 16

The abstinent run away from what they desire,
but carry their desires with them.
—*Bhagavadgita*

Directness

Isn't it kinder to be indirect? Do I have to tell the whole truth? Yep, I say that direct honesty is the only answer. Indirectness can easily cause confusion and pain as people try to figure out what we mean. Such communication can prolong the inevitable pain and even deepen it. I think many of us choose indirectness because we worry about hurting someone else's feelings. But this method never keeps people from having hurt feelings.

I have learned that I cannot make everyone happy. Once I got over the shock of this, I felt great relief. My job is to be compassionate, loving, honest, and respectful to myself and other people. Sometimes this means sharing my sadness or disappointment in a relationship. The person may not enjoy what I say, but at least they know where I'm coming from. If I am true to myself, I am true to my relationships. Directness is a gift that builds trust.

For today, make a commitment to be direct in your interactions with other people to meet your needs for honesty and compassion.

APRIL 17

The journey, not the arrival, matters;
the voyage, not the landing.
—Paul Theroux

Taking a Leap

Sometimes we are dissatisfied in our primary relationship, yet the thought of making a change is scary, so we stay in it. Sometimes we think we're afraid to learn the truth, so we don't ask direct questions. Several years ago, I was in a relationship that lasted a year. My gut told me that my partner wasn't that interested in the relationship, but I kept plugging along, hoping that it would change. In the end, I found out that he was seeing someone else. Because I went against my gut instincts, I spent a year with someone who wasn't present for me, and I created a lot of pain for myself.

Take a risk. Ask the question you are afraid to ask. Then listen for the answer. Don't just listen for the words; hear the tone of voice and body language. How do you feel after hearing the answer? Don't fool yourself into thinking that ignorance is bliss. It really isn't. Being honest with yourself and others is bliss.

Today, ask a question to which you
have wanted an answer.

APRIL 18

We see the same colors; we hear the same sounds,
but not in the same way.
—*Simone Weil*

Meeting Our Need for Order

I used to work with a man who didn't use file cabinets. He had stacks and stacks of files and paperwork on his desk and credenza. I felt overwhelmed when I came into his office and I was filled with judgment about his disorganization. Then I noticed that I could ask him for a particular document that may have been prepared the day before, a few months before, or even several years earlier. In each case, he could go directly to a stack of papers and within minutes produce the document. He did this often enough that soon my need for confidence in his order was fully met. After a while, I expected him to find whatever I was looking for. His method of order was entirely different from mine. My file cabinets are full, each file has a label, and each file drawer lists its contents on the outside. Both of us, however, meet our needs for order. We simply choose different methods. Do not assume that someone else is disorderly if their strategy for order is different than yours.

Be aware today of the variety of ways
people meet their need for order.

APRIL 19

Listen to your own Self. If you listen to that
Self within, then you find the Truth.
—Kabir

You're Not Too Much

I used to feel guilty if I had a need that somebody else didn't have. I told myself that if I wanted intimacy and my partner didn't, then there must be something wrong with me. Or, if I wanted fun and my partner wanted to rest, then I was too much, too needy, or too selfish. It did not occur to me that everyone has needs for intimacy, fun, and rest. Sometimes we simply have these needs at different times. Nobody has more needs than another, but our circumstances might cause us to alter our priorities. If money is low, I might need more resources, so I work a few more hours. Another time, money might flow more easily, so my greatest need might be fun. One day my need for intimacy might be strong. Another day I might prefer learning to intimacy. Similarly, I might really want to spend time with a particular friend, so I'll be open to a variety of activities. Other times I might really want to be physical and have fun, so if my friend wants to do something more sedate like seeing a movie, I might decide to call other people for that night's activities.

If you're telling yourself that you're "too much," look at the people you are playing with. Rather than blaming them for not having enough energy or yourself for having too much, why not find other ways to express your energy, like skating, dancing, or hiking. Once you meet that need, you will be more likely to enjoy your friends.

Remind yourself today that everyone has
their own priority of needs.

APRIL 20

Show love to all creatures and you will be happy . . .
—*Tulsidas*

Focusing on Where We Are the Same

In Compassionate Communication, we believe that everyone
has the same needs, no matter how they strive to meet
them. Can you imagine what needs the terrorists were
trying to meet when they flew airplanes into the World
Trade Center in 2001? To some, it seems unfathomable
that they were meeting needs. But think about it. Don't you
think it's possible that they did that to meet their needs for
sovereignty, autonomy, and safety? Doesn't everybody share
these needs? Our differences are not in our needs, but in
how we attempt to meet them. This simple truth can help
you lessen the conflicts in your life and your judgments of
other people. Rather than focus on where you disagree, focus
on where you are the same. This shift can make a profound
difference in your ability to understand yourself and other
people, and to bring unity to your life.

Notice today how everyone has the same needs.

APRIL 21

Do not weep; do not wax indignant. Understand.
—Baruch Spinoza

Hearing the Yes Behind the No

Persisting is when we actively attempt to meet our needs by continuing to connect with another person. *Demanding* is when we insist that someone do something, or else there will be negative repercussions. Say you ask your teenage son to mow the lawn this afternoon, and he says: "Oh Mom! I wanted to play ball with the guys." Often, when faced with this kind of resistance, we can only think of two responses—either give in to his needs and forget about the lawn, or demand that he mow the lawn. Neither option feels good to both people. Instead, how about listening for what he said yes to. Did you hear a yes? I heard him say yes to playing ball with his friends. I didn't hear a flat no to mowing the lawn. So respond to his yes, "You're excited about playing ball with your friends, huh?" "Yeah, I am. We haven't played all week." "It's especially important to you because you haven't played this week?" "Yeah. Can't someone else mow the lawn?" At this point, he probably feels a little more relaxed because you have shown that you understand his situation. Just being heard can cause people to be willing to work with you, so you might say: "Well, unfortunately, there isn't anyone else. Look, I really want you to have time to play ball today. I can tell it's very important to you. I'd also like the lawn mowed. How would you feel about playing ball with your friends today and mowing the lawn first thing tomorrow morning?" Again, you're showing that you care about him and that you're willing to work with him.

In reality, he might balk because he doesn't want to get up early or he has other reasons. Each time, acknowledge what he's saying yes to (sleeping in or doing something else), and persist towards a resolution that values both your needs. Such an approach can calm the waters for easy conflict resolution.

> Today, notice what the people in
> your life are saying yes to.

APRIL 22

Respect is love. The heart is also love—and so are you.
—*Swami Chidvilasananda*

The Value of Change

I often hear parents express sheer hopelessness that their relationship with their teenage children will ever change. They have tried everything they can think of and still there is unrest in the family. If you are in a similar situation, consider looking at things from the teenager's perspective. What needs is he trying to meet in his life? How do those needs resemble or differ from those you are trying to meet? Say you have been after your son to clean his room for weeks and all you have managed to accomplish is an ongoing fight with him. What needs do you think he is trying to meet through his actions? I would guess autonomy, ease, and fun. Your needs are probably fairness, ease, and contribution to the family. What is one thing you can do that will demonstrate that you value his needs as much as yours? How about having a conversation about your frustrations and listening to his? After you have both been heard, consider discussing all the household chores and see if you can come to an agreement on how to divide the work. Be specific about the scope of the jobs, when they will be done, and how. Then make an appointment to talk the following week to see how things went. Keep in mind that one of a teenager's primary needs is autonomy. The more he is involved in the decision-making process and the less he senses someone else's demand, the more likely he will be to respond.

Be aware today of another person's needs, and let him know that you value his needs as much as your own.

APRIL 23

There is a place where words are born of silence,
A place where the whispers of the heart arise.
—*Rumi*

I Want to Connect More Than I Want to Be Right

What do you value most? I value connection more than anything. If I connect with people, all of us have a better chance of getting our needs met. The alternative is to try to win or be right. I used to do this with a vengeance. Years ago, I was working with a woman who was learning fund-raising techniques from me. She mentioned how scared she was about asking someone to make a donation and I said: "Oh, it's not hard. You just have to get out there and do it." I thought I was right about fund-raising being easy and so I set out to convince her of my rightness, rather than connecting to her feelings and needs. We ended up in an argument over whether fund-raising was easy or hard. Had I simply connected with her feelings and needs, the conversation would have gone entirely differently. "Oh, so you want to learn to do this, but you're scared that it will be hard?" I don't feel at peace when I am trying to be right. Deeply connecting instead helps me open the possibility that everyone's needs will be met. Consider making your goal connection rather than winning. I think you'll be amazed at the results. Such a simple shift will bring abundance and hope into your relationships.

Remind yourself at least three times today that you want to connect more than you want to be right. Notice how this feels to you.

APRIL 24

Stand up and play the melody. I am God.
—*Rumi*

Supporting Our Loved Ones to Live Authentically

So you finally figured out how to live authentically. That is, you are more likely to do things because they meet your needs than because you think other people want you to. What a relief! You might also feel some frustration because the people in your life are still trying to figure *you* out, rather than making decisions that meet *their* needs. It might be hard for them to connect to and express their own. It is helpful in these moments to remind yourself that you are only responsible for your own feelings, and then to help your loved ones connect to theirs.

Suppose you come home from work and your friend calls and says, "Hey, do you want to go to dinner tonight?" "Sure. How about Mexican?" "Oh, are you sure you want Mexican?" This moment can feel frustrating, especially if you would prefer your friend to say what she wants rather than trying to manipulate you into doing something. So, you could check out your assumption. "Hmmm. Are you asking me that because you would prefer to go someplace else?" "Yeah, I guess I'm not in the mood for Mexican because I had Mexican for lunch yesterday." "OK, what *are* you in the mood for?" "How about Italian?" "Sure!"

Sometimes, the people in our lives don't yet have the skills to connect with their own needs. If we're willing to take the time to help them, we all win.

Take the time to help at least one person connect with her feelings and needs today. Notice if this deepens your relationship.

APRIL 25

*To say yes, you have to sweat and roll up your sleeves
and plunge both hands into life up to the elbows. It is
easy to say no, even if saying no means death.*
—Jean Anouilh

Getting On With Things

Not long ago I was asked to attend a party. At first I was
excited because I imagined I'd meet new people, and I wanted
to expand my circle of friends. Then, when the evening of the
party rolled around, I could feel the urge to stay home grow
by the minute. It got to the point that I was starting to justify
it. "Well, it is an hour away and it could rain. After all, I don't
really need to meet these people. My life is full as it is. They
won't notice whether I go or not. It's not a big deal." My
needs to have quiet time and to expand my circle of friends
were at odds. In the moment, my need for rest was taking
precedence so I considered backing out of my commitment
to myself and my friend who had invited me.

Do you ever do this? You want something so badly, but
then you don't show up to receive it? Sometimes saying
no is easier. We don't have to learn anything new or feel
uncomfortable in an unfamiliar situation, and we can keep
telling ourselves that the reason we don't have what we want
is because the Universe hasn't provided it. Saying yes
means showing up and all that that entails. Saying yes
means creating the possibility for change simply because
we show up.

I went to the party and enjoyed myself immensely. I met
some new people who share my values and I connected to
a new community of people who are working toward world

peace. How abundant is that? If I'd stayed home, I would have met my television. Hmmm. Where's the choice?

**Be aware of opportunities today to say yes
to enhance your personal growth.**

APRIL 26

To me, every hour of the light and dark is a miracle.
Every cubic inch of space is a miracle.
—*Walt Whitman*

Celebrate Your Progress!

Do you ever find yourself feeling overwhelmed with all that you want to do, rather than celebrating what you've already done? I started jogging recently. The first day I jogged for two minutes and walked for four minutes, and then repeated this cycle four times. To keep my heart rate at a safe level, I had to jog at a slower pace than I walked! Within three days, I was jogging faster than I walked. I could see quantifiable change in only three days. Wouldn't it be great if we could see our progress this easily when we're trying to shift our consciousness or change a behavior we have exhibited since we were five years old? Here is my suggestion. Take a moment to ponder what you are working to change. Notice whether it's a behavior or a consciousness. Consider where you were with this issue when you first decided to create change. Now where are you? I wanted to stop judging other people and connect with them instead, so I focused on shifting that one area of my consciousness. In the beginning, it didn't seem like much was happening, but I kept up with the process. Three months went by and I noticed that I made fewer judgments than before. Each week's change didn't seem that noticeable, but it was huge compared to where I started. Four months after that, I noticed the change in my consciousness even more. Celebrate your progress because it will encourage you to keep trying. You wouldn't expect to jump on a treadmill and jog three miles the first time. Try not to have the same expectations for your emotional fitness either!

> Celebrate your progress today because it
> will encourage you to keep trying.

APRIL 27

One doesn't discover new lands without consenting
to lose sight of the shore for a very long time.
—André Gide

Moving Out of the Hallway

When I first started to think about moving out of my hometown, I felt excited and raring to go. I wanted a change and I was convinced that I would "find myself" in a new town where no one had expectations of who I was. All my energy was about moving. I had already moved emotionally even though I still didn't know where to go. This is what I call being in the hallway of life. I had let go of my old life because I wanted adventure, but I hadn't built my new life. Or, put another way, I had moved from one room into the hallway, and I had not yet entered a new room. Shifting behaviors can also feel like this sometimes. We know we don't like the way we do things now, but it's frightening to change because we're not sure what will happen, and we're not sure how to do it. Here's my suggestion. If there's something you're not happy with, set the intention to change it. Just that simple act will start the change. Then try to do one thing that will further manifest it. You could empathize with someone else or yourself (listen for feelings and needs), look into class schedules at the local college, call a doctor, or ask a friend if she has a suggestion. The first step in creating change is to acknowledge a need and a behavior or situation you want to change. The second step is taking action—some action, any action. Just do something different.

> For today, take one action that will help you
> manifest the change you desire.

APRIL 28

*Resenting someone is as rational as trying to kill
someone by putting poison in their glass
and then drinking it!*
—*Author unknown*

Letting Go of Resentments

When we feel resentment toward others, we are harming our own emotional health. Several years ago, I broke up with my boyfriend. I was angry with him, I couldn't stand to see him, and I could hear the resentment in my voice when I spoke of him. This went on for six months. I wanted so badly to feel relief. A friend suggested that I meet with him in person and tell him my regrets for how I had shown up in our relationship. She suggested that if I owned up to my part, I would be able to let go of my resentments. It sounded far-fetched, but I was desperate to be relieved of my resentment, so I tried it. I invited him to have tea. I told him that I was disappointed because I realized that I hadn't been completely honest in our relationship and that I was also impatient and unforgiving sometimes. The entire meeting lasted ten minutes. He thanked me and we hugged when we parted. It was so easy, it shocked me. I saw him two weeks later, and I didn't even have a pang of resentment. I smiled and waved. A few hours later, I noticed how momentous that was. It's a funny thing, really, but when we own up to our part of an uncomfortable situation, we release the pain. I let go of resentments because it is healing for *me*. I own up to the times when I regret my behavior because it heals *me*. It's not about berating myself, but simply being honest. Such honesty can provide amazing healing.

Consider what resentments you are holding onto today
and whether you are willing to own up to your part
in these situations in an effort to contribute
to your own well-being.

APRIL 29

Every man takes the limits of his own field of vision
for the limits of the world.
—*Arthur Schopenhauer*

Don't Make Assumptions!

Do you ever feel certain that other people see things the way you do, only to find out they don't? Did you ever sit in a meeting feeling bored, certain that the other participants were also bored, only to discover when you mentioned it that they were totally engaged? People make assumptions all the time based on their own experience and view of the world. Several years ago when I worked at a university, my assistant dean came into my office with my bottle of sugar-free syrup. The dean's office had a very small refrigerator which several of us used. I assumed he was returning my syrup because he was frustrated with how much room it was taking in the refrigerator, so I said in a sarcastic tone, "What's the matter, is my syrup taking up too much space?" He looked shocked and said: "No! I'm returning it to you because I know it's your special syrup, and I was worried you wouldn't have it in the morning if you forgot it again. I thought you might be disappointed if it wasn't there for you in the morning." Ugh. It had never occurred to me that he was thinking of *me*. I was certain of my own reality. The next time someone does or says something that you don't like, try asking for clarity before assuming your reality is theirs.

Clarify your assumptions with at least two people today.

✳

APRIL 30

Every man has a right to be
valued by his best moment.
—*Ralph Waldo Emerson*

Keeping Our Perspective

One of my clients recently told me of a situation at her office. She had just completed her third year with her organization. She had received exemplary annual reviews every previous year. She made a mistake a few weeks earlier that caused the company to lose money, and she was reprimanded harshly. Her supervisor said they were watching her closely. My client felt hurt, angry, and disappointed. How could her three years of exemplary service be so quickly forgotten over one mistake? Her needs to be respected, considered, valued, and understood were not met in this situation. Don't we all want this, really? Don't we all want to be valued in our totality, to be loved even when we make mistakes? Wouldn't we also like to offer this to ourselves? Compassion is about seeing the humanness in everyone, including ourselves. One way to express compassion is to remember your entire relationship with someone, rather than focusing on one disappointing incident.

Be aware of opportunities today to connect to the
history of love you feel for someone in your life
even if the present situation is painful.

Meditations for
MAY

MAY 1

Those who profess to favor freedom and yet
depreciate agitation are men who want rain
without thunder and lightning.
—Frederick Douglass

Considering Everyone's Needs Brings Peace

We feel our freedom when we are willing to look at others' needs and our own, evaluate all of them, and work toward valuing everyone's needs. It sounds easy. It did to me in the beginning. However, in a charged moment, valuing other people's needs can be a challenge.

Say that your employee wants to start work at eight-thirty instead of eight each morning. Everyone else in the department arrives at eight, and you like this because it meets your needs for predictability, order, and ease. What do you do? Simply say no to the employee because you're worried that your needs won't be met? Or do you discuss the situation with him in an effort to value everyone's needs? It often only takes a few minutes to connect with someone. "Well, I enjoy the predictability and ease I have when everyone starts at eight, but I'm willing to discuss it with you, Bob. Will you tell me how adjusting your schedule to start at eight-thirty will benefit you, and how it might affect the department?" You have all the time you need in this moment to have such a discussion with someone. Everyone will benefit from your interest in valuing their needs as well as yours.

Take the time to demonstrate that you value everyone's
needs as much as your own today.

MAY 2

Tomorrow's life is too late. Live today.
—Martial

Getting Started

Take the first step today. Don't wait until tomorrow. Want to have more love in your life? Be more loving right this moment no matter who is in front of you. Want to save more money? Go to your wallet right now and take out some money to put into your savings. It doesn't matter how much or how often. The reward is in taking the first step, and then the second and third until you've attained your goal. Don't focus on your end result—that can be overwhelming. Just focus on this day. What can you do this day to begin to attain your goal?

I always wanted to be a jogger, but I had a plethora of excuses for why I didn't get started: I was too overweight, I was too out of shape, my knees weren't strong enough . . . Then one day I borrowed a friend's book on how to jog. That was the first step. The second step was to read the book, and the third was to start jogging. I started by jogging for two minutes and walking for four minutes for four repetitions, following the book's suggestion. At the end of ten weeks, if I follow the plan, I will be jogging for thirty minutes straight, just by doing a little bit each day. I will attain a lifetime goal in ten weeks! What is your goal? What small step can you take today to attain it?

Identify one goal and take one small step
toward achieving it today.

MAY 3

We live in a vastly complex society which has been able
to provide us with a multitude of material things, and
this is good, but people are beginning to suspect that
we have paid a high spiritual price for our plenty.
—Euell Gibbons

Living Our Values

Sometimes I wish everyone else would just make it easy for
me to live my values. If other people would just do their
part, I wouldn't have to work so hard at doing mine. Can
you relate to this? Here's the real truth: I support peace in
the world, which means that I want to live my life peacefully.
This is my value; no one else forces me to hold it. I own it
because it's important to me. That means that I want to
live peacefully even if someone screams in my face, or does
something that I perceive as mean. I do this because it's
important to *me*, not because it's important to *them*.

Recently, someone who was renting a house from me
told me he wanted to get out of the lease, and if I didn't let
him, he would sue me. I was tempted to get an attorney and
match his might with more of my own. I had an internal
picture of myself putting my dukes up. Then I asked myself,
"What is important to you, Mary?" The answer was to live
my values. I decided to give him everything he asked for so
that he could be happier in his life. I was also happier in mine
because I stepped aside from a potential conflict. The most
important thing is being true to ourselves, not winning, not
being right, and certainly not being the biggest and meanest.

Identify your most important value today.
Then live it. Notice how healing this can
feel even just after one day.

MAY 4

You must remember that man is noble,
man is sublime, man is divine, and can
accomplish whatever he desires.
—Swami Muktananda

Shooting for the Moon

You can have anything you want. Nothing is being held from
you. In a Compassionate Communication process, we believe
there are enough resources in the Universe to meet all of
our needs. Most people are stumped because they can only
see one strategy for meeting a need. For instance, someone
may have a need for intimacy. When she hasn't experienced
it in her past or current partnerships, she may think it is
unavailable to her. As long as she focuses solely on meeting
her needs with her partners, she misses opportunities to meet
it with friends and family. Try not to limit your success by
stopping when one particular strategy doesn't work. Focus
again on your need and try another way.

Identify one need that you would like to
experience more of and make a list of at least
five strategies for meeting it today.

MAY 5

I am at peace with the community of life.
—Louise L. Hay

Serenity as a Consciousness

Serenity doesn't mean that everything in our lives is smooth. It means that no matter what is happening, we have faith in a higher purpose. Serenity is a choice. I used to experience emotional highs and lows. Then one day, a friend said to me: "You know, I don't get it. You say that you have a full spiritual life, yet you hit these deep emotional bottoms. Where is your faith when you do that?" This hit home; she was right. Now, I *choose* to hold onto my faith that all is well in the Universe no matter how it may appear in the moment. Sometimes I view something as good, and then I find that it was harmful. Other times, I consider something to be bad, but then find that I benefit hugely from it. Now, I try not to judge anything. It is not for me to decide whether something is good or bad. My role is to decide how I feel about it and what needs it will or will not meet. I'll let the Universe do the rest.

For today, no matter what is happening in your life, choose to believe that all is well in the Universe. Choose serenity. Then take action to resolve any situations that are not enjoyable to you.

152

MAY 6

There is a vitality, a life force, an energy, a quickening, that is translated through you into action, and because there is only one of you in all time, this expression is unique. And, if you block it, it will never exist through any other medium and will be lost.
—Martha Graham

Making Requests Count

The first three components of the Nonviolent Communication process clarify our observations, feelings, and the needs we are trying to meet. The fourth component is to make a specific and doable request. The request completes the communication by stating specifically what we would like from someone else to meet our need. Without the request, our communication can be confusing and can easily be seen as a demand.

Say you come home from work and find your children watching TV. The living room has dirty dishes and clothes strewn throughout, and you say, "When I come home and see dirty dishes and laundry in the living room, I feel annoyed because I value mutual respect and orderliness." Then you walk out of the room. Now your children must decide for themselves what you want. You could want the room to be picked up right now. But when that's done, will you still be mad? Or maybe it would be OK with you if the house were picked up in a half hour. Or maybe you want something else. If you end your communication with a request, what you want is clear to everyone. Try this: "When I come home and see dirty dishes and laundry in the living room, I feel annoyed because I value mutual respect and orderliness. Would you be willing to pick up the living room within thirty minutes?" You may still need to debate the timing of when the room is picked up, but it is clear to them what you are asking. When people know what you want, you have a better chance of meeting your needs.

Make clear requests of people today, and notice if you are more successful at meeting your needs.

MAY 7

It is right and necessary that we should be individuals.
The Divine Spirit never made any two things alike—
No two rosebushes, two snowflakes, two grains of sand,
Or two persons. We are all just a little unique for each
wears A different face; but behind each is
One Presence—God
—*Ernest Holmes*

Universal Needs

Every human being has the same universal needs. For instance, we all need support but we may choose different methods to receive it. When I am under a stressful deadline, I prefer quiet, uninterrupted time to accomplish my task. In that situation, if people allow me my quiet space, my need for support is met. We all need companionship, but we choose different people to be our friends and lovers. We all need food, but we like different kinds. We all breathe the same air. We all love, cry, and grieve.

Notice the universal needs you share
with other people today.

MAY 8

We must be aware of the real problems of the world.
Then, with mindfulness, we will know what to do
and what not to do to be of help.
—*Thich Nhat Hanh*

Don't Assume You Know What Other People Need

We must listen deeply to people in an effort to understand what they need. Don't assume you know what another person's problem is or what they need. Learn by listening deeply. Have you ever listened to someone and noticed yourself becoming impatient? At that point, you may have stopped listening and started giving them advice on how to solve their problem, even though they said, "No, that won't work" in response to all your suggestions.

Often, when we feel uncomfortable about someone else's pain, we want to fix it. We want to help her solve her problem so that *we* will feel better. We can sometimes fool ourselves into believing that we want to do this to make the other person feel better, but in reality *we* are uncomfortable and *we* want to feel better. When we can express our problems to someone who is comfortable listening to us, and who believes in *our* ability to solve our issues, it is very healing.

If someone comes to you to talk about a problem they are having, try to stop and listen deeply. Resolutions come naturally to people once they know they are heard. Tell yourself that your role is not to solve her problem, but rather to hear her. Your listening presence can bring relief to both of you and provide additional opportunities for healing.

If a friend comes to you with a problem today, just listen intently. Don't try to fix it. Resolutions will come naturally once she is heard.

MAY 9

At the height of laughter, the universe is flung into a kaleidoscope of new possibilities.
—*Jean Houston*

You Just Gotta Laugh

Many years ago, one of my sisters and I traveled from northern Washington to northern California. I had taken my car in to be serviced before we left. I knew that my clutch was slipping so I planned to replace it, but the mechanic told me I could easily put it off until I returned. At one point, we were in the mountains of Oregon and I lost fourth gear and then third gear. We drove up the freeway through a mountain range with only second gear, and then we lost that! So here we were driving on the shoulder of the road, so slowly that bicyclists were passing us. We planned to keep moving until we came upon a town. At one point, my sister jumped out of our moving vehicle and walked beside it because we thought decreased weight might help. At first we were worried, but then the humor of the situation took over. We laughed hysterically as she walked alongside the car, hopping back in when she got tired. We laughed again when bicyclists passed us with a wave. Without talking about it and without planning it, we had decided to enjoy our situation. We were on vacation, after all, and we had each other's company. It wasn't what we planned, but that didn't mean we couldn't enjoy ourselves.

Sometime later, a father and son in a truck pulled over and offered to tow us to the next town, which was ten miles away. The man attached a rope to our car that was so short, I couldn't see his rear bumper. He promised to go slowly. Soon, we were going fifty mph as he drove us to a garage. He stayed with us when we spoke to the mechanic to make sure we would be OK, and he offered us a place to stay overnight. We found ourselves "stuck" in Florence, Oregon. We had a lovely day and evening in the quaint little town, and we received love in so many unexpected places. Sometimes you just don't know why something is happening or what the point of it is. But if you can lighten up a bit, you might be able to enjoy the rewards. I suggest laughter as a starting point.

Be aware of opportunities to see the
humor in a situation today.

MAY 10

The present moment is filled with joy and happiness.
If you are attentive, you will see it.
—Thich Nhat Hanh

Seeing the Beauty in This Moment

There is beauty in your life right this minute. Look around. Do you see it? Pick out eight things that meet your needs for beauty right now. Start with yourself! Some things that meet my need for beauty are seeing my cats and bunny sleeping peacefully, a dramatic sky, gardens, a smile, and certain textures. Ahhh. Sometimes, it just takes a different pair of glasses to see the world.

Notice the beauty in your life today.
Does this shift your perspective?

MAY 11

Go confidently in the direction of your dreams!
Live the life you've imagined. As you simplify your
life, the laws of the universe will be simpler.
—Henry David Thoreau

Be What You Want in the World

It's simple, really. If you want connection, connect. If you want peace in your life, be peaceful. Don't wait for the Red Sea to part. Start small. Try to remember to look the cashier in the eye when you thank him. Thank your mail carrier for her service to you and your family. Say hello to your neighbor. Or just spend time connecting with yourself. All your attempts to connect with yourself and other people will bring fruit. No effort is wasted.

Commit to living peacefully today in your interactions
with other people and yourself.

MAY 12

*The Divine Spirit is flowing through me
in an individual way and I accept
the genius of my own being.*
—Ernest Holmes

Celebrate Yourself!

Celebrate your progress, every step of it. I started my journey
of self-discovery in 1986. Many times, I felt overwhelmed
and I told myself I wasn't getting anywhere. I often felt discouraged and wanted to give up. I didn't give up because
I didn't want to live such a hopeless life. Now, my life is
mostly peaceful and joyful. Now I see how every effort I
made to shift my life has contributed to my current state
of being. I am grateful for every mistake, every victory, and
every confusing moment. They all led me here.

We all have a starting point. If you are just getting
started, hurrah to you. If you've been doing this for a while,
congratulations. No matter where you are in your life, you
have made progress. Celebrate yourself and your progress!

Celebrate your progress at least once today.

MAY 13

The fountain of beauty is the heart,
and every generous thought illustrates
the walls of your chamber.
—Francis Quarles

Making a Connection in a Difficult Situation

I often hear this question in my work: "What is the single most important thing I can do to defuse a conflict?" My answer is always the same. "Hear the feelings and needs of the people involved." Whether there is the potential of physical or emotional violence, the most effective method I have ever found to defuse a conflict is to listen deeply to the underlying needs of the people in conflict. Nothing is swifter, more direct, or more healing.

Imagine how you would feel if your partner told you that she had invited her family to visit for a week during your vacation. You could be furious with her because you thought you would spend your vacation differently. Perhaps you only get two weeks of vacation a year and you really want a break. In exasperation you say to her: "How dare you invite your family to share in our vacation without discussing it with me? Did it even occur to you to consider my needs or to include me in the discussion of this?" She replies, "It sounds like you're angry because you wanted to do something else on our vacation and you would have liked to be involved in the decision." "Yes! How could you make a decision that affects my life so greatly without discussing it with me?" "So, besides being mad that I invited them, you're also baffled about why I did it." "Yes. I'm baffled and frustrated." You begin to calm down because you know she has heard your needs. Then she asks, "Are you also kind of hurt because you wanted to spend time with just me?" "Yes. And, I really wanted a break. I wanted quiet time with you. I was so looking forward to it." Now that she thinks you have been heard fully, she shares what's going on with her. "I'm feeling really sad. I didn't know that you needed the down time so much. I know that you like my family, so when Mom asked if she could come, I just said OK. Now that I see how upset you are because you want quiet time with me, I would like to revisit this. I'm open to changing my plans if we can create a vacation that works for both of us. Would you be willing to brainstorm this with me for a few minutes?" "Sure." Within moments, anger is defused and the opportunity exists to create a solution that will value both people's needs. It's miraculous.

Be aware of opportunities to defuse conflicts by
reflecting the feelings and needs of the other person.

MAY 14

God is our refuge and strength,
a very present help in trouble.
—Psalms 46:1

How to Know if Someone Has Been Heard

Often people ask me how they can tell if the other person has been heard. Many times you can feel a release of tension in your own body. Other times you may notice that the other person responds in a calm tone with few words, such as "Yeah" or "Uh huh." Two minutes before, he may have had a lot more to say or perhaps he expressed himself loudly.

Another thing I look for is body language. When people are angry, they often sit or stand taller. They literally seem bigger. Once they have been heard, you may notice their shoulders or jaw relax; maybe they uncross their arms or tear up a little. In essence, people tend to look, act, and sound softer when they have been fully heard. If you are not sure whether someone has been heard and you want to be cautious, you may ask the person, "Is there anything else you'd like me to hear?" In any case, if you try to reason with or educate someone before he feels he has been heard, he will likely respond negatively to you. After he is heard, you may notice a willingness on his part to listen and proceed.

Be aware of how you feel today when someone tries to reason with you before you have been heard.

MAY 15

He who cannot forgive others breaks the bridge
over which he must pass himself.
—*George Herbert*

Getting Beyond Our Judgments So We May Connect

Any time we enter a conversation harboring ill will or judgment about the other person, we are part of the problem. How can we truly connect with another if we simultaneously think he is bad, wrong, or evil? It is important to remember that all actions are attempts to meet needs. People are not inherently evil. Nevertheless, sometimes we do judge other people, so what do we do? Consider the needs the other person is trying to meet through his actions. For example, someone might say to you, "I am done discussing this with you!" Can you imagine what his feelings and needs might be? You could say, "Are you worried that continuing this conversation won't lead to resolution because of our past experiences?" "Yes! And you don't listen, so what's the point?" "So, you're also frustrated and want to know that I will really hear you this time?" "Yeah." If we focus on what we think is wrong with the other person, we stay in the problem or conflict. The minute we step out of judgment and listen for their underlying needs, we begin working for the solution. Put your focus in the direction of the result you want.

> Be aware of opportunities to consciously direct
> your focus toward the result you want.

MAY 16

Adversity introduces a man to himself.
—Anonymous

Sometimes I Can't Get Past My Judgments

Don't you just want to say "Ugh!" sometimes? "Ugh" comes to mind for me when I intend to connect with someone while my brain works overtime telling me all the reasons why this person is bad or wrong. This recently came up for me when a woman called me to lodge a complaint about an interaction we had. I let her talk for about ten minutes. In that time, she told me I had botched the job, that I had lied, and that I didn't care about her or her family. None of this was true from my perspective. In fact, I had gone out of my way to help her family meet all its needs. Nevertheless, here she was on the phone full of rage and disappointment. My initial thoughts were judgments about her. I thought she was narcissistic, mean, and completely unreasonable.

Then I caught myself judging her. I asked myself, "Mary, what do you value?" The answer, as always, was, "To connect!" I was able to connect to my unmet needs in this conversation—respect, consideration, connection, and integrity. Once I was connected to them, I could simultaneously connect to this woman's desire for fairness and consideration. That was when I could release my judgments of her, see her humanness, and begin to hear her. Sometimes, it is way too hard to connect to other people if we don't first connect to ourselves. It doesn't matter whether you listen to yourself or the other person first, as long as you do both you will ultimately connect.

Be aware today of times when you are judging someone. Then be aware of your own needs to improve your connection to them.

MAY 17

Let me tell you the secret that has led me to my goal.
My strength lies solely in my tenacity.
—Louis Pasteur

Learning From Our Regrets

Changing our focus from trying to win and be right to connecting is a paradigm shift. We are bound to make mistakes in the beginning, which may cause discomfort. Consider the times when you didn't respond the way you wanted. How could you have handled that situation differently? What would have better met your needs? Try not to judge your behavior, but learn from it. Each time we review our actions, we come closer to meeting our ideal.

When I first started to learn Compassionate Communication, I would review my own situations and other people's. I would translate the words of newscasters, grocery cashiers, my mother, and even my cat's behaviors into feelings and needs. Each time, I learned something and I became a little more adept with my new skills. Habit is an amazing thing— we develop habits that either serve us or don't. I decided that I wanted a new paradigm that would better serve my life. Through the habit of translating comments into feelings and needs, I achieved this. You can too.

Today, practice translating people's words into feelings
and needs wherever opportunities exist.

MAY 18

The wisdom of life consists in the elimination of nonessentials.
—Lin Yutang

Creating More Efficient Meetings

I often hear people express their discontent with meetings. They say meetings are long and unproductive. In my experience, meetings are unproductive when the participants aren't clear about their needs or what they want from the group. If five people hold a meeting and they all express an opinion without expressing a need or informing the group of what they want, the meeting lacks clarity.

Say a Homeowners' Association meets and the topic is whether people should be permitted to build a fence around their home. The first person who talks says, "I think we should be able to build fences." The second person says, "We should be able to build fences that are six feet or lower." Someone else says, "We should only build white fences." Another doesn't think we should build fences at all. Not one person has expressed a need or made a request and the conversation circles with little hope for resolution.

How about if the first person changes his statement to: "Well, I would like it if we could build fences because it would help protect our pets. Does anyone object to this?" Notice that he expresses his needs—*to protect pets*, and he makes a direct request—*Does anyone object to this?* Somebody else raises her hand and says: "I like the idea of fences to protect our animals but I would like them to be six feet or lower so that we don't lose our views. Does anyone object to this?" Again, she expresses her need—*to protect*

166

pets and maintain the view, and a request—*Does anyone object to this?*

When participants focus on expressing their needs and making clear requests, meetings become more efficient and enjoyable. If a participant is unfamiliar with this process, anyone can ask her for clarity about her needs and what she would like back from the group. In this way, a single attendee can support the group in creating a productive and enjoyable meeting.

Be aware today of opportunities to clarify your needs and requests in group discussions to maintain an efficient and fun process.

MAY 19

*Our physical body possesses a wisdom which we
who inhabit the body lack. We give it orders
which make no sense.*
—Henry Miller

Living Peacefully, Starting With Our Physical Selves

I spent years abusing my physical self with alcohol, cigarettes, and food. I believe I do not live peacefully if I am not at peace with my body. I have not had a cigarette in twelve years, or alcohol in seven years, yet I still struggle to feed my body nurturing food. I am certain that I choose food that doesn't nurture my system because of my needs for safety, predictability, and relief. To meet those needs, I am creating new strategies that are more in harmony with my values of integrity, nurturing, and love. Some of these are to limit my sugar and carbohydrate intake and significantly increase the quantity of vegetables I eat each day. The human body is an awesome and complicated system. It supports us no matter what we do to it. It loves us no matter how we feel about it. Please join me in living in harmony with our bodies. If you make loving your body as natural as brushing your teeth or making your bed in the morning, you can bring even deeper peace into your life.

Be aware of all the ways your body
supports your life today.

MAY 20

Satisfaction of one's curiosity is one of the
greatest sources of happiness in life.
—Linus Pauling

Engage Your Curiosity

Try to be curious rather than judgmental. If a person does something that you can't fathom, ask *them* about it rather than telling your guess about it to yourself and other people—"What could he be thinking?" If your teenage son agrees to mow the lawn once a week, but continuously doesn't do it, don't focus on your own anger; ask him what keeps him from following through on his commitment. If you have a friend who interrupts you more than you like, ask her if she's worried about not having enough time to share. Develop curiosity about people and their behaviors. Don't be afraid to ask questions. You may be surprised by what you learn.

Adopt an attitude of curiosity today and ask questions!

---- ✳ ----

MAY 21

If you judge people, you have no time to love them.
—Mother Teresa

Losing Our Judgments

Consider the situation when your mother calls you on the phone and you become increasingly agitated as the conversation continues. You consider never calling her again—or at least not for a month. You're convinced that no matter what you do, nothing will help you connect with her. You may be relieved to know that there are other solutions. Whenever you feel frustrated, agitated, judgmental, or critical, listen for the feelings and needs of the other, and you will be amazed at the results.

If your mother talks critically about your sister and you feel agitated, you could say, "Mom, are you feeling worried about Beth because you want her to be happy?" Anytime we connect to the feelings and needs of another person, we can't help but lose our judgments and criticisms. This is called empathy. It may sound too simple to accomplish such a radical transformation, but honestly, it isn't. When we focus on feelings and needs, our feelings about others and ourselves improve, our perspective shifts, and our ability to be compassionate increases. It is a simple, transformative, profound truth.

Empathize with at least one person today rather than judging her. Notice if doing this shifts your feelings.

MAY 22

Tenacity is when you follow your heart—when the whole world is screaming to get back into your head.
—Sonia Choquette

Setting the Intention

Not long ago, I was talking with a friend who told me that he wanted to come to a mutually satisfying resolution with another friend, but didn't think it was possible. He was thinking about calling his friend even though he had no hope that the friend would be able to hear him. This expectation was a setup. He convinced himself that he wouldn't succeed before he even started. When we enter into conversations with this attitude, we contribute to our lack of success. When we start conversations that might be challenging with the intention of success, we shift the energy immediately toward it. We will not always be successful by starting with this attitude, but we will have greater opportunity to succeed if we do.

Set your intention before starting a conversation today.

MAY 23

In the middle of difficulty lies opportunity.
—Albert Einstein

Striving for Win-Win Resolutions

In Nonviolent Communication, we strive for win-win resolutions. That means that no one loses. We don't decide things by the majority, because that would mean that the minority loses. Compromise is similar. In fact, in a compromise both people could feel dissatisfied with the resolution because it usually involves an element of *giving in.*

An alternative is shifting; both people connect to the needs they are trying to meet, and in doing so, one person makes an honest shift to contribute to the other person's needs. For instance, a young woman recently asked me for a large discount on one of my classes. At first I was reluctant because I had already given many discounts. But she began to tell me how much she wanted to take the class and how much she wanted to learn new tools to communicate with her child. Her money was very tight because she was a single mom earning less than she needed to support herself and her son. Her passion and earnestness shone through like a beacon. Seeing this, I shifted and agreed to let her take the class at no charge. I didn't begrudge this decision. I did this joyfully because, although I still have a need for financial security, I also have a need to contribute to young parents who want to learn effective ways to communicate with their children. I shifted from my original need for financial security to a desire to contribute to her and her family. My decision met both our needs.

Be aware of opportunities to shift to a different need in order to contribute to someone else's life today.

MAY 24

When you really listen to yourself,
you can heal yourself.
—Ceanna DeRohan

Self-Empathy: A Direct Route to Personal Healing

It is true that we cannot fully understand other people until we understand ourselves. I tried to escape this for years. I told people that I was a caring and loving person. But deep down, I struggled to feel compassion. I was consumed with anger, resentment, and an overriding belief that I was never going to be happy. It wasn't until I looked at my own inner critic (known as the jackal in Compassionate Communication) that I started to heal. The more inner healing I received, the greater my compassion for other people grew; this result increased exponentially. Inner peace creates outward peace.

I gained much of my healing through self-empathy within the Compassionate Communication process. I focused on this process for several months before I started to experience noticeable changes in my attitude and greater inner peace. It led to a remarkable shift toward the happiness and peace I now experience on a daily basis. The self-empathy process has four steps:

Enjoy your inner critic. Acknowledge what the jackal says without censorship or judgment.

Acknowledge your feelings. How do you feel about this situation? List all of your feelings.

Acknowledge your needs. What do you need—love, support, kindness, courtesy, or something else?

Make a request of yourself and others. Do you feel better simply by acknowledging your feelings and needs? Or would you like to make a request of yourself or someone else to rectify the situation?

Commit to practicing self-empathy at least once today.

MAY 25

Should you shield the canyons from the windstorms,
you would never see the beauty of their carvings.
—Dr. Elisabeth Kübler-Ross

Mourning Our Losses

Do you ever tell yourself that you shouldn't feel bad because things could be worse, or because someone else is worse off, or that your situation just isn't so bad that you need to carry on about it? Every time we tell ourselves that our sadness and grief are not worth mourning, we cut ourselves off from potential healing and life. Mourning, in a Nonviolent Communication process, involves allowing ourselves to feel the pain of the unmet needs in our life. In some ways, this process is about recognizing the depth and sadness of our unmet needs, which can't happen when we tell ourselves that we shouldn't feel that way. Our level of grief will depend on the situation. However, no matter the depth of our sadness, mourning enables us to heal the pain and gain clarity about how to meet our needs in the present moment.

The mourning process in Nonviolent Communication involves four steps:

Identify the feelings—sadness, disappointment, worry—
  you have about your unmet need
Identify the need—support, fun, friendship, intimacy.
Imagine how you would feel if the need were met.
Look for additional strategies to meet the need.

Be aware of any sadness, disappointment,
or hurt you feel today and take a moment
to mourn your unmet needs.

MAY 26

This is how a human being can change:
There's a worm addicted to eating grape leaves.
Suddenly, he wakes up, call it grace, whatever,
Something wakes him, and he's no longer a worm.
He's the entire vineyard, and the orchard too,
The fruit, the trunks, a growing wisdom and joy
That doesn't need to devour.
—*Rumi*

Sustaining Our World

The world's people are consuming its resources at an alarming rate. We consume more than we replenish at astronomical speed. This is a form of violence, of not valuing everyone's needs. It is not OK with me if my needs are met while people in other countries, or even in the house next door, do not have enough to sustain themselves. People can feel overwhelmed imagining a shift in this course we are on, so I suggest we simply shift our own over-consumption. Consider how you can change your life so that you take less from the earth's resources and replenish more. Respect everything that lives. Consider how you can support its life and yours. Shift your consciousness to consider how you *contribute* to the *earth's* ability to flourish. No action is too small. Start today.

Take an action today to better support
the earth's sustainability.

MAY 27

Friend, there's a window that opens from heart to heart
And there are ways of closing it . . .
—*Rumi*

Keeping Ourselves Open

One of the swiftest ways to close the heart is critical or judgmental thinking. How open are you when you are judging another person? The goal in peaceful living is to approach our relationships with an open heart. Years ago, I asked another trainer of Nonviolent Communication to help me come up with a request that would help me meet my needs for intimacy in my relationship. I wanted to create a dialogue that would help me get what I wanted. The trainer said: "Mary, I hope that you are entering this conversation with a desire to *connect* to your partner. Your goal should always be to *connect* with someone, not simply to get your own way." I realized in that moment that I hardly ever had conversations with people simply to connect with them or understand them. My motivation was to get what I wanted. No wonder so many people saw me as manipulative and questioned my motives.

Now, when I want to talk to someone about an issue that might be emotional, I start with the intention to connect and a desire to find ways to value both our needs. I try to keep my heart open to all the possible ways we can do this. The truth is, I have had years of training on how to close my heart. Now I am learning new behaviors to keep it open. I have achieved such great happiness in this new paradigm.

Start conversations today with an intention
to connect with other people.

MAY 28

Don't just do something, stand there.
—*Buddha*

The Power of Empathy

People often need empathy when they are in the most pain. In these situations, we may hear their words as critical and judgmental. It is important in such moments to remember that everything they say or do is an attempt to meet their needs. When they are in pain, sometimes the methods they use to meet their needs are ineffective and hurtful to others. When we attempt empathy in these charged moments, we may receive the gift of connection—of truly understanding the other person. In this way, empathizing with those in pain is one of the most healing things we can do for them and for ourselves.

Be aware of opportunities to empathize with someone who is in emotional pain today.

MAY 29

*To be successful, the first thing to do
is fall in love with your work.*
—Sister Mary Lauretta

Living in Joy

We all have daily activities that don't seem fun. Mine are cooking, lighting a fire, and cleaning the cat box. For years I grumbled about these things and I could find no joy in them at all, until I started to connect to the needs I was trying to meet with each activity. Each morning for several months, when I heard my inner critic grumble about cooking, I would say, "I cook because I value nourishment." When building a fire, I would say, "I'm building this fire because I value sustainability and warmth." And when cleaning the cat box, I would say to myself, "I am cleaning the cat box because I want my cats to have a happy and clean environment." Then after each statement, I would ask myself if I still wanted to complete the task. Some mornings I decided that I could go out for breakfast and the litter could go one more day, or I could put on another layer of clothes instead of making a fire. Each day I connected to the need I was trying to meet, and then I decided whether I wanted to do the activity. It was a simple process that only took a few minutes, and it taught me that I have choices. I don't have to do anything. I choose to do some tasks because they meet my needs. By taking the demand out of these tasks and connecting to my needs, I feel more empowered and joyful.

Connect to your values or needs
when doing daily tasks today.

MAY 30

*Until you make peace with who you are, you'll
never be content with what you have.*
—*Doris Mortman*

Clarifying What You Value

Make a clear, conscious decision about what's important to you, and then live from that place. I used to strive to be liked.

I measured my success by other people's opinions of me. I was in pain for years using this strategy. If someone didn't like me, I felt bad and I tried to be the kind of person they wanted me to be. If someone didn't want to spend time with me, I was certain it was because I wasn't a likeable person. It did not occur to me to clarify my own values and to live from them. For instance, I value authenticity so I began to speak up when something was important to me, rather than keep quiet so that people would like me. Once I truly understood what was important to me, I began to live more peacefully. Sometimes people still don't like me, but I know that if I act in harmony with my values, I can be at peace even in the face of conflict.

Live from your values today.

MAY 31

What's terrible is to pretend that the second-rate is the first-rate. To pretend that you don't need love when you do; or you like your work when you know quite well you're capable of better.
—Doris Lessing

Denying Our Needs

It is painful spending our days pretending we're not who we are. For years I tried not to be passionate because I thought my passion turned people off. And I tried not to be intense because I thought I was "too much" for people. Each day, for years, I would try figuratively to squeeze myself into small spaces. Sometimes, I simply couldn't breathe fully in my life, and often I had no hope that I could let all my bigness out and still be loved. Finally, at about age thirty-five, I began to break out of the box I had built around myself by speaking my truth and choosing different people to share my passion with. I liberated myself and I could breathe fully again.

We all have needs. We all have feelings. It doesn't serve anyone to hide ourselves or deny our needs. The world isn't a better place if we're unhappy. The best hope for peace is for every person to notice what they need and to work actively to meet their needs. This alone will dramatically diminish the frustration, anger, judgments, and violence in our world.

Today, decide to be yourself and meet
your genuine needs.

Meditations for
JUNE

JUNE 1

If you are all wrapped up in yourself,
you are overdressed.
—Kate Halverson

Considering the Needs of Other People

If you only focus on what you want, you are only halfway there. One of the basic principles of Nonviolent Communication is valuing everyone's needs *equally*. Remember that needs are the underlying reasons why we do things. You might go to the store to pick up food to feed your family. Your need is to *feed your family* and your strategy is to *go to the store*. If you didn't have enough food to feed everyone in your family tonight, would you like to eat your fill and let others go hungry? Or would you like to find a way to meet everyone's need for food? Most of us would want to find a way to feed everyone in our family. We are not always able to meet everyone's needs, but we certainly value them. If we focus on other people's needs at our own expense, we focus too much on others. If we focus on our own needs at the expense of others, we focus too much on ourselves. The consciousness we strive for is to value everyone's needs *equally*. We feel the power of this consciousness when we realize that there are creative ways to meet many people's needs simultaneously. Indeed, the Universe is abundant with resources to do this if we are willing to be present to them.

Today, notice when it is easy for you to value everyone's
needs and when you are limited in doing this.

JUNE 2

The body does not lie.
—*Martha Graham*

Meeting Our Need for Rest

I was astounded to discover that a friend of mine renews herself by being with people. She feels more restful and relaxed when she is with people than when she is alone. I, on the other hand, meet my need for rest when I am alone and quiet. I spend much of my work life listening and talking with people, which I enjoy very much. However, when the day is done, I need a little quiet time to myself. How much quiet time I need and how much time with other people my friend needs depend on how depleted we are in the moment. We all have different ways to meet our need for rest. The important thing is to notice when we need that time. You might know you need rest when you find yourself snapping at people on the phone, when you snap at your cat, or when you ignore your partner. Rather than behave in ways that you might regret, consider doing something that will help you meet your need for rest. Everyone in your life will benefit.

Be aware today of times when you have a need for rest,
and do something to help you meet it.

JUNE 3

The Eskimo has fifty-two names for snow because it is
important to them; there ought to be as many for love.
—Margaret Atwood

What's Love Got to Do With It?

We tend to talk about the things that are important to us,
or the things we experience the most in our lives. I used to
talk often about the abuse I received. It was the focal point of
my life and experience, and remained my focal point until I
started talking about other things, such as compassion, love,
and peace. Once I shifted my focus, I started to receive those
things, rather than violence. Place your attention on the
positive things you want in your life. If you want more love,
shift your focus from grumbling about how lonely you are
to noticing the times when you feel loved. Express gratitude
for the times that reflect your ideals for love. You may start
with only a few moments in which you feel grateful, but I
am confident they will increase if you continue this practice.

For today, focus your attention on the enjoyable things
in your life that you would like to increase.

JUNE 4

True feeling justifies whatever it may cost.
—May Sarton

Being Open to Feeling

If someone accidentally stepped on your finger, it would hurt, right? You would feel and probably express pain. Few of us would endure the pain without asking the person to step off our finger simply because we thought we shouldn't complain. Pain is pain. It's not good or bad; it is simply how we feel. Maybe the person didn't intend to cause pain, but they did. Emotional pain is similar. If someone says something to us that stimulates pain in us, it is OK to acknowledge it, even if the other person didn't intend for us to be hurt. We don't need to justify our feelings, hide them, pretend they don't exist, or be embarrassed. It is OK, in fact it is exciting, to be a feeling person.

Today, feel more alive by acknowledging your feelings freely to yourself and to other people.

JUNE 5

A caress is better than a career.
—*Elisabeth Marbury*

Noticing What Is Important

I woke up one day and I realized that I had a lucrative career in higher education. I was paid a good salary and I had attained some freedom and a good reputation. I also had very few friends, was in little contact with my family, and wasn't in a significant relationship. Most of my life was devoted to my career. Then I began to think: "Is this it? Is this enough?"

I decided it wasn't. Building a career never kept my bed warm at night and it never gave me someone to lean on when I was overwhelmed. It never gave me a hug or offered love. It did tap into my intellect, which I was comfortable showing to the world. Relationships, on the other hand, tapped into my heart, which I was ill at ease showing to myself or other people. That was five years ago. Today, I have many dear friends, I am close and connected to my family, and my life is filled with love and joy. Now when I ask myself: "Is this it? Is this enough?" The answer is, "Yes."

Be aware of where you focus your life today, and
shift the focus if you are not happy with it.

JUNE 6

Each contact with a human being is so rare,
and so precious. One should preserve it.
—Anaïs Nin

Seeing the God in All of Us

Every life is precious. There isn't a person or creature that is here by mistake. Something greater than all life combined has determined our place on Earth. Simply put your energy where you feel the most joy, and know that the Universe will take care of the rest. Do this without judging other people and you will take one step toward world peace.

Be aware of your worth and your place on earth today.

JUNE 7

*One's life has value so long as one attributes value
to the life of others, by means of love, friendship,
indignation, and compassion.*
—Simone de Beauvoir

Valuing the Whole Community

Just getting what I want isn't enough. I also value the needs of
my community and the world, so I don't want my needs to be
met at the expense of others. I don't want to buy clothes that
were made in a sweatshop in a Third World country. I don't
want to frequent large chain stores that have a reputation
for mistreating their employees. I don't want to buy gasoline
from companies that have a history of polluting the world's
oceans. It's not that I protest these organizations or rebel
against them. Instead, I make choices that meet my needs
for integrity and valuing the world's community. I value my
needs and the world's needs simultaneously. Consider how
your actions value the world community's needs.

Today, find ways to meet your needs that are in
harmony with the needs of the world's people.

JUNE 8

*There is nothing more thrilling in this world, I
think, than having a child that is yours, and yet is
mysteriously a stranger.*
—Agatha Christie

Loving Our Role as Parent

Parenthood is a paradox. If you do your job well, your children leave you. I met an English woman once who told me that for the first twenty-four hours of her son's life, he was her child. She savored that first day with him, knowing he was all hers. The morning of the second day, she began the process of helping him leave her successfully. Parenting can be painful. We want our children to love us, and we know that ultimately we will have to let them go their own way. We want the very best for them; we want them to be happy, healthy, safe, and full of love. Yet, as we nurture them, we also teach them how to live on their own, how to be independent, and how to leave us well. Remember the ultimate *need* you are trying to meet when raising your children—*contributing* to their ability to live independently.

Today, focus on the paradoxical needs you try to
meet through parenting, such as contributing to your
children's ability to live independently.

JUNE 9

In an effort to give good and comforting answers to the young questioners whom we love, we very often arrive at good and comforting answers for ourselves.
—Ruth Goode

If You Want It, Give It Away

If you feel overwhelmed, hopeless, or sad, consider empathizing with someone else. You'll feel better immediately. It may seem like a contradiction, but connecting with other people can be a catalyst for sweet connection with ourselves. Many times when I have felt overwhelmed in my own life, a friend has called to talk about her struggles. My first instinct is to say: "I can't talk right now. Would it be OK if I called you back in a couple of hours?" to allow myself time to deal with my own overload before talking with someone else. However, I have learned that very often, connecting deeply with someone else's struggle helps *me* connect to *mine*. The act of giving love to someone else helps me remember what is most important to me—connecting with people and living peacefully. If you want more money, make a donation to someone else. If you want more love, extend your love to another person. If you long for peace, offer peace to others. If you want understanding, take the time to understand another. Give it away, and you will receive it back threefold.

Determine what you want most today, and then commit to giving it away to at least one person.

JUNE 10

If you want to be listened to, you should
put in time listening.
—Marge Piercy

Getting Out of Ourselves

I spent most of my life obsessing about myself and my needs. I thought I was a caring person, but I rarely contributed to anyone else's life unless it was convenient for me. I had a mentor once who told me that I spent too much time thinking about my own comfort and not enough time considering other people's feelings. At the time, I was attending a series of meetings. I felt uncomfortable every day, so I wouldn't talk to people or participate much. My mentor suggested that I reach out to someone because *they* might be feeling uncomfortable too. This was a revelation. It had never occurred to me to reach out to *other people* when *I* felt uncomfortable. My mentor assigned me to go to the meeting each day, say hello, and chat with at least two people. In a few short weeks, I had met several people, I felt comfortable participating, and I even started to enjoy going. If you're uncomfortable in a situation, consider reaching out to someone else. You may be surprised at how this simple action can shift your experience and help you feel more connected.

Consider reaching out to someone today,
especially if you feel uncomfortable.

JUNE 11

The healthy and strong individual is the one who asks
for help when he needs it, whether he's got an abscess
on his knee or in his soul.
—Rona Barrett

Making Requests to Enrich Our Lives

Contrary to popular belief, when you make a request of someone, you do not diminish your relationship; you enhance it. It is laborious, frustrating, and futile to search for the perfect person who will automatically know what you want without being told. However, simply asking for what you want can provide instant relief. If you want more intimacy in your relationship, what specifically could the other person do to help you meet that need? You could say: "Honey, I've been feeling a little lonely lately, and I would really like more intimacy in our relationship. Would you be willing to plan a time this week when we spend an entire evening alone together without the TV or telephones?" Or maybe you want sex: "Honey, I've been feeling lonely and I'm really missing our lovemaking. How would you feel about taking a couple of hours tonight and creating one of our famous long lovemaking sessions?" If she says no to either of these requests, consider brainstorming a different strategy that would meet both your needs. It isn't a sign of weakness to clarify what you would like. It helps you commit to living a full and joyful life!

Be aware of opportunities to clarify your requests to
your partner and other people in your life today.

JUNE 12

The mere sense of living is joy enough.
—*Emily Dickinson*

Living in the Present

Live for this moment. When you worry, you are focusing on the future. When you feel regret, you are dwelling in the past. What is happening right now? Do you have enough food, friends, and love right now? If so, celebrate! If not, what can you do to shift your experience? Tomorrow will come soon enough. Try to enjoy the process of getting there.

Each time you catch yourself worrying or feeling regret today, ask if there is anything you can do to resolve the situation. If there is nothing you can do, celebrate all you have in this moment. If there is something, take action immediately.

JUNE 13

Whoever is happy will make others happy too.
—*Anne Frank*

Connecting to Your Needs in Relationships

Many people evaluate their relationships based on their perception of how the other person feels. I did this for years. I would decide that a relationship was good or bad based on whether my partner was enjoying it. This left me feeling insecure and confused. A more effective way to evaluate relationships is to check in with *your* feelings and needs. How do *you* feel and what needs of *yours* are met when you spend time with someone? Do you feel happy, free, and relaxed? Or do you tend to feel worried, confused, or on edge? Once you have connected with your own feelings and needs, consider whether this relationship is working for you. If it isn't, be specific about which of your needs are unmet. Notice if you can do anything to help meet them.

Connect with your feelings and needs in
one of your relationships today.

JUNE 14

*The excursion is the same when you go looking for
your sorrow as when you go looking for your joy.*
—*Eudora Welty*

Shifting Our Perceptions to
Change Our Experience

I recently assisted a friend in mediating a situation. When we talked afterward, I was overflowing with how pleased I was with the outcome, how open and honest the participants were, and how hopeful I felt about the future of this group. My friend talked about her uncomfortable feelings, how certain situations annoyed her, and how much distrust she felt. We both participated in the same event. We even remembered the same facts of the situation. However, we perceived them differently. Was either of us right? No. Everyone is entitled to their own experience.

How do you generally experience life situations? Does your experience contribute to joy or despair? If you want to change your experience, consider shifting your perspective. To learn how, ask someone else how they experienced a situation you both shared. As you listen to his perceptions and learn how they differ from yours, you can begin to shift your view of your own life. Choose to perceive your life from different perspectives and with a joyful heart.

Today, make a choice to change your experience
by joyfully shifting your perception.

JUNE 15

People who fight with fire usually end up with ashes.
—*Abigail Van Buren*

Living Peacefully

As scary as it can be sometimes, put down your fists. Stop fighting. Give up your urge to be right and to win. Instead, approach any charged situations you find yourself in with a sincere desire to be honest, to value everyone's needs, and to meet your own need for fairness. When we match might with might, we create discord, frustration, and separation from other people. Do you want to promote this in your life? Try peace instead. You can only control *yourself,* and the way you show up is your most valuable asset. No matter how other people act, if you feel good about your part, you have succeeded. In the end, you may not get what you asked for but you will be more likely to meet your needs for integrity, valuing life, and relief.

Be aware today of the times when you are tempted to use might to get what you want, and instead choose integrity and authenticity.

JUNE 16

Could we all just admit when we're crabby?
—*Sark*

Using Anger as a Beacon

I used to be afraid of my anger because I didn't know how to express it, and I had an underlying fear that once I opened the lid on it, I would overwhelm myself and the people in my life. Consequently, I rarely allowed myself to examine my anger. I have come to appreciate it because it tells me when something is up. In a sense, it serves as a beacon. When something stimulates pain in us, our anger beacon lights up, whether we want it to or not, and warns us that we have an unmet need. What if your spouse has filled the garage with old stuff until there is limited space remaining for your cars? You may have felt a little annoyed when she started this process, and as time went on, you became more angry about it, but you just didn't want to admit it to yourself. Then, one day, her old typewriter appears in the garage and somehow that just tips you over the edge. What if you had simply checked in with yourself and noticed how you were feeling when the first box appeared in the garage? Had you addressed your feelings then, you would have been in a better position to resolve the situation with more ease and you wouldn't have suffered annoyance for several weeks or months. By acknowledging our feelings immediately, we can deal with them before we react in ways we may regret later.

Try to notice the point at which you first feel angry. Then take a moment to acknowledge your feelings and unmet needs associated with the situation that sparked your anger before you respond to the other person.

JUNE 17

*I have come to the conclusion, after many years
of sometimes-sad experience, that you cannot
come to any conclusion at all.*
—Vita Sackville-West

Enjoying the Process

In Compassionate Communication, we strive to stop judging situations and people. Instead, we look at how we feel and whether our needs are met. For example, if our partnership does not meet our need for intimacy, we talk with our partner about our feelings and what we need *without blaming her for lacking intimacy.* Instead, we focus on ways to meet our need for intimacy as well as the other person's needs. We might say: "Honey, I have noticed that we haven't made love in three weeks and I'm feeling disappointed and confused about this. I miss that aspect of our intimate life. Do you miss it too?" Notice that we express our need (intimate life) without placing blame on either party. The request (do you miss it too?) opens the conversation so we can hear the other person's needs. When we approach situations without preconceived ideas and take the time to check in with the other person, we enhance our opportunity to resolve situations in mutually beneficial ways.

> Focus on your feelings and needs today
> rather than on judging other people.

JUNE 18

*While others may argue about whether the world
ends with a bang or a whimper, I just want to
make sure mine doesn't end with a whine.*
—Barbara Gordon

Enjoying Your Life

The surest way to enjoy life is to do things that meet our needs. If we don't enjoy a particular activity, let's consider the need we hope to meet by doing it. Recently, I had a number of projects with looming deadlines that were weighing on me. I started to feel overwhelmed and I told myself, "I have to get these things done!" Then, I noticed that I no longer enjoyed the projects because I was focused on completing them no matter what. So, I took a few minutes and considered the needs I was trying to meet with each project. Once I connected to them, I asked myself this question for each project: "How would I feel if I delayed the completion of this project?" I found I had a strong desire to continue with many of the projects, but I decided to finish a few of them later.

This simple exercise offered me two things: the opportunity to connect to the needs I was trying to meet project by project, thereby connecting to my joy in each, and the chance to reshuffle priorities based on my current needs for ease and relief. Do you like what you're doing right now? If not, consider the needs you are trying to meet and whether you want to continue. I once heard a poem about a man who was looking at a tombstone that listed the date of a person's birth, then a dash, and then the date of his death. The poem asked how well the dead person had lived "his dash." We all have a beginning and an end. The challenge is to enjoy the middle. When we live our life conscious of our needs, we have a greater opportunity to enjoy our dash.

Be aware of how you are living your dash today.

JUNE 19

What I want in my life is compassion,
a flow between myself and others based
on a mutual giving from the heart.
—*Marshall B. Rosenberg, PhD*

Enriching Life

In Compassionate Communication, we believe that *enriching life* is the most satisfying motivation for our actions. If you are motivated by fear, guilt, blame, or shame, you may act only to avoid suffering the consequences of not doing what you have been asked. The best way to experience permanent, lifelong change is to instead focus on how your life will improve when you make a change. For example, you are more likely to succeed at losing weight and maintaining your weight loss if you connect to the needs you want to meet, such as health and beauty. This offers stronger motivation than if you connect to the shame or blame you feel about being overweight.

Be aware of times when you attempt to motivate
yourself and others with guilt, blame, or shame today,
and then look for motivations that enrich life instead.

JUNE 20

*When we submit to doing something solely for the
purpose of avoiding punishment, our attention is
distracted from the value of the action itself . . .
If a worker's performance is promoted by fear of
punishment, the job gets done, but morale suffers;
sooner or later, productivity will decrease.*
—Marshall B. Rosenberg, PhD

Protective vs. Punitive Use of Force

Our society spends a great deal of time punishing people for their misdeeds. This is called punitive use of force. This stems from a belief that people behave in certain ways because they are bad or evil, and that they need to be punished to mend their ways.

Suppose you see your child run into a busy street. If you pull her from the street and berate her for being careless, you are using *punitive force.* Your focus is on judging her behavior. *Protective use of force,* on the other hand, stems from the belief that sometimes people do things because they don't know any better. It represents a desire to prevent injury or injustice. It focuses on protecting people's rights and well-being, not judging their behavior. If you use protective force you would still grab your child, not because you believed she was bad, but because you want to protect her. When we punish people, they focus on avoiding the consequences of their actions, not on their values in relation to their actions. Focusing on avoiding consequences is unlikely to encourage change.

Focus on protective use of force today by adopting an attitude that people sometimes do things that cause them pain because they don't know better.

JUNE 21

*It seems obvious to me right now that rhetoric and
blaming don't solve anything.*
—D.W., prison inmate

Taking Responsibility for Your Choices

Sometimes, it just seems easier for us to blame others for our
choices. We think that if we place the blame on someone else,
we won't look as bad. Our primary motivation may be the
desire to be accepted and valued; however, it's an awkward
strategy to meet those needs. If we don't take responsibility
for our actions, others no longer trust us.

We all have choices. You may think that you *have* to
follow the rules at work. You don't; you *choose* to follow
the rules. You can choose to quit, or confront the system,
or rebel. Because none of these choices feels satisfying, you
might *choose* to follow the rules to meet your needs for
ease, financial security, or your position in the company.
Ultimately, though, it's your choice. Once we begin taking
responsibility for our choices, we empower ourselves, regain
others' trust, and enhance our ability to maintain satisfying
relationships.

Be aware of the times when you don't take
responsibility for your choices, then notice
the choices you have.

JUNE 22

*I particularly hope to address parents' yearning for
deeper connection with themselves, their partners,
and their children, and their desire to contribute,
through parenting, to fostering peace in the world.*
—Inbal Kashtan

Parenting With a Focus on the Long-Term Goal

Parents are often tempted to wield their enormous physical, emotional, and intellectual power in order to coerce their children into doing what they want. This strategy may meet the immediate need for ease, but it can be counterproductive in the long term.

If you find yourself coercing your child into doing something, ask yourself two questions: "What do I want my child to do?" and "What do I want my child's reasons for doing it to be?" Often, a parent wants her children to be self-motivated, but she limits their opportunity for this when she forces them to do things they don't want to do.

When children are motivated by guilt, fear, or shame, they begin to lose touch with themselves because they focus on *your* reactions, not on *their* needs. When this happens, they create a paradigm that it is OK to do certain things as long as they aren't caught. When they live in this paradigm, they are no longer connecting to their own needs to belong or to contribute to their family or community. They lose their connection to self.

Be aware of the times you are coercing or forcing
your child to do things today, then consider
other methods that will help her connect to
her intrinsic motivation for doing them.

JUNE 23

*I believe that only genuine mutual understanding
can sustain peace . . .*
—Lucy Leu

Empathy for Children

The empathy process in Nonviolent Communication
involves listening for the feelings and needs of another
person. We can do this with children as well as adults.
Say your child is not eating his dinner. You can choose to
understand what is going on with him rather than try to
change his behavior. He could be having fun and doesn't
want to stop to eat, or maybe he doesn't like the food you
offer, or maybe his stomach hurts. Consider empathizing
with him by saying, "Are you disappointed because you
wanted to keep playing?" Or, "Are you mad because you
don't like spaghetti?" By doing this, you expand your child's
emotional vocabulary and give your child the message that
his needs are important to you. Once you have discovered
what is going on with him, try to create a strategy that values
both your needs. Avoid getting stuck on the specific strategy
you hoped for, which might be to get your son to eat his
dinner by six o'clock The better you connect with your

child's needs, the more you will defuse the power struggle that often occurs in parent/child relationships, and the more you will build trust.

> Be aware today of opportunities to
> empathize with your children.

———————— ✳ ————————

JUNE 24

> *I wish with all my heart that we had been able*
> *to give the previous generation of students these*
> *(Nonviolent Communication) skills. I'm certain if*
> *we had, they would have had other means for*
> *resolving their differences than violence.*
> —*A teacher in Belgrade, Yugoslavia*

Modeling Behaviors You'd Like to Receive

The ways that we interact with our children shape the way they will interact in their world. Our actions either increase or decrease our children's ability to understand themselves and their behaviors. When we take the time to connect to their feelings and needs, we demonstrate a way of being that is thoughtful, compassionate, and effective. Our children will learn from our modeling, and approach their life situations better able to choose strategies that will best meet their needs and those of the other people in their lives. All of us will enjoy a more peaceful world as a result.

> Be aware today of how your actions model compassion,
> tolerance, and love for your children.

JUNE 25

Courage is the price that life exacts
for granting peace.
—Amelia Earhart

Communicating With People Who
Don't Share Our Values

Nonviolent Communication works with everyone, even people who aren't familiar with the process or don't share our values for connection and compassion. In fact, compassion automatically blossoms when we stay true to the principles of Nonviolent Communication. We don't try to convince anyone to do it our way or to value the same things we value. We merely focus on what *we* value: compassion among people and valuing everyone's needs.

Some time ago, I worked with a realtor in a very difficult and challenging situation. At one point, I became worried that he would remove himself from the situation before it was resolved, and I was terrified that I would be left on my own to manage it, so I said to him: "You must feel overwhelmed and wonder how you got yourself into this mess. Am I right?" "Yes! I have asked myself that question numerous times. This couple is outrageous and I'm afraid I'll be dragged into a lawsuit." "Yeah, it really is overwhelming, isn't it?" "Yes it is." "I would certainly understand if you chose to remove yourself, and when I think about that possibility, I feel terrified about handling this on my own. Can you think of anything that I could do that would make it more appealing for you to see this through resolution?" "You know, Mary, the only reason I'm still here is because of you. So the only thing you need to do is to keep doing what you're doing. This is an awful situation, but you are very pleasant to work with."

In the past, I might have tried to bully the realtor into staying on the project by insisting that he honor the contract. This time, I acknowledged his unmet needs, expressed my own fears, and asked him how I could make it more worthwhile for him to stick it out. I would have let him out of his contract in a heartbeat if that was what he wanted. He stood by me for two more months until the issue was resolved, even though the pressure grew more intense. No matter what we face, no matter how tempting it is to match might with might, we strive to meet our needs without negatively affecting others. By doing this we are actually more likely to meet our own needs and we are better able to live peacefully.

**Be aware today of your needs and
find harmonious ways to meet them.**

JUNE 26

*Observe!! There are few things as
important or as religious as that.*
—Frederick Buechner, minister

Observing Reality

How often do we see something and then make up a whole story about it? My mother was famous for this. We would be driving down the road and she would see a woman doing something, anything, and my mother would make up a whole story about this woman and her life. We all do this throughout our day. It is one of the ways we bring pain into our lives.

For instance, your partner is two hours late for your date. What do you do? You may begin to make up stories about her lateness. You might think that she's inconsiderate, or that she's probably hurt, or maybe that she values her work more than her time with you. Stories like this cause us pain, and we really have no idea if any of them are true.

Here's another strategy. Simply *observe* what you know—that *she is two hours later than we had agreed to meet*. From there, decide what would best meet your needs given the circumstances. You could call her to find out what's going on, you could decide to go to a movie and leave a note for her in case she shows up, or you could call a friend to commiserate about your situation. There are many choices available to you. Any of the latter choices are less likely to induce pain. Why, then, do we spend so much time torturing ourselves with stories about what *might* be happening? Instead, commit yourself to only observing the facts and then making decisions that are likely to give you relief and joy, rather than making up stories that will surely cause you pain.

Be aware of the times that you make up a story about why something is happening today. Then, bring yourself back to simply observing the facts.

JUNE 27

I've never seen a stupid kid;
I've seen a kid who sometimes did
things I didn't understand
Or things in ways, I hadn't planned;
I've seen a kid who hadn't seen
the same places where I had been,
But he was not a stupid kid.
Before you call him stupid,
think, was he a stupid kid or did he just
know different things than you did?
—*Ruth Bebermeyer*

Separating Observations and Evaluations

Often times we blend an observation—the facts of a situation—with our own opinion. Here is an example: Say your brother spent all of Saturday helping a friend put a new roof on his house. An observation mixed with an evaluation would sound like this: "You are going to wear yourself out!" An observation that is separate from an evaluation would look like this: "When I see you spending all day Saturday roofing your friend's house and I know how hard you work during the week too, I feel worried that you might wear yourself out."

In the first example, the speaker judges her brother's behavior: he's going to wear himself out. In the second example, she acknowledges the facts—her brother helped a friend roof his house on Saturday—and acknowledges her own fears about how this might affect his life. The difference is subtle, but the results are not. Often times, when we mix an evaluation and observation, we promote defensiveness in other people. When we are able to separate the two, we are more likely to promote an open dialogue about our concerns.

Be aware of your evaluations and observations today.
Try to separate the two to create more
opportunities for open dialogue.

JUNE 28

*Creative minds have always been known to
survive any kind of bad training.*
—*Anna Freud*

Attending to Our Feelings

Many of us have received little or no training in expressing our feelings. We have been taught to focus more on other people than ourselves. Rather than noticing how *we* feel in a relationship, we focus our attention on wondering if the other person enjoys it. Rather than notice how we feel about our work performance, we wonder what our boss thinks of it. This lack of attention to our own feelings tends to keep us disconnected from ourselves and creates confusion. When we shift our focus to our own feelings and needs, we connect back to ourselves and receive clarity about what we need to be happy in the moment.

Be aware of the times you focus your attention
on other people's feelings today, and then shift
the focus back to your own.

JUNE 29

*To keep a lamp burning we have
to keep putting oil in it.*
—Mother Teresa

Meeting Our Need for Exercise

I used to hike up a small mountain before work several mornings a week. I could complete this rugged, six-mile hike in an hour and a half. Then, I would take a quick shower and start my workday. Today, I walk or jog for thirty minutes and do a thirty-minute yoga workout four to five mornings a week. In both cases, my need for exercise has been well met. In my younger days, it was fun to work my body hard and to feel powerful because of what I could accomplish. Today, much less activity feels good to me.

We all have different strategies and different degrees of endurance for exercise or movement. When I have focused on working out in ways that experts suggest, I have felt overwhelmed and had a hard time sticking to the program. When I instead focus on my desire to meet my needs for physical well-being, exercise, and serenity, I enjoy my morning workouts. Are you meeting your needs for exercise? Consider which activities would help you meet your needs for physical and emotional health and fun, rather than focusing on what expert opinion says.

Be aware today of whether your need for exercise is
met and if you would like to tweak your program.

JUNE 30

*Fortunately, analysis is not the only way to resolve
inner conflicts. Life itself still remains
a very effective therapist.*
—*Karen Horney*

Building a Feelings Vocabulary

Many years ago, I was so disconnected from myself that it was difficult for me to identify or express my feelings. At the time, I worked with a therapist who took the time to teach me a feelings vocabulary. I would tell her what happened, and she would help me connect to my feelings about the situation. I thought we were wasting a lot of valuable time doing this. Really, wasn't it more important that *she* knew what I was feeling? Why was it important for *me* to know? Now, years later, I am grateful for the hours she spent helping me connect to my feelings. Now I know that until I could do so, I couldn't live fully present, I couldn't take care of myself, and I couldn't make sound decisions. My initial plan of relying on my therapist's ability to know what I was feeling only worked when I was with her. The minute I left her office, I was left with my disconnected self and my inability to deal with situations. Today, I easily connect with my feelings and so I know it is possible for anyone to expand their feelings vocabulary. At the beginning of this book, there is a list of feelings. If it is difficult for you to know what you feel and to express it, consider reviewing the list and spend some time expanding your feelings vocabulary.

Be aware of your feelings and name them today.

Meditations for
JULY

JULY 1

The ability to accept responsibility
is the measure of the man.
—Roy L. Smith

Taking Responsibility for Our Feelings

What a relief it is to finally understand that other people are not responsible for our feelings. I used to think that this was a cliché, and that it simply didn't make sense. Now I know that our feelings are the result of our underlying needs. Let's say that your teenage daughter invites a friend home for dinner without asking you ahead of time. Sometimes, you would enjoy the addition to your family gathering because it met your needs for fun and diversity, and because it contributes to your daughter's life. On another night, you might feel very tired and overwhelmed, and you might not enjoy having a guest at your table because of your needs for ease and rest. In both scenarios, the stimulus is the same— *your daughter invites a friend home without asking you first.* However, you respond to the situation very differently depending on how this meets your needs.

When we know that others are not responsible for our feelings, we can stop blaming them, and start acknowledging what we truly need. This shift in consciousness can have a dramatic impact and improve the quality of your life and relationships. If your daughter surprises you with a dinner guest, for instance, you can order pizza for the kids and spend the evening in your room if you need rest and ease, or you can invite her friend to come back another evening. There are numerous options available to you. If you focus on blaming your daughter, however, your choices are limited and you can experience hurt feelings and strain in your relationship.

> Be aware of the underlying needs that
> cause your feelings today.

JULY 2

See into life—don't just look at it.
—Anne Baxter

Connecting to Humanity

Consider the possibility that everyone on the planet has the same basic needs—that in fact, having the same needs is part of what makes us human. We all need love, shelter, food, water, connection, fulfillment, and to be valued. In each household, culture, or country, the ways we go about meeting these needs might vary, but not the needs themselves.

I have a need for family, so I stay in weekly contact with them and visit them once or twice a year. In some cultures, people live with their extended families to meet this need. In others, elderly parents move in with their grown children. We all try to meet our need for family in one way or another. Similarly, we all need shelter, but we may live in houses, tents, huts, or castles. Our strategies differ, but our needs are the same. This is what connects human beings across all cultures and lifestyles. The next time you are in conflict and catch yourself thinking that the other person doesn't care about the same things you do, consider what needs she may be trying to meet with her actions. You may be surprised to find that both of you choose different strategies to meet the same needs.

> Today, consider the underlying needs people
> strive to meet through their actions.

————————————— ✳ —————————————

JULY 3

Standing in the middle of the road is very dangerous;
you get knocked down by traffic from both sides.
—*Margaret Thatcher*

When It's Hard for Us to Express Our Needs

When I first discovered that I had needs, I talked about them to anyone who would listen. I was so filled with grief over spending the first forty years of my life unaware of them that I started a personal mission to be conscious of them and work to meet them. Often, the expression of my needs sounded like a demand or a criticism. "Well, you know I worked till nine last night and I've got a full day today, so how about if *you* . . . " I tried to meet my need for support, but my request sounded like a demand, and it was difficult for people to want to contribute to my life.

I gradually became able to grieve for all the years that I hadn't paid attention to my needs and I increasingly believed that my needs would be met, so I could release much of the charge behind my requests. I don't regret the initial stages of learning these concepts or making my charged requests because they contributed to my eventual success. It can be challenging to shift our paradigms, but the peace we experience afterward is well worth the effort.

Today, pay attention to how you express your needs.

※

JULY 4

As long as one keeps searching, the answers come.
—*Joan Baez*

Stages of Emotional Maturity

Many of us begin our personal journey thinking that we are responsible for everyone's feelings, and strive to keep everyone happy. At this stage, we are afraid of losing ourselves in relationships, and may think we are abused. In the next stage of development, we come to understand that we are not responsible for other people's feelings and they aren't responsible for ours. In this stage we feel a mixture of emotions: joy because we now have the power to make ourselves happy, relief in knowing that we don't have to make others happy, and grief about the anguish we experienced before we made this discovery. The third stage is emotional maturity; we take responsibility for our actions. This consciousness allows for creativity in problem solving and a depth of intimacy we had not known previously. In the fourth stage, we learn to value everyone's needs equally.

Be aware of what stage of emotional
maturity you are in today.

JULY 5

Minor things can become moments of great revelation
when encountered for the first time.
—Margot Fonteyn

Tips on Making a Request

Many of us have rarely asked for what we want, so a few tips on how to do this are in order.

Tip number one: Ask for what you want, not what you don't want. One time I was in a car with two young boys. One of them kicked his brother, so I said: "Jake, when you kick your brother I feel sad because I value everyone's safety. So please don't kick your brother." He said, "OK," and then hit his brother! I once drove for miles on a highway looking for a speed limit sign. Finally, one appeared and it said, "No longer a forty-five-mph zone." I burst out laughing. All I knew was that I shouldn't drive forty-five, but I had no idea what the actual speed limit was.

Tip number two: Be specific. If you want the house to be tidied up in thirty minutes, say so. Otherwise, you leave yourself open to frustration and disappointment. People may interpret "soon" in different ways. You may have experienced this already. Have the confidence to be specific.

Tip number three: Make the request doable. Avoid asking someone to do something they simply cannot do, such as asking a person to write a thirty-page report in an evening, or your partner to bring in the garbage can if he'll be out of town. When you make a request in a compassionate relationship, everyone's needs are considered and valued equally.

The final tip is to get into the habit of making requests. Everyone wants to give and receive compassionately. Don't you enjoy contributing to people's lives? They want to contribute to yours as well. Give them the gift of your request. The worst thing that can happen is they'll say no.

Make a specific, doable request of
at least two people today.

--- ✳ ---

JULY 6

The real voyage of discovery consists not in seeking
new landscapes but in having new eyes.
—Marcel Proust

Living Autonomously

Many people consider autonomy, or free choice, to be a need. That is, they believe that we all need it to live happily. I see autonomy more as something we already have, as a way of living. Let's imagine that a friend of yours works for someone who wants her to start her workday at seven in the morning. She is often up until late at night with her children so she would rather start at eight-thirty. It might be tempting for her to complain, "I have to be at work at seven." By expressing the situation in that language, she chooses not to live autonomously—she says she doesn't have a choice about what time she goes to work. In reality, she could quit her job, look for another job, or talk to her children about going to bed earlier. Maybe she wants to keep this job because it provides health insurance and meets her need for financial security, or the short commute may meet her need for ease. Whatever her reasons, she chooses to stay in the job. In making that choice, she does not meet some needs, such as for rest. We always have choices in our lives. Sometimes none of them appeal to us, but we still choose. The more we recognize that autonomy is a way of living, the more joy and empowerment we will feel.

> Today, notice when you say that you "have"
> to do something, and acknowledge the needs
> you meet by choosing to do it.

JULY 7

*The problems that exist in the world today cannot be
solved by the level of thinking that created them.*
—*Albert Einstein*

Life Is a Cabaret!

Don't do anything that isn't play. Learn to make clear choices, and only do those things that bring you satisfaction. Sound impossible? The best way I have found to bring joy into my life is to connect to the reasons I do things. It may seem hard to imagine much joy associated with cleaning the cat box or telling someone that I'm unhappy in our relationship. However, once I connect with the life-enriching purpose behind these activities, I can feel renewed joy in the task. While the actual cleaning of the cat box isn't much fun for me, the joy I feel contributing to my cats' clean environment is obvious to me. And although I don't enjoy telling someone I'm not happy in our relationship, I enjoy how it meets my needs for honesty, integrity, and the hope that we can make changes that meet both our needs. Joy isn't always hoop-hollerin' fun. Sometimes it is merely knowing we contribute to another's life, or that we meet our own need for integrity. If you don't look forward to an activity, see if you can uncover the underlying needs it meets. Is it worth it to you to do it? If so, do it with the benefit of this new understanding. If it's not worth it to you, consider other ways to make it more fun. Once you shift the energy behind an action, you will be more connected to why you do things, and you will feel more joy.

> For today, clarify the needs you want
> to meet through your activities.

JULY 8

Love involves a peculiar unfathomable combination
of understanding and misunderstanding.
—Diane Arbus

Making Sure We Are Heard

Isn't it amazing how people can witness the same thing, but interpret it differently? I used to marvel at this, get into arguments about how others didn't hear things correctly, or feel angry because I thought they weren't being honest. Now, I accept the fact that we all hear things through our own filters, and because of this, we may sometimes miss what someone wants to tell us. For this reason, I frequently check to make sure that the other person hears me. I do this in a number of ways. Sometimes I might just ask, "Do you understand?" or "Is that clear?" Other times I want more information, so I might say, "I really want to make sure I was being clear, so would you tell me what you heard me say?" If the person didn't hear what I wanted to convey, I might say: "Thank you for telling me what you heard. That wasn't exactly what I intended," and then try again. Asking for such a reflection can be critical in a charged situation because we often find it difficult to hear others when we are in pain ourselves. When someone takes the time to reflect what they heard, they may realize that they don't know what the other person has been trying to tell them after all. This simple process can help both people stay connected to each other and resolve their differences amicably.

Be aware today of opportunities to ask someone to reflect what they heard you say in order to meet your own needs for clarity and being heard.

JULY 9

No partner in a love relationship . . . should feel that he has to give up an essential part of himself to make it viable.
—*May Sarton*

Listening, the Next Step

Often, in our effort to be heard, we forget to listen to others. If we want to ensure that we are heard, we can ask the other person to reflect what they heard us say. Then it is our turn to hear what is going on with them. We might ask, "How do you feel about what I've said?" or "What comes up for you around this topic?" Both of these questions offer opportunities for the other person to express his feelings. If the conversation is challenging, you might want to reflect back what he says to ensure that you hear him accurately. It is important to remember that a dialogue is not complete until both people have been heard. In fact, your need to be heard will not be met completely until you have heard how what you said affects the other person.

> Reflect what someone says to you today
> to be sure that you have heard him.

JULY 10

*I think the one lesson I have learned is that there
is no substitute for paying attention.*
—Diane Sawyer

Creating Productive Group Gatherings

How many times have we attended meetings at work or in our personal lives that left us feeling overwhelmed, hopeless, and annoyed? When we learn to clarify our needs, we create efficient and successful meetings. Several years ago, I attended a training of sixty people. One morning in our big group session, a man made a request that there be a small group session that day on a specific topic. Someone else responded by saying that he didn't want it to happen at three in the afternoon. because he wanted to do something else then. Another person said that she didn't think we should be spending our time on that topic at all, and yet another suggested that we cover it at one, whereupon someone else said that one wouldn't work for her. Before long, ten people had spoken and we were no closer to a solution. Can you relate to this? We could have spent hours tossing around ideas, but we found a solution when I asked, "How many people here are interested in this topic?" Two people raised their hands. Then I asked the gentlemen who had made the request, "When you see that only two people are interested in this topic, do you still want to pursue this?" He said no.

In an efficient group process, clarity is key. To enhance clarity, try to only say things if you are clear *what you want back from the group.* Then be sure and *ask for what you want* so people don't have to figure it out for you. Any one person in a group can assist the process with a moment of clarity. If a person says something and you're not sure what he wants back from the group, try saying this: "I'm confused about what you would like from us. Would you help us clarify what kind of a response you're looking for?"

Be aware of when you are not clear about
your requests in group settings today.

JULY 11

*There are two ways of spreading light: to be the
candle or the mirror that reflects it.*
—Edith Wharton

Releasing Our Judgments

An underlying theme in a Nonviolent Communication
consciousness is to translate our judgments into feelings
and needs. It is impossible to value other people's needs
and remain compassionate if we simultaneously harbor
judgments. Releasing judgments, however, can feel like a
monumental task. It seemed that way for me at first. My
mind seemed to lodge a judgment per second in an effort
to organize data into good or bad categories. My thoughts
would go like this: This dress is pretty and that one isn't,
this person drives well and that person doesn't, this yard is
well kept and that one isn't, this road is in bad condition,
this person is a bad boss—and on it went. The smallest of
details had to be judged and categorized.

Finally I became willing to shift this behavior. I started to
translate my judgments into acknowledging how something
affected me. So when I caught myself thinking, "What a
crummy road," I would translate it into "This road is a lot
rougher than I'm used to, and I'm a little worried about
my tires." I would translate "What a grumpy mother" into
"When I see that woman talk to her children in that way,
I feel sad because I value more patience." Or sometimes I
would empathize with the mother in my mind by saying, "I
bet that mother is feeling overwhelmed and needs a break."
Once I got into the habit of this, my judgments began to
subside dramatically. It became easy to love people and feel

compassion for them, and I experienced a freedom I had never known before. This kind of a shift takes focus and commitment, but the rewards are many.

Be aware of your judgments today and try to translate them into how the situation affects your state of needs.

JULY 12

I have a simple philosophy. Fill what's empty.
Empty what's full. And scratch where it itches.
—Alice Roosevelt Longworth

Taking Responsibility for Our Requests

Do you ever wonder if the reason your needs don't often get met has something to do with you? I used to think this, but I would reassure myself that there was nothing wrong with me. Somehow it seemed more comfortable to blame other people for their inability to meet my needs properly. Then I started to notice that people did exactly what I'd asked, and my needs still did not get met. This was the stage of my emotional recovery in which I became acutely aware of how important it is to design requests to fit specific needs. One time I wanted to ensure that I was heard, so I asked my friend how he felt about what I said. It was a clear request, but it didn't meet *my need for being heard*. A more effective request would have been to ask him to *tell me what he heard me say*. Another time, I asked a friend to go to a movie with me and I went home that night feeling unsatisfied. Then I realized that what I *really wanted* was time to talk, which was not possible in a movie theater. Before you make a request of someone, notice if the strategy you are considering is likely to meet your needs. If not, consider making a different request that may be more satisfying to you.

Be aware of your requests today and
notice if they meet your needs.

JULY 13

The hearing that is only in the ears is one thing. The hearing of the understanding is another. But the hearing of the spirit is not limited to any one faculty, to the ear, or to the mind. Hence it demands the emptiness of all the faculties. And when the faculties are empty, then the whole being listens. There is then a direct grasp of what is right there before you that can never be heard with the ear or understood with the mind.
—Chuang-Tzu

The Presence of Hearing Someone Deeply

In Compassionate Communication, empathy is the respectful understanding of what others are experiencing. It does not mean agreeing or even sharing the same experience as the other person. It is a process in which we acknowledge and understand their experience without judging or bringing up our own life experience. It is a moment in which we offer our presence to another human being to contribute

226

to her life and meet our own needs for contribution and connection. It is priceless, powerful, and healing. It can defuse a violent situation in a few seconds and provide a level of clarity that catapults someone to a deeper level of personal understanding. It is what most people long for, but few know how to get.

The process is simple; listen for the feelings and needs of the other person. If your spouse is screaming at you because you were an hour late for your date, empathizing means that you listen for her feelings and needs without bringing your story into the picture: "Sounds like you're furious and maybe scared because you value commitment and respect." That's it. Simply listen for the underlying feelings and needs of the other person and reflect them back to her. It is amazing how healing it is to be deeply understood when one is angry. It only takes a few words, but it can move mountains of pain. Once the other person is heard, it is then your turn to express yourself.

Be aware of opportunities to express a respectful understanding of what others are experiencing today.

JULY 14

Life is not a problem to be solved but a
reality to be experienced.
—Søren Kierkegaard

We Don't Need to Fix Other People

When empathizing with someone, we listen for their feelings and needs and don't try to fix their problem for them. The very process of giving someone space to talk about their issue without our judgment, to be truly understood by us, and to be deeply heard is very healing, enough so that most people will organically find their own creative ways to resolve their issues. Rely on this process and you will lose all desire to fix people's problems. Instead, you will learn to trust their ability to resolve their issues. All it takes is your presence and your desire to hear their feelings and needs. Amazing!

Be aware of opportunities to listen to someone
without trying to fix their problem today.

JULY 15

The more faithfully you listen to the voice within you,
the better you will hear what is happening outside.
—*Dag Hammarskjöld*

When Our Own Pain Keeps Us
From Empathizing With Another

At the beginning of a flight, flight attendants advise that if the plane loses air pressure, passengers should put on their own oxygen masks before putting them on their children. This is because an adult who dies of suffocation is of no help to a small child. So it is with empathy. Sometimes, we are in so much pain ourselves that we find it impossible to empathize with another. This usually means that we are in need of empathy ourselves. In this case, consider telling the person with whom you are talking: "I am noticing that I am in distress and so I am struggling to be present for you. Would you consider empathizing with me a few moments so that I can become more present for you?" If the person is unwilling to do this, or if you are uncomfortable making this request, consider removing yourself from the situation until you can fill your own empathy tank. It is important to take the time to do so before attempting to help someone else fill theirs. You are doing no one a favor if you pretend to be present when you are not.

Be aware of moments today when you struggle
to be present with another person, and take
steps to fill your own empathy tank.

JULY 16

*"I think patience is what love is," he said, "because
how could you love somebody without it?"*
—Jane Howard

Bringing the Topic of a Conversation
Back to Your Needs

You pop into your colleague's office to say hi and ask what time it is. He offers a lengthy dissertation on how clocks work. You think you could walk out the door without him noticing, but deep down, you respect him and you want to maintain a cordial relationship. On the other hand, you really don't care how clocks work; you just wanted to know the time. What do you do? The topic isn't interesting to you, but your relationship with your colleague is. If you can't find interest in the topic, connect with the needs he is trying to meet with the information and make a request that will help you to meet your needs. You might say: "So, Bob, I can tell that the topic of how clocks work is very interesting to you. I appreciate your desire to contribute to me in that way, and I would prefer you contribute to a more immediate need I have, which is to know what time it is. Would you be willing to tell me what it is, and then I'll see if I have time to stay for your story?" When you demonstrate that you understand why the issue is personally important to him and reassert the needs you are trying to meet, you show that you value both your needs, and you have a greater opportunity to meet them in the moment.

Be aware of opportunities today to reassert your needs while also valuing someone else's needs.

JULY 17

Empathize with silence by listening to the
feelings and needs behind it.
—Marshall B. Rosenberg, PhD

Empathizing With Someone Who Is Silent

Sometimes in a conversation a person becomes silent. When this happens, it is easy for us make up stories or create judgments about what we think is going on with her. We may feel annoyed and lose hope that we can come to resolution if the other person doesn't express herself. Rather than creating your own version of what might be going on with the other person, or becoming angry at her, consider empathizing with her. That is, reflect what you think her feelings and needs might be. You might say, "When you are silent I wonder if you are feeling angry and want some consideration." Or, "When you are silent I wonder if you feel hurt and want to know that I care about your needs as much as my own." Or, "Are you worried that if you open your mouth, you will say something you will regret later?" If the person is in enough pain, it might take more than one round of empathy. It may also be that she needs some space to clarify her thoughts. Try to consider her needs along with your own and create solutions that will allow both your needs to be met.

Be aware of opportunities to empathize
with someone who is silent today.

JULY 18

*Life appears to me too short to be spent in nursing
animosity or registering wrongs.*
—Charlotte Brontë

Stimulus or Cause

Violence is a result of thinking that others *caused* our pain and deserve to be punished. When living from this consciousness, we believe that our anger is justified.

Consider road rage. A driver who engages in it believes that the other person is driving badly or is trying to tick him off, so he tailgates, makes hand gestures, or worse yet, shoots at them. He often feels justified in his anger. Two weeks before, however, he may have driven down that same road in the same traffic but didn't behave violently. Why? Maybe because he had an easier day at work, or left work earlier and had more time to get home, or it was his anniversary and he was excited about the evening ahead. *The stimulus was the same*—traffic on a particular road—but his *feelings were quite different* depending on his needs.

The *cause* of our feelings is *our own needs in the moment*. What happens is simply the *stimulus*. In order to maintain serenity in our life, it is important to understand this distinction.

Be aware today of times when you are tempted to
blame other people for your feelings, and try to
discover your unmet needs.

JULY 19

You give but little when you give of your possessions.
It is when you give of yourself that you truly give.
—Kahlil Gibran

Protective Use of Force

In most situations, if both people have a chance to be heard, peaceful resolution is possible. However, situations sometimes arise that involve imminent danger with little time for dialogue, or in which one person may not be willing to communicate. When this happens, and there is the potential for physical harm, protective use of force may be necessary—the use of force to restrain someone. It is important when resorting to this action that we maintain awareness that we are not punishing the person. We are merely keeping them or others safe.

For example, if you work in a hospital, you may need to apply protective use of force if you see that a health professional is accidentally administering a life-threatening drug. Similarly, if your child is running out into a street full of oncoming traffic, your use of physical force to remove her from danger would be the protective use of force. In both cases, it is important to maintain the consciousness that you have taken the action to protect life, not as punishment for bad behavior. Such a consciousness is based on the belief that people take actions that are dangerous to themselves and others out of ignorance, not because they are bad. We desire to serve life and act accordingly.

For today, be aware of your attitude toward others who do things that are dangerous to themselves or other people. Make a decision to serve life in the situation, rather than to judge the people involved.

JULY 20

Think for yourself and let others enjoy
the right to do the same.
—Voltaire

Punitive Use of Force

Punitive use of force takes place when we punish people because we deem their behavior to be bad or wrong and the only way to change their behavior is to make them ashamed about doing it or feel afraid of doing it again. This consciousness arises from the belief that people do things that are dangerous to themselves or others because they are bad. It also assumes that we are in a position to determine what is good and what is bad, and that we have the power to enforce our views of this.

For instance, if you refuse to make dinner to punish your spouse for being late, you are operating in a punitive use of force model, punishing someone for perceived bad behavior. If you take the kids out to dinner without her because they are hungry, free of any judgment about your spouse's lateness, you are operating in a protective use of force model because you focus on supporting your children, not punishing your wife. This consciousness serves life without judgment and blame.

Be aware today of when you are using
force in a punitive way.

JULY 21

*If you fear something, you set yourself up to
experience it again and again. As Job said,
"What I have feared has come upon me."*
—*Gloria Karpinski*

Focusing on What You Want

Nonviolent Communication teaches us that it is more
productive and satisfying to focus on what we want than
on what we don't have or don't like. For example, say
your partner spanked your five-year-old child, and you
feel strongly that spanking is harmful to children. When
faced with this, some people might focus on blaming their
partner for harming the child, or on how this incident has
harmed the child's emotional and physical health. Instead, I
suggest that you focus on what you *want* instead of what we
don't want or what we *don't like*. What will help rectify the
situation right now? What would you like your partner to do
next time a similar situation occurs? And what will help your
child right now? By focusing directly on what you want, you
eliminate much of the emotional pain caused by berating
yourself or others.

Where is your focus right now? If it is on what is wrong
with your life, take a moment to shift it to what you want.

Be aware of the times when you focus on what you
don't want today, and shift to what you do want.

235

JULY 22

*The fragrance always stays in the hand
that gives the rose.*
—Hada Bejar

Expressing Appreciation in a Life-Serving Way

"You are such a good girl." "You are great." "You did a good job on that project." These statements are an attempt to express appreciation, but they convey that the speaker is in a position to judge the other person. This may sound extreme, but whenever we judge someone, we demonstrate that we sit in judgment. A way to express appreciation without judgment is to state what they did, how you feel about what they did, and which of your needs are met by their behavior. For example, say your father helped you lay a new kitchen floor. You want to express appreciation without judgment, so you might say: "You know, Dad, when you give up your Saturday to help me lay the floor and you explain every step to me in ways I can understand, I feel such gratitude. My needs for support, ease, and accomplishment are well met. Thanks for helping me with this today." Notice that the speaker states an observation—*when you give up your Saturday to help me lay the floor and you explain every step to me in ways I can understand*; their feelings—*I feel such gratitude*; and their needs that were met—*support, ease, and accomplishment.* Such an expression of appreciation clearly states how your life was enriched by your father's support, without judging him in any way.

Be aware today of opportunities to express your
appreciation without judgment.

236

JULY 23

Never bend your head, always hold it high.
Look the world straight in the face.
—Helen Keller

Receiving Appreciation With Grace

Many of us struggle with receiving appreciation. We either belittle our accomplishment by saying things such as "Oh, it wasn't that big of a deal," or we let our ego expand by thinking that we are better than other people. Sometimes we show this by saying something like, "Yeah, these people really needed us, didn't they!" Either way, we miss the boat. A more satisfying way to receive appreciation is to *connect to how we have contributed to another person's life:* to connect to the other person, not ourselves. A response in this model could be, "Oh, I feel excited hearing that my talk stimulated hope in you." Notice that the person receiving the appreciation reflects back the need that was met in the other person—hope. I am the same person even if half of my audience enjoys my talk and the other half doesn't. I am no better or worse. It does, however, bring me great joy to hear that people's lives have been changed by my talk.

Find opportunities today to receive appreciation
by connecting to the other person's needs
that your actions met.

JULY 24

We are here to help each other through life,
this is why we are in partnership.
—Hugh Prather

A Hunger for Appreciation

Despite our difficulty in receiving appreciation, or maybe partially because of it, many of us long for it. This is a quandary because many of us have not found a comfortable way to ask that our need for appreciation be met, so our longing becomes even more pronounced. If you are in this situation, consider asking this question, "Would you be willing to tell me three specific reasons why you enjoy working with me (or why you enjoy having me in your life)?" Try to be as specific as possible with this request. It doesn't tell you much if the response is: "Oh, you know I love you. I just like spending time with you." Or, "What do you mean? You're one of my favorite employees!" While these comments are intended to be supportive, they reveal very little. If you receive responses like this and you do not feel satisfied, simply ask another question: "Really? Can you tell me what I do and what needs it meets that makes me one of your favorite employees?" This connection will be revealing to both of you. Many people don't stop to consider the underlying reasons why they enjoy someone's company, or why they enjoy an employee. Taking this time can deepen your relationship, while helping you meet your need for appreciation.

Ask one person today what they enjoy
about having you in their life.

JULY 25

*The only difference between the beauty of
one person and the beauty of another is the
concept of beauty that people have.*
—Don Miguel Ruiz

Getting Past Our Judgments

Do you sometimes feel overwhelmed with your judgments of self and others? Once when I was driving, I noticed a woman walking down the street. Without being aware at first, I thought, "Well, that's a particularly ugly outfit she's wearing." A few minutes later, I caught myself thinking, "Who would drive a car like that?" I started to get a glimpse into how fast and unrelenting my judgments of others were. I vowed to myself that I was going to relieve myself of this pattern. I asked God to help me be aware of my judgments in the moment. Then whenever I caught myself judging, either aloud or silently, I immediately translated it. When I caught myself thinking, "Well, that's a particularly ugly outfit," I would translate it into, "When I see orange and red together, I feel annoyed because it doesn't meet my need for beauty." Later, I started shortening it to "Orange and red don't meet my need for beauty." In this way, I am acknowledging my own feelings and needs without judging or blaming someone else. Learning to do this took time, but after a while I began to notice that I was less judgmental, which allowed more room for compassion.

Notice how many judgments you have of yourself
and other people today and begin translating those
judgments into your feelings and needs.

JULY 26

Is it not by love alone that we succeed in
penetrating the very essence of a being?
—Igor Stravinsky

Mediating Conflicts

When mediating conflicts using Nonviolent Communication, I focus on establishing a quality of connection that involves trust and a sincere desire to resolve the situation peacefully. This involves listening for the needs that each person is trying to meet. I reflect back to them what I think their feelings and needs are until they feel heard.

"So, you're furious with your neighbor because he built a fence that is so high it blocks your view?" "Yes, and he said he wouldn't do it!" "You're also mad because your need for trust wasn't met?" "Yeah."

To the other party: "Would you tell me what needs you hear your neighbor express?" "He's calling me a liar." "Hmmm. Thanks for reflecting that. I heard him say that he thinks you agreed not to build a fence so high that it blocked his view and his need for trust wasn't met when you did this. Would you mind telling me what needs you heard that time?" "It seems like he misses his view, and he's ticked because he needs to trust that people will keep their agreements." "Yes, I think that's it. What are your issues?" "I've wanted him to get rid of his old junky cars in the front lawn for months. I'm sick of looking at his junk." "So, you'd like the neighborhood to maintain a more beautiful appearance?" "Well, yeah. It looks like a junk yard right next door to my house!" "And you would like to maintain your image?" "Yeah."

"First Party, will you tell me what needs you hear your neighbor speaking of?" "He's ticked because he thinks my cars are making the neighborhood look bad, and he wants to maintain his image." "Yes, thank you."

Connecting to everyone's needs can take several hours. It is precious time, though, because once this quality of connection is established, creating strategies that values both their needs can come quickly. When using the Nonviolent Communication process, all parties will probably be satisfied with the results.

I avoid the mistake of starting with solutions. I realize that focusing on a resolution before the parties have established a level of trust is futile. If you are involved with or mediating any dispute, set the intention to connect first. Once a connection is established, then begin the process of creating strategies.

> If you find yourself in a conflict today,
> set the intention to connect first, and create
> strategies for resolving the issue second.

JULY 27

*Managing conflict for mutual benefit moves
people away from assuming that co-workers
are arrogant and untrustworthy to seeing
them as reliable colleagues.*
—Dean Tjosvold and Mary Tjosvold

Conflict Resolution

When there is conflict, the chances are good that people are arguing over a particular strategy. When we focus on our needs, the opportunities for peaceful resolution that values everyone's needs are much greater. For instance, if a couple is arguing over whether they will get to their vacation spot by train or plane, they are arguing over strategy. What do you suppose both people's needs are? I guess taking the train would meet needs for adventure and fun, while the plane might meet needs for efficiency about the use of vacation time. Looking at the predicament in these terms, can you think of anything this couple could do to meet both of their needs? How about taking the train one way and the plane the other? Or taking the train for part of the journey both ways, and the plane for the rest of the trip? How about extending the length of the trip so there is time for the train ride and ample time at the vacation spot? When we look at our conflicts from the perspective of needs rather than strategies, we open the possibility for creative resolution that meets everyone's needs.

Be aware of opportunities to shift the focus from strategies to needs today to resolve a conflict.

JULY 28

Humility is to make a right estimate of one's self.
—*Charles Haddon Spurgeon*

Self-Empathy

Sometimes our behaviors keep us from meeting our greatest needs. Let's say you long for deep connection with others, but you are also afraid of it, so you push people away. Then you tell yourself that no one likes you. Often the result is depression, loneliness, and self-criticism. The process of self-empathy can help us become clearer about what we truly want and can help us behave in ways that are more likely to meet our needs. Self-empathy also encourages us to focus on what we desire, rather than on what is wrong with others or ourselves. Let's assume that your joints are very sore. Rather than criticize yourself because of what you did or didn't do, focus on what it will take to make your joints feel better. Your focus, then, is not on what's wrong, but rather on what you need to rectify the situation.

There are four steps to the self-empathy process:

Enjoy the jackal show: Give your jackal an opportunity to say all it wants to say. Do not try to restrain or censor it, because you might miss the full wisdom and healing it holds for you.

Identify your feelings: Be aware of your feelings associated with the stimulus.

Identify your needs: Be sure to identify your unmet needs.

Make a request: Once you have identified your unmet needs, make a request that will help you meet those needs.

If you don't get past your judgments and identify your feelings and needs, you are unlikely to receive the relief and healing you desire.

Be aware of opportunities today to empathize with
yourself to help clarify your feelings and needs.

JULY 29

I find the great thing in this world is not so much
where we stand, as in what direction we are moving.
—*Goethe*

Mediating With a Group

When you mediate a group conflict, the principles of listening
for needs are the same as with one-on-one conflicts. Start the
mediation by telling everyone that the group will not begin
looking at strategies until everyone's needs have been heard.

Dedicate the first portion of the mediation solely to
hearing needs. Then encourage one person to start the
process by stating her needs in the situation. Many people
aren't connected to their needs, so they often express their
judgments. Your role as the mediator is to hear the needs no
matter how they are expressed. Repeat the needs you hear
from the first person. Then ask someone else in the group
to reflect the needs that he heard from her. When she feels
heard, ask someone else to express her needs and begin the
process again, where you reflect the needs first and someone
else from the group reflects them second. If someone
interrupts the process to express his own judgments, ask him
to hold that thought until it is his turn. Be sure that everyone
in the group knows they will have a turn. Once everyone is
confident that their needs have been heard, you will notice
the energy in the room relaxing.

At this point, start brainstorming strategies that will value everyone's needs. Be sure they are expressed in positive, doable language. That is, ask the participants to focus on what they want to happen, rather than what they don't want to happen.

The initial time spent hearing needs is critical to the process. It is only when everyone's needs have been heard that people are ready to consider strategies that value everyone's needs. If you doubt this, think about a time in your life when you were annoyed with someone and the two of you were trying to come up with a resolution to the situation. How willing were you to consider a solution that would meet both your needs when the other person wasn't hearing you? Whether you're in a group or working one on one, the principle is the same: People struggle to come to agreement when they don't feel heard.

Be aware of opportunities today to help people discover the underlying needs behind their actions.

JULY 30

A humble knowledge of one's self is a surer road to God than a deep searching of the sciences.
—Thomas à Kempis

Mindfulness

What do you feel and need right now? Take a moment to ponder this. Mindfulness of being is the foundation of Compassionate Communication. That means that we try to stay present in each moment, focusing on what is happening right now. Thich Nhat Hanh, a Buddhist scholar, teacher, and poet, teaches that the goal is to be present in the moment no matter what you are doing, even if you are simply brushing your teeth. Most of us are unable to maintain constant mindfulness, but the more present we are, the greater the likelihood that we will be aware of our needs and meet them, thus the greater opportunity for joy. You may be surprised how enlightening mindfulness can be.

Connect to your feelings and needs at least four times today. Notice how differently you conduct your day when you are mindful.

JULY 31

I hope I shall possess firmness and virtue enough to maintain what I consider the most enviable of all titles, the character of an honest man.
—*George Washington*

The Gift of You

Every one of us is a gift to the people in our lives. But how often, when someone asks us how we are doing, do we respond with a flat "Fine"? Is this an honest statement? Sometimes it is. But often, we are so used to telling people that we are fine, we forget to notice that we're not! Being fully present to the moment when we are with other people is the gift of ourselves. Hiding ourselves is the anti-gift. Come out today. The next time someone asks you how you are doing, consider checking in with yourself and offering an honest answer. You don't have to tell them a fifteen-minute story about it. You could simply say: "Hmmm. I'm actually feeling a little tired and overwhelmed by this project I'm working on. I'm certain that it will work itself out. I'm just worrying about it right now. How are you?" If you can't imagine being that honest with someone else, then at the very least be honest with yourself. You are a gift. Being fully present to how you are will help you acknowledge and live within this consciousness.

For today, respond to each "How are you?"
with an honest, thoughtful answer.

Meditations for
AUGUST

AUGUST 1

*The heart of him who truly loves is a paradise on
earth; he has God in himself, for God is love.*
—Felicité Robert de Lamennais

I See the Spirit in You

When we see others as spiritual beings, we connect to their
divine energy. I have believed this for years. But for many of
those years, I would forget the Spirit in another person if we
were in conflict. To *know* that a person is a spiritual being,
but then *think* they are an insensitive slob or an egotistical
bore, is a contradiction. It just doesn't fit. Today, I know that
I may not always enjoy someone's behavior, but I don't have
to judge them. I can honestly acknowledge my feelings about
a situation without denying the Divine in the other person.
In fact, just being honest about my feelings is an act of love.

I recently said to a friend, in a tone of utter exasperation:
"I am so frustrated right now, and I'd really like to know
that we can come to a resolution that works for both us.
Would you be willing to take a break for an hour so I can
calm myself? I think this would help me be more willing
to proceed." I expressed my frustration without judging or
blaming her. When we came back together, we were able to
resolve the situation and deepen our friendship. Seeing the
spiritual being in another person does not mean you never
feel angry; it means you know that they are a spiritual being
and can still express your feelings. If you struggle to see the
Divine in another person, focus on the needs she is trying
to meet through her behavior. Remember that behind every
action is a desire to meet a need.

Be aware of the spiritual being in everyone
you meet today—and in yourself.

AUGUST 2

*I care not so much what I am in the opinion of
others as what I am in my own; I would be rich
of myself, and not by borrowing.*
—Michel Eyquem de Montaigne

One More Thing About Strategies

Remember what I have said about needs being universal
and strategies specific? Well, the process of Compassionate
Communication is also a strategy. The needs I try to meet
by living and teaching this process are harmony, peace, fun,
love, safety, joy, and deeper connection to my life. The needs
are universal, and the strategy I have found that best meets
those needs is Compassionate Communication. There are
many ways to meet our needs in life, and we all choose the
path that best suits us. The more open we are to creative
ways to meet those needs, the more peaceful our life and the
world will be.

Be aware of your strategies for living peacefully today.
Notice if they are working for you or if you
would like to consider new ones.

AUGUST 3

My goal is to change the world one heart at a time.
—Mary Mackenzie

Inspiring Social Change

People ask me all the time how they can change a situation. Activists who work for peace and social change want the answer. Many of us are looking for the big over-arching answers. We want the quick fix. If you want social change, act in harmony with the values toward which you are working. "Be the change you seek," as Gandhi put it. If you want peace, work *toward peace*; don't rally *against war*. Don't spend your days working for peace while harboring enemy images of people who support different causes than yours; don't go home and spank your child or yell at your partner. *Be peace*. Living from your values does not mean that you are perfect. When you act in ways that aren't in harmony with your values, own up to it and try to do it differently next time. Set a course that is in alignment with your values and do your very best to stay headed in that direction. This is social change.

For today, make a conscious effort to be
that which you want in your world.

AUGUST 4

We want facts to fit the preconceptions.
When they don't, it is easier to ignore the facts
than to change the preconceptions.
—Jessamyn West

It's All About Please and Thank You

If I told you that every communication is either a please or
a thank you, would you believe me? This was an enormous
revelation to me. Think about the please behind a neighbor's
words when he says, "What will it take for you to keep your
stupid dog out of my yard?" I'd guess that he needs peace,
respect, and consideration. He might also need cleanliness if
the dog does you-know-what in his yard. So in essence, he
is saying *please*, will you help me meet my needs for peace,
respect, consideration, and cleanliness?

If someone says, "You're great," this sounds like a *thank
you* to me. Maybe what he's saying is *thank you* for building
a fence so the dog will stay in your yard. Or, *thank you* for
meeting his needs for the dog's safety and his peace of mind.
Sometimes, people's choice of words may be difficult to
hear. In fact, we may feel downright aggravated by them.
I don't suggest that we can suddenly start to enjoy these
conversations, only that we begin to recognize that behind
each statement is a desire to meet needs, either by saying
please or thank you. In this way, we are more likely to feel
compassion because we have connected to their humanness.

Listen for the please or thank you
in your conversations today.

AUGUST 5

If God seems far away, who moved?
—*Unknown*

Connecting With Others

Do you sometimes struggle to connect authentically and vulnerably with others? If you find yourself in a relationship that is unsatisfying to you, look at how you participate in it. What are you doing to meet your need for connection? Is there anything you can do differently? I used to feel very lonely and sad because my relationships weren't as satisfying as I wanted them to be. When I looked at my part in them, though, I realized that I kept myself protected. That meant that I always looked good. No matter how sad, hurt, or angry I felt, I maintained my composure and I rarely asked for support. I wasn't vulnerable or authentically connected with other people, although I wanted them to be that way for me. I met my need for protection but at the same time I prevented myself from meeting my needs for connection, support, and intimacy.

If you are struggling in a relationship, look at your own behavior and the needs behind it, and see if you can make some changes in your strategies that will positively affect your experience.

Look at your relationships today and see if there are things you can do to positively shift your experience.

AUGUST 6

When people are bored, it is primarily with
their own selves that they are bored.
—Eric Hoffer

No Matter Where You Go, There You Are

I spent the first thirty-five years or so of my life unhappy and dissatisfied. Then one day I realized that the only common denominator was me. I was unhappy because *I* was there! It was hard for me to imagine that my unhappiness was my doing, but I could not deny that in every situation, I was there. The best I could do was act as if I understood this, and I set an intention to build a happy life. One day at a time, I tried to see things through new lenses. I tried to be more authentic, to be in touch with my feelings and needs, and to live more closely in alignment with my values. Actually, I had to define my values before I could live in alignment with them.

We all start somewhere. Some people have made great progress toward a happy life; others have many obstacles to overcome. Wherever you are in your emotional and spiritual recovery, it is not too late to begin. If you are bored with your predicament, take time to get in touch with your feelings and needs and come up with new strategies and new ways of behaving.

Do one thing differently today to promote
positive change in your life.

AUGUST 7

*The problem comes when we want to cling to a
particular thought or idea. The mind always wants
to cling. I'm sixty years old, and if I'm still clinging
to being forty, then I'm in trouble.*
—Ram Dass

Being Compassionate or Doing Compassion

Sometimes I hear people say things like, "I didn't do
Compassionate Communication this week." Or "I tried
Compassionate Communication when I was arguing with
my wife last week." Compassionate Communication is not
a thing to do, or to pull out of our bag of tricks once in
a while. Compassionate Communication is a consciousness
of valuing everyone's needs and of valuing connection more
than being right, winning, or protecting ourselves. It is a
way of living. It's true that sometimes as a result of our old
conditioning or our pain, our inner critic may chatter loudly
or vehemently, or we may snap at our spouse, children, or
co-workers. However, our goal is to increasingly transform
our way of handling these situations into a Compassionate
Communication consciousness. Shifting our paradigm of the
world takes time and we all have a different learning process.
I recommend that you set the intention each morning to live
the Compassionate Communication process to the best of
your ability. By simply setting the intention, you can live the
consciousness.

Make a conscious decision to *be* Compassionate
Communication today.

AUGUST 8

We are dangerous when we are not conscious of our
responsibility for how we behave, think, and feel
—*Marshall B. Rosenberg, PhD*

Taking Responsibility for Our Actions

Some time ago, I was visiting my family in the Seattle area. I was on I-5 heading south. The traffic was much slower than I had anticipated, and what I expected to be a one-hour drive became a two-hour drive. I could not detect any reason the traffic was so slow, so I decided to blame the hundreds of people in the fast lane who were driving slowly, and who didn't move into a slower lane to allow the traffic to flow more easily (or the way I wanted it to flow!). I became increasingly exasperated and I started to drive more aggressively by switching lanes, cutting in front of people, and tailgating. I kept telling myself that if everyone else just drove better, I wouldn't have to be so aggressive. I pulled off the freeway and into a gas station. When I got out of my car, a young man came up to me and said, "This is a public service announcement." I said, "What?" He said: "This is a free public service announcement. Cutting in front of vehicles and doing multiple lane changes on the freeway is hazardous to everyone on the freeway." I stopped cold. This young man followed me off the freeway and into the gas station to let me know that he felt afraid of my driving! I thought about saying that I had to drive that way because other people wouldn't relinquish the fast lane. That it was really their fault. But I stopped myself. I knew that I had felt impatient and wanted more ease on the freeway, and of the countless ways in which I could have handled the situation,

I had chosen to drive aggressively. I was quite shocked by what this man said to me, and shocked at my own behavior, so I simply said: "You're right. Thank you for reminding me." "You're welcome," he said as he walked off.

Even if all the choices we ponder are unpleasant, we are always responsible for our own actions, and we always have a choice.

> Be aware of times today when you do not take responsibility for your actions. Own up to your responsibility in that moment.

AUGUST 9

If one does not know to which port
one is sailing, no wind is favorable
—*Seneca*

To Confess or Not

In Nonviolent Communication, we strive to value everyone's needs equally. This can be a confusing concept in situations that stimulate pain. Suppose you have had a brief affair. You feel guilty so you're tempted to tell your husband about it. Before taking action, consider your motivation for telling him. Or, put another way, consider what needs you want to meet by telling him. Do you want to assuage your own feelings of guilt? If so, would this meet your needs for honesty or relief? Do you think telling him will contribute positively to his life?

Our goal is to try to meet our own needs without sacrificing those of others. In situations like this, I suggest that you consider which needs, yours and his, will be met by being honest, especially when the information will likely stimulate pain. I'm not suggesting that you decide to keep the secret. Every situation is different. I am only suggesting that you seriously consider everyone's needs before taking action. And, consider if there are other ways in which you can meet your own need for relief that would better value your husband's needs.

> Be aware today of how often you
> do not consider everyone's needs.

AUGUST 10

My whole goal is to keep my spirit intact. If that
doesn't happen, none of this is worth it.
—Jewel

Honesty as a Means to Connect

Not long ago, I was sitting in church listening to the choir. One of the gentlemen in the choir stepped up to the mike to sing a brief solo. He sang off key sometimes and his voice shook. I thought he was very nervous. I wondered, should I tell him that he sang off key? It would have been honest—at least from my perspective. Instead, I told him that I admired his courage in doing something he enjoyed so much, and that his courage helped me muster the strength to sing in public as well. This also was an honest statement. He teared up a bit and told me that he sang so beautifully when he was alone, and that he was really trying to free his voice in front of other people. We both gained an expanded appreciation for each other, and I walked away feeling gratitude that my church community offered such opportunities to its members. Talking with my church friend in this way met many needs for me: honesty, connection, consideration, respect, and learning. And it helped me remember that honesty is an important tool that can be used to connect, rather than stimulate pain in others.

Notice the opportunities you have today to use honesty as a means to connect with someone else.

AUGUST 11

Nothing is unthinkable, nothing impossible to the balanced person, provided it arises out of the needs of life and is dedicated to life's further developments.
—Lewis Mumford

Power Over vs. Power With

Power over refers to people using their power or authority to get what they want. Examples include corporate leaders who wield their power to influence legislation that benefits them and parents who use coercion or punishment to get their children to behave in desired ways. Usually, this system sets up a dynamic in which a few hold power over many.

In contrast, *power with* refers to power that seeks to meet everyone's needs. Examples of this include parents who discuss vacation plans with the rest of the family, corporations that seek participation and decision-making from all employees, and neighborhood associations that invite input from community members. A *power with* system values the input and needs of everyone who will be affected by decisions. The most powerful change agent known to human beings is an *intrinsic* desire to change. The attempt to force people to change out of fear of consequences can promote an *extrinsic* desire for momentary compliance. It rarely, if ever, promotes long-term change.

If you notice you are using a *power over* paradigm to achieve a result, shift the focus to *power with*. Notice how this shift in consciousness affects the results.

AUGUST 12

The most exhausting thing in life is being insincere.
—*Anne Morrow Lindbergh*

The Relief of Authenticity

Sometimes I hear people say that they don't have the energy to be authentic, and that it is easier to ignore their truth to keep the peace. I understand this sentiment because I lived this way for many years. I thought it took less energy to censor myself, to go along with what other people wanted, and even to keep myself from having opinions. Now I know that stuffing my feelings, needs, desires, and truth took a tremendous amount of energy every day. It took years for me to acquire the skills to do this—to automatically deny my needs without thinking about what I was doing.

When I began to change this habit, it seemed overwhelming because it was different, and I was unaccustomed to focusing on my feelings and needs. I left the familiar territory of trying to figure out what others wanted. I had to learn a whole new vocabulary that acknowledged my feelings and allowed me to speak up for my needs. It took some time to develop these new skills, but I discovered the most amazing thing: it took far less energy than stuffing my feelings! Today, I feel free. The energy I once used to deny myself is now available to let me experience joy, love, happiness, and hope. It is an expansive opening that I could never have experienced before. The possibilities are endless.

> Notice how often you censor yourself to
> keep the peace. Then, become willing to
> express your true feelings and needs.

AUGUST 13

Until he extends his circle of compassion to
all living things, man will not himself find peace.
—*Albert Schweitzer*

Expressing Big Emotions Compassionately

Sometimes we find ourselves in situations where we become extremely frustrated, angry, or exasperated. It happens to all of us from time to time. The difference for me now is that I express my intense feelings by owning them. This is called screaming in giraffe. In the old days, I might have said in an angry voice: "I am so sick and tired of you! Is it possible for you to think of anyone else but yourself?" Notice that my focus was on the other person. Today, even in highly charged situations, I use all four components of Compassionate Communication (observation, feeling, need, request). I may say them in a loud voice, but the final result is quite different. It might be: "You know, when I notice that you have been talking about your feelings and needs for the past fifteen minutes but haven't asked me what is going on with me, I feel annoyed and hurt because I'd like to know that you value my needs as much as your own. Would you be willing to listen to what's going on with me for a few minutes?" Notice that I made a specific request—*to listen to what's going on with me for a few minutes.* I am not asking him to give up his needs, simply to focus on mine for a few minutes. When we express frustration without blaming others and by clarifying our own needs and requests, we diminish the possibility of hurt feelings and separation in our relationships.

If you feel very agitated or angry today, try screaming in giraffe rather than blaming the other person.

AUGUST 14

The moment you have in your heart this
extraordinary thing called love and feel the depth,
the delight, the ecstasy of it, you will discover that
for you the world is transformed.
—J. Krishnamurti

Love as a Need

In Nonviolent Communication, we consider love to be a need. Remember that needs are universal; everyone has the same ones. We all need love, but the ways in which we express it can be very different. Spending quiet, focused time connecting with another is a common way that I meet my need for love. I have dated people who meet their need for love by buying me things. Neither of these methods is right or wrong – they are just different. Some people express love through sex, others would prefer physical closeness, such as hugging, snuggling, and massage. Some people fix things for others or help them analyze their struggles. One friend of mine expresses her love by reading to me when we travel together. I love how nurturing this feels, but I can only stay awake for a few minutes because her voice is so calming and soothing! There are literally unlimited ways to meet our need for love. How do you meet your need for love?

Notice whether your need for love is met today. If it
is not, consider ways that you could meet it.

AUGUST 15

By perseverance, the snail reached the ark.
—*Charles Haddon Spurgeon*

Being Persistent About Getting Our Needs Met

Do you ever find yourself in an argument that doesn't seem to have a solution? Consider this couple's situation. The husband picks up after himself and he likes a neat home; the wife tends to put things down and leave them there. Their arguments usually involve the husband accusing the wife of being lazy and uncaring, and the wife accusing the husband of being rigid. The only two strategies that they can come up with are either the husband picks up for both of them or the wife tries to pick up for herself. But she usually doesn't stick with it for long and the argument starts over. Sometimes people get stuck in this kind of argument for years.

How about a different approach? Let's consider the needs. The husband may need orderliness and cooperation, while the wife may need spontaneity and autonomy. Suppose he says to her: "You know, when I come home and see your clothes on the floor from the living room to the bedroom, I feel confused and annoyed because yesterday I heard you say that you would start picking up your things. Did I hear you correctly yesterday?" "Well, yeah, but you know I came home and jumped in the shower. I meant to pick up the clothes, but then I started reading the paper and just forgot." "So, your intention was to pick up your clothes, but then you got distracted?" "Yeah. That's it." "You know, when I hear that I feel annoyed because I'd really like to trust that you'll follow through on your commitments. Do you think you heard my request to pick up your things as a demand?"

"Of course it's a demand. If I don't do it your way, I'm in trouble." "I can see how you'd think that because I have been really upset about this issue for a long time. But I'd like you to hear it differently now. I really do value orderliness, but I also value your need for autonomy and spontaneity. I'd truly like for us to create a solution that meets both of our needs. Would you be willing to brainstorm ideas with me that might accomplish that?"

Can you imagine new solutions to this ongoing conflict? It's especially difficult to be creative when you are emotionally charged by the situation. Here are a few ideas: She pays someone to clean the house weekly; they put a box by the front door for all the clothes she takes off; she has one room in the house designated hers where she can be as untidy as she likes; he has one room that's his and keeps it as tidy as he likes; or he continues to tidy the house for both of them and she adds other duties to her list, such as the laundry or yard work. The point is that there are numerous ways to meet these needs. The trick is to be creative and flexible in choosing strategies.

Be aware of your needs today and be creative
and flexible about getting them met.

AUGUST 16

*We know that when people learn to communicate
effectively with each other, their lives and their
relationships can be truly transformed.*
—Dr. Thomas Gordon

Clarifying Our Requests to Meet Our Needs

Consider these common complaints: "My husband never listens to me." "My wife is always talking about her feelings, and then she wants me to talk about my feelings too!" We understand the frustration behind statements like these, but if you find yourself making them, *what specifically do you want?* Or, put another way, what could your partner do in order to meet your needs? If your husband listens to you once a week, is that enough? Or would it need to be three times a week? Would it meet your needs if your wife only asked you to talk about your feelings twice a week? Or would you like her to never ask you how you are feeling? What is enough?

Our job is to clarify the requests we make of ourselves and the people in our life. In doing so, we should make our requests specific, doable, and immediate. For instance, a wife could say something like: "Honey, I've really had a rough day today, and I'd just like to be heard. *Would you be willing to listen to me for fifteen minutes—just listen—without giving me advice or trying to solve the problem?*" A husband could say: "You know, when you ask me how I'm feeling, I'm worried that if I don't know, or if I don't say it right, you'll be upset with me. *Would you be willing to hear me say how I'm feeling in my own words, without correcting me or commenting on my use of words?*" In these examples, both

266

speakers make it completely clear what they want from each other. In doing so, they both have a much greater chance of meeting their needs.

Take the opportunity to be very clear about what you would like from at least one person today.

AUGUST 17

When we fear punishment, we focus on consequences, not on our own values.
—Marshall B. Rosenberg, PhD

Intrinsic vs. Extrinsic Motivation

Are you motivated by fear of punishment or negative consequences? Or are you motivated by a true inner desire? Research shows that long-lasting, permanent change comes when people have an intrinsic desire to change. Extrinsic motivation is temporary and often only lasts while one is being observed (such as driving the speed limit when a police officer is present). Do you call your mother because you truly want to connect with her? Or do you call her because you're worried she'll feel hurt if you don't? If the latter is your motivation, it is not likely that you call often, or that you enjoy the conversations.

When I started working for the Flagstaff Center for Compassionate Communication, they told me that we didn't have set work hours, and that our pay was not dependent on a specific number of hours worked per week. I was flabbergasted, and I spent the first year trying to figure out how to gauge my effectiveness, usefulness, and contribution. I went from thinking I was working too hard to comparing my work habits with my colleagues and thinking I wasn't working enough. After about a year of agonizing over this, I started to come to work because I truly valued and enjoyed it. Now I work longer hours than I ever worked in higher education, I rarely feel tired or overworked, and I'm not preoccupied with wondering if I'm doing enough. Through this process, my motivation has shifted from extrinsic to intrinsic, and I am more productive and peaceful in my work.

Notice whether you are primarily intrinsically or extrinsically motivated today. How does this information feel to you?

AUGUST 18

Our faith must be alive, always growing, like a tree.
—*Thich Nhat Hanh*

Serenity Is a Choice

Serenity is a state of being and a universal need that is peaceful, tranquil, and clear. We can be serene even in a catastrophe, or when life is challenging, or when we are scared, hurt, angry, or sad. This happens when we are able to connect to what we value most, and to act in harmony with those values. In Compassionate Communication, many of us hold a deep value to connect with people. When we are open to connecting even if we are triggered, angry, sad, or hurt, we can achieve serenity in that moment.

Let's say you volunteer your time by working at your local soup kitchen. You are excited about the quality of food it provides and how it supports your community. Each week when you go to work there, one of the other volunteers talks to homeless people in ways that don't meet your needs for respect and consideration. You can choose to lose your serenity by gossiping about your colleague to other volunteers, not saying hello to him when you see him, or ignoring him. If you choose these behaviors, however, you will probably also lose connection to the joy you feel through your volunteer work and your respect for the soup kitchen. There is another option you can use to maintain your serenity. You can say hello to your colleague when you see him, talk to him honestly about how you feel, connect with him about how he feels, and focus on the needs you try to meet by working at the kitchen each week. The more we focus attention on our greatest needs, the more serenity we will enjoy in our lives from day to day.

Make a decision to live with serenity even if challenging situations arise in your life today.

AUGUST 19

Keep your eye on the sunshine,
and you will not see the shadows.
—Helen Keller

Observing Without Judgment

You're in a store and you see someone you haven't seen in a while. She walks past you without saying anything. You think, "What a snob" or "She doesn't like me." Later you find out that she didn't recognize you, or that she was in a hurry to get her mother's medication at the pharmacy. On another day, you call a colleague to ask for advice. He doesn't return your call, so you start to think, "I call him too much" or "He is so insensitive. He should know how important this is to me." Later, you find out that he was out of town for two weeks, or that he and his wife had just separated, and he was very upset. Many times, what happened and the story we make up about why it happened are two different things. Whenever we create a story about a person's actions, we create drama and pain in our own life.

Before you spend even a moment creating a story about someone's behavior, stop yourself and clarify what actually happened. Try your best not to add any of your own evaluations or judgments. For instance, in our first example, you were in a store and someone you know walked past you without saying anything. That is all you know. In the second example, you only know that you called your colleague and he hasn't called you back. Once you have clarity about what actually happened, consider connecting with the person about what was going on with them. You will find that the more you observe life without judgment and evaluation, the more open you will be to hearing and connecting with other people.

Today, stick to the facts and don't make up stories about why people behave in certain ways.

AUGUST 20

There is no way to peace; peace is the way.
—A.J. Muste

Getting Beyond Our Self-Defeating Behaviors

Have you ever noticed yourself doing something that shakes the serenity of your colleagues, your family, or yourself? We have become so used to conflict that we hardly know how to handle some situations without it. Not long ago, I participated in a committee of Nonviolent Communication trainers. I was starting to tell myself that I wasn't being heard or valued. Then I came up with an idea that I was sure the committee would want to hear. The more I thought about it, though, the more it became clear to me that probably none of them would like my idea. In fact, it could very likely be the stimulus for discontent in the group. In that moment, I saw one of my behaviors that keep me from meeting my needs: When my needs for being heard and valued are not met, I do something to be seen, even if it causes conflict in the group. This behavior never helps me meet my original needs of being heard and valued. So in this situation, rather than share my idea, which I thought would create conflict, I expressed that my needs to be seen and valued were not being met. Then I asked everyone in the group to tell me how my participation in this committee met needs they had. This request brought clarity, warmth, support, and love, along with meeting my needs to be heard and valued.

> Today, pick one self-defeating behavior you would like to change. Notice the needs you are trying to meet before taking action. Then ask yourself if your action is likely to have the desired effect.

AUGUST 21

We have to understand in order to be of help.
We all have pain, but we tend to suppress it because
we don't want it to come up to our living room.
The most important thing is that we need to be
understood. We need someone to be able to
listen to us and to understand us.

Then, we will suffer less.
—Thich Nhat Hanh

Move In to Conflict—Don't Back Up!

Have you ever noticed how often we back up when we find ourselves in a conflict? Or how much we try to pull away when someone is angry or in emotional pain? Can you imagine seeing someone bleeding on the street, and then walking right past him? We can be so attuned and ready to help someone in physical pain, and yet we often recoil from a person who is in emotional pain. I suggest that we begin to retrain ourselves to "move in" when someone is in emotional pain, rather than pulling back.

Here's an example of how this might look. Your partner might say to you: "You're never on time. Never!" If you were to argue with him, or list all the times that you were punctual, or explain that you were late because of traffic, you would be backing away. To move in sometimes takes courage and often takes a clear desire for connection. In this instance, you could move in by saying, "Are you annoyed because you'd like to trust me when I say I'll meet you at a specific time?" It's a simple process, really, but the rewards can be increased intimacy, joy, understanding, connection, and deeper relationships. When we back away, the results are often anger, resentment, hurt, and disconnection. These feelings are similar to how you would feel if you were injured and someone walked on by, and similar to the feelings you would have walking past a physically injured person. How about setting a goal of moving in to someone's emotional pain—maybe even your own!

For today, empathize with at least one person in emotional pain rather than backing up.

AUGUST 22

No one can make you feel inferior
without your consent.
—Eleanor Roosevelt

You Are Not Responsible for Other People's Feelings

How many times have we heard this? It may sound trite, but it's true! Everyone's feelings are a result of met or unmet needs. It's important that we take responsibility for our actions and acknowledge that our behaviors are sometimes a stimulus for other people's pain. It is equally important that we acknowledge to ourselves that other people are responsible for their own feelings.

Say that you are telling a story about your younger brother's childhood, which you think is hysterical and clearly demonstrates his quick wit. He, on the other hand, feels hurt and embarrassed because he wants respect and consideration, especially while his girlfriend is visiting the family. In this situation, your brother doesn't appreciate that you are trying to contribute to his relationship with his girlfriend. Are you responsible for how he feels? Absolutely not. Should you acknowledge that you were the stimulus for his pain, and express your regret? Absolutely. If you can remember this simple philosophy, it can be easier for you to take responsibility for your actions, without taking responsibility for other people's feelings. This will enhance and deepen your relationships.

Notice if you are taking responsibility for other
people's feelings today and be aware that
they are responsible instead.

Competence, like truth, beauty and a contact lens,
is in the eye of the beholder.
—Laurence J. Peter

Making Comparisons

She is so beautiful; I wish I could look that way. He is so athletic; I could never do that. She is much smarter than he is; she's really the brains of the family. I know this job better than he does! Feeling joyful today? Consider comparing your body to a supermodel, or comparing your professional skills to a leader in your field. This activity is sure to overwhelm anyone with feelings of shame, guilt, or disappointment, and knock the joy right out of them.

Anytime we compare ourselves to other people, or compare others, we open the door to pain and despair, and we separate ourselves from others. Learn to evaluate yourself without comparisons. For instance, acknowledge your disappointment because you would have liked a project you worked on to have more depth, or acknowledge your excitement that it came together with such ease. Consider that you'd really rather be twenty pounds lighter to meet your need for beauty, or that someone else's weight gain doesn't meet your need for beauty. Own your feelings and needs without comparisons. Believe me, everyone in your life will feel the relief of this simple change.

Notice how often you compare yourself to other people
and how you feel when you do this.

AUGUST 24

Honesty is the first chapter of the book of wisdom.
—*Thomas Jefferson*

When Someone Doesn't Appreciate Our Honesty

Not everyone will receive your honesty with joy. If they seem unhappy, this is an indication that they have unmet needs, not that you have made them unhappy. Remember that feelings are a result of met or unmet needs; a situation is only the stimulus of feelings, not the cause. When someone doesn't appreciate your honesty, try empathizing with them. What if your partner has body odor that you find offensive? You could say to him: "Honey, when we are physically close and I smell your body odor, I feel kind of grossed out, and it's hard for me to want to be intimate with you. Would you be willing to start wearing deodorant?" Maybe your partner won't enjoy hearing this, so he might say: "Oh come on. It can't be that bad!" Now is the time for you to empathize. "Are you feeling hurt and embarrassed because you value tolerance?" "Well, yeah. Plus, you know that I don't like to put unnatural crap on my body!" "So, you'd really like understanding that you don't wear deodorant because you value your health?" "Yeah!" "You know, I hear that you show respect for your body by not putting chemicals on yourself. I respect that too. At the same time, I am concerned because your body odor is strong enough that I resist being close to you. Would you be willing to go to the health food store and look for a more natural deodorant? Or, maybe would you be willing to take a shower and change your clothes every day?" "Well, yeah, I guess I could go the health food store and look for a natural alternative to deodorant. I'll do that tomorrow after work. And, I'll go take a shower right now."

When we withhold our truth or lie, we can create emotional and physical distance in our relationships. By being honest, we can strengthen them.

Be aware today of how your actions stimulate feelings in other people but are not the cause of their feelings.

AUGUST 25

We are all born for love. It is the principle of existence, and its only end.
—Benjamin Disraeli

Love as a Feeling and a Need

Love can be both a feeling and a need in Nonviolent Communication. It can be seen as a need if we do something to meet our need for love, such as reading to someone, helping someone with his homework, snuggling, or helping our elderly mother comb her hair. For many of us, any of these activities would meet our need for love. We can also experience love as a feeling, just as warmth, affection, and excitement are feelings. We might feel love when we hear our child let out a big belly laugh, when we see our dogs curled up on the floor sleeping soundly, when our best friend calls us after being gone for a period of time, or when our partner comes home with our DVD because he knows we're feeling blue. Often, but not always, we can feel love and meet our need for love at the same time.

Notice when you feel love and when your need for love is met today and what caused this.

AUGUST 26

I've had a wonderful evening, but this wasn't it.
—*Groucho Marx*

Getting Our Need for Love Met

Sometimes you might find yourself in a situation where your need for love is not met. Perhaps your partner expresses his love by helping you come up with solutions for your problems, but all you really want is for him to listen to you. Or perhaps your cat, which you brought into your life to love, just vomited on your new, very expensive rug and left a stain. In both these situations, your need for love is not met.

Now what do we do? I suggest you consider ways in which a partner or friend could meet your need for love. Be sure to request something the other person is capable of doing. How about asking your partner for thirty minutes of his time? Make it clear to him that you don't want him to try to fix your problems, just to listen to you. If it is difficult for him to connect to his feelings, I would avoid asking him to connect to yours! Instead, ask for what you think he is capable of doing. Now, about the cat. You could ask her to stop vomiting on your favorite rug, but is it likely she'll comply? Probably not. Instead, how about asking her to snuggle with you? Whatever the situation, it is our responsibility to clarify how we can meet our need for love, while also considering the abilities of our loved ones to comply with our requests.

Make a request of at least one person today in
an attempt to meet your need for love.

AUGUST 27

If a man speaks or acts with pure thought, happiness
follows him like a shadow that never leaves him.
—Buddha

Choosing Our Response

We have four choices of how to respond to someone, even when they say things that are hard to hear. If someone says to you, "You shouldn't have done that, it was inappropriate," consider your four options. The first one is to blame the speaker. "What do *you* know about what's appropriate? You are the last person who should be talking to me about appropriate!" The second option is to blame yourself. "Oh he's right. I shouldn't have done that. What was I thinking? I'm always doing the wrong thing." A third choice is to empathize with yourself by acknowledging your feelings and needs. "When I hear him say that, *I feel hurt and angry* because *I need understanding and acknowledgment* for how much effort I have put into this." The fourth option is to empathize with the speaker, listening to his feelings and needs. "Are you *worried* because you *value this project* so much, and you wanted *to make sure it goes well?*" It seems astonishing, but every time someone communicates with us, we have four choices on how to respond. Choose your response based on the needs you want to meet in the moment.

Today, be aware of the four options you have
when you respond to someone, and consciously make
your choice based on the needs you want to meet.

279

AUGUST 28

We never know how high we are—till
we are called to rise.
—Emily Dickinson

Expressing Ourselves Honestly

You have something that you want to say to someone, but you're worried they won't enjoy hearing it. What do you do? Say it anyway or keep it to yourself to maintain peace in the relationship? If you bottle it up, you will begin to resent the other person, so being honest is the best way to maintain the relationship. Consider expressing yourself using the four steps of Compassionate Communication.

Let's say that you want to tell your partner that she talks more than you enjoy hearing.

Step 1 is the observation:	"Honey, when you talk for this long
Step 2 expresses a feeling:	I feel overwhelmed
Step 3 expresses a need:	because I need more time to integrate new information, and I just can't let this much information in at once.
Step 4 makes a request:	Would you be willing to let me tell you what I've heard so far to make sure I understand what you want me to know?"

This kind of communication is short, direct, and respectful, and you will increase your chances of being heard. If she doesn't enjoy hearing this from you, consider empathizing with her by listening to her feelings and needs. Here are a few tips: An observation is just the facts; avoid adding your judgments about the situation. Talk about your own feelings; avoid talking about the other person's feelings. Needs are universal; every human being has the same needs. Strategies are specific; ask someone for a specific action to help you meet your need.

Be aware of opportunities to be honest with people using the four steps of Compassionate Communication.

AUGUST 29

Few blame themselves until they have
exhausted all other possibilities.
—Anonymous

Being Honest About Our Anger

When I am angry, it is likely that I am not getting something that I want and that I think I should get, and I am about to say something that will ensure I won't get it. When we blame other people, we place ourselves in a dangerous position of not meeting our needs in that relationship. Instead, take a deep breath and don't say anything. While taking this breath, quietly acknowledge to yourself *your* unmet needs and feelings in the situation. Only when you have connected to your feelings and needs should you consider speaking to the other person.

Here is how it works. Let's say your boss just told you:

"This proposal is completely unacceptable. You have a half hour to fix it!" Take a breath and think to yourself: "Ugh. I am so ticked at him. He is so demanding and impossible to please because he gives such vague information." Then connect to the feelings and needs beneath these judgments, "I really *feel annoyed* (feelings) because I'd like *clarity about what he specifically wants* (needs)." Then, say aloud: "You know when I hear that I feel frustrated because I created the proposal based on your specifications. I need some clarity here. Would you be willing to tell me exactly what parts are unacceptable to you?" Such a communication is more likely to meet your needs for clarity, respect, and being valued.

Be aware of opportunities today to practice
connecting with yourself before responding
to another person in anger.

AUGUST 30

Happiness itself is a kind of gratitude.
—*Joseph Wood Krutch*

How Are You Feeling?

How are you feeling right this minute? Here is a list of words that may describe how you feel when *your needs are being met*: loving, happy, satisfied, content, excited, joyful, peaceful, confident, elated, vibrant, delighted, amused, or hopeful. Here is a list of feelings you may have if *your needs are not being met*: scared, worried, pain, confused, annoyed, frustrated, angry, ticked off, tired, weary, embarrassed, lost, irritated, impatient, or resentful. Remember that your feelings are the result of whether your needs are met or not. It is helpful to be aware of how we feel and then uncover our underlying needs. When we do this, we are in a better position to live joyfully.

> Be aware of how your feelings are
> connected to your needs today.

AUGUST 31

Hating people is like burning down
your house to get rid of a rat.
—*Harry Emerson Fosdick*

Self-Righteous Anger

Have you ever noticed that some of your behaviors ensure that your needs for peace and relief *won't* be met? Take judgments for instance. The more we have, the less peaceful and happy we feel. The same is true for resentment and anger. Don't you just feel awful when you are filled with them? How does feeling that way meet your needs for peace and relief? Sometimes I think we are seduced by self-righteous anger, but it's an empty seduction, an illusion. It doesn't meet a single universal need. In fact, it is the anti-solution because it causes pain and eliminates the opportunity to meet our needs. Stay focused on the needs you are trying to meet in your life, and then choose behaviors that are geared towards meeting them.

It's not that judgment, resentment, and anger are wrong; it is simply that they will not support you in meeting your needs. Let them go with love and choose a different behavior.

Be aware today of opportunities to release your judgment, anger, and resentment to better meet your needs.

Meditations for
SEPTEMBER

SEPTEMBER 1

We don't get to know people when they come to us;
we must go to them to find out what they are like.
—Goethe

Focus on Connecting

I think my early friends had incredible stamina. I had built such a high wall around my heart that they had to chip away at it to connect with me. I greatly appreciate their attempts to connect, but now the people in my life no longer have to make this effort. I receive the connection I desire because *I focus on connecting* with people. When I see someone in pain, I make myself available to them. When I see someone in the store whom I know, I go out of my way to greet them. I express appreciation to people when they have contributed to my life, and I let them know when I wish things had happened differently. I am present, loving, and available for a connection, not because I think other people want it (although I believe they do), but because *I want it*. I want to live in a world where people care for one another, so I actively create that world. If you want to get to know someone, let her know you. If you want someone to connect with you, connect with her. Take the first step and you will change your life.

Be aware today of opportunities to
create what you want by living it.

SEPTEMBER 2

Fanaticism consists in redoubling your effort
when you have forgotten your aim.
—George Santayana

Focusing on Needs to Enrich Your Life

Strategies are the means we use to meet our underlying needs. Many of us are less than successful at meeting our needs because we become stuck on strategies that rarely work. Perhaps we are so focused on getting a specific job or promotion that we lose sight of the needs we want to meet with the new position. In this case, the job or promotion is the strategy. What is the need? Is it financial security, a challenge, belonging to a different group, or ease? Will this job meet the needs we are focused on? Are there other ways we can meet them?

When I worked in higher education, I went to bat for pay increases and promotions. My goal was to make more money, I thought. Now, I think my deep underlying need was reassurance that I was valued in the organization and that I made a difference. Now, I make less money but I am better off financially, I am much happier, and I know that I am valued in my organization. If I had stayed focused solely on my salary, I never would have discovered the joy of meeting my need to be valued. I would not have known that there are many ways to meet my need for financial security.

Rather than focus on your strategies, focus on the needs you wish to meet. You might see a strategy that you would not have thought of, but if it will head you in the direction of your underlying need, go with it. Then feel the joy of living in ways that meet your needs.

Today, focus on your needs, rather than your strategies.
It just might open new possibilities for change.

SEPTEMBER 3

Live each day as if your life had just begun.
—Goethe

Doing Something Different

This is it. Today is the day to be open to others. Maybe it's scary to be vulnerable, but what is the alternative? Keep doing the same things, and you will have the same results. Make a change right now. Do something different. What is your greatest need at this moment? Is it love, support, compassion, financial security, hope, family, friendship, shelter, food, or something I haven't mentioned? Name one thing you can do right now that will bring you closer to meeting that need. Do it today. Don't put it off. This is your life.

Commit to doing one thing that will bring
you closer to meeting a need today.

SEPTEMBER 4

Whenever you have seen God pass, mark it,
and go and sit in that window again.
—Henry Ward Beecher

Shedding Light on What Works

What works in your life right now? What do you enjoy? Notice what you have done to make this area of your life a success. Can you use the same principles to shed light on another area of your life that you would like to change? If a strategy works, take note, and do it again. So much of the time, we focus on what doesn't work. But there is just as much wisdom in noticing what does work and why. This awareness serves two purposes: It allows us to clarify how we currently meet our needs, and it allows us to feel gratitude for the aspects of our lives we enjoy. When we do this, we shift our attitude toward success and celebration, and experience both relief and joy.

> Notice what is working in your life and how you
> manifest your success. Then find ways to use this
> information to create more joy.

SEPTEMBER 5

Some people are always grumbling that roses have
thorns; I am thankful that thorns have roses.
—*Alphonse Karr*

Manifesting What We Love

We manifest whatever we focus on. If you focus on the negative, you will receive negativity. If you focus on what works, you will experience success. In a way, focusing on what we love is a form of affirmation.

Years ago, I learned to use affirmations, so I would spend three minutes each day affirming that my life was abundant with love. I felt silly doing this because I didn't believe it. My life wasn't full of love, so why did it help to lie about it? That form of affirmation just didn't work for me. Today, I affirm the needs and values I love. Even if I don't have what I love, I can honestly say I love it. For example, if I am struggling with someone, I affirm, "I love ease, compassion, and openness in relationships." I may not experience this in the moment, but I affirm what I love. By doing this, I tell the Universe what I want in my life.

What needs and values do you want to manifest in your life? Tell yourself that you love these, and then allow the manifestation to appear.

Express what you love today
and then let it come to you.

SEPTEMBER 6

Mere survival is an affliction. What is of interest
is life, and the direction of that life.
—*Guy Frégault*

Loving Life

I spent much of my first thirty-five years just getting by. I didn't feel much joy. I didn't have many friends. I didn't feel passion. I just got through each day. In essence, I spent my life reacting to my perception of other people's feelings and needs, rather than being in touch with my own. Now, I understand that what is interesting about being alive is living. If I'm just getting by, unaware of what I feel or need, I do not fully experience life. It is the difference between living life in black and white, and experiencing full color. Why just get by when you can experience living color? Be aware. Be vibrant! This is your life. Make it work for you.

Commit to living today in full awareness of
what you feel and need in each moment.

SEPTEMBER 7

*We must always change, renew,
rejuvenate ourselves; otherwise we harden.*
—*Goethe*

Change Happens

I used to think that people were supposed to feel and show little emotion. So I set out to be "even," as I put it. I thought the best way to achieve this was to be "stable," which to me meant to stagnate. I felt joy about things only for a short while. Then I wondered if I would ever be happy and if I was just difficult to please. It never occurred to me that trying new things and discovering what I enjoyed or didn't enjoy was part of experiencing life. Indeed, to stagnate is to limit life. Life *is* change. Thank goodness for that! Try new things and enjoy them. Notice which needs you meet with each activity, and which you do not. Stay connected to your life in ways that meet your needs, be willing to adopt strategies that best serve you, and you will find more joy and interest in life. It is inevitable.

Be open to changing your strategies
to best serve your needs today.

SEPTEMBER 8

The greatest mistake you can make in life is to be
continually fearing you will make one.
—Elbert Hubbard

Take the Leap!

Go ahead. Take the leap. What is the worst thing that can happen? Often we are reluctant to make changes that will enhance our lives because of our need for predictability. We may not enjoy the way we live but at least we know what to expect. However, if we don't try new things that could help us meet our needs, we miss opportunities for joy, love, and fun. Our need for predictability seems at odds with our need to enjoy life.

But our needs are never in conflict. It is possible to meet all our needs with carefully chosen strategies. Do you have a dream that you tell yourself can never come true? Think of one thing you can do today to move toward your dream and still meet your need for predictability. Are you willing to take that first step? If not, why? Empathize with yourself—listen to your feelings and needs and uncover what holds you back from manifesting your dream. Once you feel relief through the empathy process, go ahead and take that first step.

Today, identify a dream you have and take
one step toward achieving it.

SEPTEMBER 9

Never think you've seen the last of anything . . .
—Eudora Welty

Our Actions Impact Others

Have you ever noticed that we all breathe the same air? Literally, each time we exhale, our breath goes out to the world. Where does it go? Your neighbor's house, Utah, China? Sooner or later, it probably makes its way to all those places. Similarly, each action we take has an affect on the world. Sometimes the way our actions affect others is obvious, but often, like our breath, they spread invisibly. If we don't see an impact, we easily forget that we have one. This is dangerous because in the forgetting we lose touch with our role in creating peace in the world.

Say that you have had a frustrating day and when you go home, you yell at your kids or kick your dog. Your kids learn from your behavior and your modeling, and when they feel frustrated they yell at someone else. When people feel frustrated or angry they may snap at the bank clerk or store cashier. Maybe those people will go home and snap at their children. We can affect people without knowing that we do.

It is important to be aware of this and choose to act in ways that are in harmony with the results we want.

For today, consider how your actions with the people you encounter will ripple through the world.

SEPTEMBER 10

It is well to give when asked, but it is better to give unasked, through understanding.
—*Kahil Gibran*

The Gift of Understanding

All people long for understanding. It is such an easy thing to give, yet rarely do we see its importance in creating peace of mind. Consider a situation in which you have just heard that your boyfriend is dating one of your friends. You call another friend to tell her about it and she says, "You must be feeling so hurt because you'd like to trust that your friends will be honest with you." When someone simply reflects our feelings and needs without aggravating the situation, we feel instant relief because they "got" us. I'd rather be "got" than to have people commiserate with me. Commiseration can sound like: "Oh my! I can't believe this. How utterly insensitive and thoughtless of both of them. What a betrayal!" This can sound supportive, but it plays into the problem and stimulates more pain. On the other hand, when we offer understanding to another person, *we receive the gift of connection.* Everyone wins.

Today, be aware of your desire to commiserate
and see if you can turn it into an opportunity
to empathize with another person.

SEPTEMBER 11

*The greatest thing in the world is
to know how to be one's own self.*
—Michel Eyquem de Montaigne

Finding Our True Self

Many years ago, I reached an all-time low in my self-esteem. I really thought that I didn't deserve love. I realized that I had spent years running from this belief, striving for more promotions and recognition so that I could hide my deep fear that I was a worthless human being. I was terrified of being "found out." Then, one day I decided to stop the race. I wanted to face up to the fear. If I was a worthless person, then I wanted to accept this fact and figure out how to live within that reality. Or, if I was a valuable human being, I wanted to know that, so I could stop the messages of worthlessness that ran incessantly through my head. In a sense, I longed to know who I was, not who I told myself I was. I began to face myself honestly that day, and embarked on a journey of discovering my feelings, needs, and values. I learned that everyone is valuable, lovable, and important to our world's evolution. Now I concern myself more with living in harmony with my needs and values, which I see as my true self.

Be aware of your value today, and act accordingly.

SEPTEMBER 12

The shortest and surest way to live with honor in the world is to be in reality what we would appear to be.
—Socrates

Living Authentically

Have you ever heard comments like these? "I didn't know you were angry!" "Really? You were enjoying the party?" The true test of living authentically is when people perceive your feelings accurately. It sounds easy, but it takes courage, honesty, and an ability to be in the present moment. It is so natural for many of us to lie about who we are and what we feel. Say that a woman you wanted to date calls you to ask if you want to go skiing. You might say, "Oh sure, I love to ski," when in reality you gave up skiing years ago because you didn't enjoy it. You tell yourself that if she discovers you don't like skiing she won't like you, so you lie to *meet your need for acceptance and love.* At the same time, you *deny your need for authenticity, honesty, and fun.*

It is a total relief to be authentic. No more hiding out, making up excuses, or lying to people. It can feel like a weight has been lifted from your chest. Imagine just being you, without worrying about how other people will receive you.

Be aware today of opportunities to be honest with people because you desire to live authentically.

SEPTEMBER 13

You may find the worst enemy
or best friend within yourself.
—English proverb

Knowing Ourselves

The question is not what other people think of you, but what you think of yourself. Who are you, really? Often, we don't take the time to consider what we value. We think we know, yet our behaviors are often contrary to our values. We long to be heard, so we yell louder. If we thought it through, however, we would see that yelling is not an effective way to be heard. We may get attention, but we are rarely heard or enjoyed. What is your greatest need? Maybe it is for acceptance, understanding, love, connection, or to be heard. What are you doing to manifest the satisfaction of this need? Consider whether your behaviors are likely to help you succeed. When your behaviors are in alignment with your needs, you have greater opportunities for joy.

Today, notice whether your behaviors
are in alignment with your deepest values.

SEPTEMBER 14

*I always say to myself, what is the most
important thing we can think about
at this extraordinary moment.*
—R. Buckminster Fuller

Being Present in This Moment

Have you ever noticed a tendency for your attention to be everywhere but where you actually are? You may be doing the dishes and stewing over a task you have tomorrow. Or changing the baby's diaper while fretting about something you said earlier that day. You may be talking to a friend while worrying about your trip next week. Where is your attention right now as you read this meditation? Take a moment to connect with yourself. Tomorrow will come later and yesterday already happened. This is your moment to live. How can you spend it in the way that you most enjoy? Be conscious and present as much as possible in your life, and you will feel more connection and joy in all of your activities.

Commit to being present as much as possible
in each moment of your life today.

SEPTEMBER 15

*I've never sought success in order to get
fame and money; it's the talent and
passion that count in success.*
—Ingrid Bergman

No Sacrifices, Please

When someone suffers for my success, we both lose. It is anti-success. In a win-lose situation *everyone loses*. My goal is to live in a world where no one's success depends on anyone else's pain and where no one's needs are sacrificed. There is enough love, space, and time in the Universe to meet everyone's needs. Many skeptics tell me that empathizing, listening for the other person's feelings and needs, is too time-consuming. In reality, it often takes only a few minutes. Afterward, resolution can be swift and simple. On the other hand, trying to convince others to do things our way even though they strongly disagree can be very time-consuming. If they give in, it will take more time to encourage, motivate, and push them to stay on our course. Take the time to connect, gain consensus, and inspire buy-in, and your life will run more smoothly and with greater ease.

Be aware of opportunities today to inspire consensus.

SEPTEMBER 16

The beginning of love is to let those we love be
perfectly themselves, and not to twist them to fit our
own image. Otherwise, we love only the reflection
of ourselves we find in them.
—*Thomas Merton*

Perceiving Reality

Often, when we start a new relationship, we twist reality to suit our needs. We like most of the qualities of our new girlfriend, so we pretend that her incessant swearing and burping are intriguing qualities that prove she lives authentically. Or we have just accepted a big promotion, so we tend to ignore the fact that our boss belittles us in public. Instead, we choose to think that the situation isn't *that* bad. When we try to make another person fit into a reality that we prefer in order to meet our own needs—whether for love, connection, or financial security—everyone suffers. Instead, bring your focus back to yourself. Notice which of your needs are met or unmet when you spend time with someone. Don't judge *them*; just focus on *your* feelings and needs. Then, decide whether continuing the relationship will meet them.

Be honest with yourself today about
the people and situations in your life.

SEPTEMBER 17

Somebody's boring me . . . I think it's me.
—*Dylan Thomas*

Creating Your Experience

It is so easy to say, "What a boring speaker." Whenever we judge someone else, rather than acknowledge our own feelings, we miss the boat. Judging another person will not make our experience more interesting. In fact, it renders us powerless. Our best chance to shift from bored to intrigued is to focus on our unmet needs. Maybe we're tired and struggle to be interested in the topic, or maybe we don't understand its relevance to our lives. Once we connect to our unmet need, we can find ways to meet it. We could step outside and take a short nap to meet our need for rest, then be more able to stay present. Or perhaps we could ask the speaker how this topic relates to our life so that we can sustain our interest. Once we connect to our unmet need, we may even decide that it would be best for us to leave. Only after we connect to our unmet need can we make sound decisions that will transform our experience.

If you feel bored today, connect to your unmet needs
and then look for strategies that will meet them.

SEPTEMBER 18

Just because everything is different doesn't
mean anything has changed.
—Irene Peter

Changing Our Perspective

Many years ago, I was renting a house with an absurdly low rent. I lived in this house for many years and my landlord had never raised it. Then one day he told me that our local utility company offered him three times the rent I paid to lease the house. He apologized profusely as he told me he simply couldn't pass up this opportunity. At first I was upset, and worried that I wouldn't be able to afford a house of similar quality, so I prayed for an answer to my dilemma. In the meantime, I answered countless ads for rentals. I found that even a much more modest home would double my rent. Everyone I talked to about this said, "You should look into buying your own house." And each time I said, "Oh, I can't do that!" Then I would go home and again pray for an answer. After about two weeks, I began to get angry and my prayers turned into demands: "Hey! I need help here. Are you paying attention?" After a few days, a thought ran through my head: *"Mary, maybe you should buy your own house!"* Ah, maybe *that* was the answer to my prayers! Although I didn't think it was possible, I found a way to buy my first house before I had to move out of the rental. My mortgage payment was less than it would have been if I had rented a house, and I was nurturing an investment in my future.

Often times we have exactly what we need; we just don't recognize it. You don't always have to change your

302

situation; sometimes changing your view of things is all you need.

Focus on an area of your life that you are not enjoying and try to view it differently to change your experience.

SEPTEMBER 19

If I am faithful to the duties of the present,
God will provide for the future.
—*Gregory T. Bedell*

Staying Present in the Moment

How do you feel and what do you need right now? Don't worry about tomorrow or fret about yesterday. Just be here in this moment. When you are present to your needs and act in harmony with your values, everything else will fall into place. Your life is like a symphony—as long as each note is played in harmony with the score, the music will be beautiful. It is inevitable.

Several times today, notice if you are present to the moment. If you are not, notice how you feel and what you might need. This will help you stay present.

SEPTEMBER 20

The tragedy is not so much what men suffer,
but rather what they miss.
—*Thomas Carlyle*

Taking Action to Change Our Experience

Sometimes when we are unhappy with an aspect of our life, it seems too painful to change; thus, our continued unhappiness is the result of our inaction rather than our action. When I was in high school, I was terribly shy and uncomfortable with people, so I kept my distance. This met my need for protection and ease. I developed a few close friends, but I didn't mingle or talk with people easily. When I was in my thirties, I began to realize how the decision not to deal with my shyness in high school had kept me isolated from people. My loneliness and discomfort with people went on for more than ten years after high school because I hadn't taken the risk then to overcome them. Later, my needs for intimacy, fun, and connection became more pressing than my needs for protection and ease, so I began to create strategies that would help me learn how to connect with people *and* protect myself.

Reflect on an area of your life that stimulates pain in you. Is the pain caused by something that is happening, or by your own inaction? Without judging yourself or your decisions, consider whether you are now in a better position to take action to change your experience.

Ponder one area of your life that you are unhappy
with today. Consider whether the cause is
your action or inaction.

SEPTEMBER 21

*The only tyrant I accept in this world is
the still small voice within me.*
—Mahatma Gandhi

Acknowledging Our Inner Critic

In Compassionate Communication, some of us call the critical
voice inside our heads our jackal. The jackal says you *should*
or *shouldn't* do something; it judges you and other people;
and it is the most likely to get scared when you begin to make
a change. I used to be embarrassed by my jackal because I
thought I *should* be more compassionate and less judgmental,
so I tried my best to ignore the voice. That just caused it to
howl louder. After many years, I learned to love that voice
because when it howls, I know I have an unmet need.

I may not always enjoy the jackal's methods for alerting
me to this. One time, I gave a training to forty-five military
men who made it clear that they weren't interested in
Compassionate Communication. About halfway through
the workshop, my inner jackal started to say: "You have
got to get out of here! These people aren't interested in
what you have to say. This is a waste of your time!" Had
I ignored this voice, I believe it would have gotten louder
and my ability to continue with the workshop would have

been severely limited. Instead, I empathized with the voice by thinking: "Are you embarrassed and feeling hopeless that you are unable to contribute to the participants' lives? Do you need ease and respect?" Once I was able to connect to those underlying needs, I recognized that I could not expect everyone I encountered to meet them. I might not meet those needs in this group at all, but one of the participants might. Once I looked for people who appeared to enjoy the workshop, I found several who did. In fact, after empathizing with my jackal, I was able to notice that most of the participants seemed to be enjoying themselves. Before connecting to my jackal voice, I had focused on the few who didn't want to be there.

Our inner jackals hold wisdom for us if we are willing to listen. When we acknowledge our jackal and empathize with its need, we gain insights into ourselves and we clear the way for resolution.

Be aware of your jackal today and consider
the wisdom it is trying to share with you.

SEPTEMBER 22

*If we could read the secret history of our enemies,
we should find in each man's life sorrow and
suffering enough to disarm all hostility.*
—*Henry Wadsworth Longfellow*

Connecting to Our Humanity

Human beings are basically the same. We all have the same needs for love, support, food, water, appreciation, and caring for our families. We all suffer. We all laugh. We all feel joy. We all feel sorrow. We all bleed, and we grieve when our loved ones are injured or in pain. We feel scared if we're in danger and hopeless when we can't find ways to live safely. If you are in conflict with someone, try to forget your differences. Connect to your similarities, your universal needs, and the humanity that you share with that person. When we connect to the humanity in other people, we can eliminate violence.

Be aware of the humanity you share
with other people today.

SEPTEMBER 23

*Happiness is not a state to arrive at
but a manner of traveling.*
—Samuel Johnson

Enjoyment Redefined

The purpose of life is not to get somewhere, but to enjoy the ride. I used to live my life just "getting through" things. I was miserable most of the time but I kept telling myself that someday I would be happy. I forced myself to accept jobs I didn't enjoy, to date men who didn't meet my need for respect, to maintain friendships with people I didn't enjoy because I thought that by doing this, I would benefit down the line. The problem was, "down the line" never happened. I never felt joy because I was doing things that gave me no pleasure. One day I realized that if I didn't start to enjoy my life now, I never would. Today is what you have. Consider what you can do to enjoy it.

Do something that you enjoy today.
There is nothing more precious than this moment.

SEPTEMBER 24

That kind of life is most happy which affords us most opportunities of gaining our esteem.
—*Samuel Johnson*

Forget About Being Nice

Nonviolent Communication does not teach people to be nice. On the contrary, we empower others to ask for what they want in ways that are more likely be heard and respected. I used to have an image in my head of what nice looked like. It was saying "OK" through clenched teeth. To me, nice meant doing what someone else wanted at my expense. I thought I *should* be nice. Indeed, I believed that if I didn't consider your needs to be more important than mine, I was being selfish. Now I think it is selfish not to consider my own needs. If I do not value myself, I do not value my relationships. It is impossible for two people to enjoy a relationship if one of them is miserable. So forget about being nice. Instead, consider connecting to the needs of everyone you are in relationship with. Do this to meet your own needs for respect, love, connection, and intimacy.

Be aware today of how your relationships suffer when you are not present for yourself.

SEPTEMBER 25

Not knowing when the dawn will come
I open every door.
—Emily Dickinson

If It Ain't Broke, Don't Fix It

Have you heard the saying, "If it ain't broke, don't fix it"? Communication is like that too. Don't try to adjust your communication and behaviors if they already work for you. However, if you are struggling in your relationships, the chances are good that how you communicate is part of the problem. It may even be the biggest part.

I used to think communication meant the way I talked to people. Consequently, because I was bright and articulate, I didn't think I needed to learn more about it. What a misconception that was! After several years learning and teaching Nonviolent Communication, I know now that communication is the totality of how we express ourselves. It includes our use of words, our inner voice, our body language, our attitudes, and the way we view life. All of these affect our communication and our ability to interact with others and with ourselves. A shift in any aspect of our communication can affect the way we present ourselves and the way others perceive us.

If you suspect that you could learn more about how to communicate, consider learning Nonviolent Communication. It is a way of living that has had a dramatic impact on thousands of people worldwide.

Be aware today if your communication with yourself
and other people is as satisfying as it might be.

SEPTEMBER 26

*Jealousy sees things always with magnifying
glasses which make little things large,
of dwarfs giants, of suspicions truths.*
—*Miguel de Cervantes*

Give Up Your Assumptions

Can we all just agree to stop making assumptions? When enough people stop making assumptions, the violence in our world will diminish significantly. Every living being is the totality of their experience. Every experience we have shapes our current reality. If you were raised in a peaceful, loving home and someone else was raised in a home where violence was the norm, your experiences of life will differ. If you have a doctorate and spent two years traveling abroad while someone else dropped out of school in the ninth grade and spent two years living on the street, your experiences will be dissimilar. Recognizing your differences does not mean you judge people and their experiences; rather, you acknowledge that each person sees life through a different lens. Don't believe that other people see things your way or that they will experience events the way you do. The chances are good that your assumptions about the other person, no matter who it is, are inaccurate.

Years ago, I dated a man and I made the assumption that we were both monogamous. I was surprised to discover that this assumption wasn't accurate. At first I was hurt and angry because my need for respect had not been met. But when I thought about it, I realized that we had never discussed this. I had assumed that he valued monogamy the same way I did; and he assumed that I held the same values he did. This caused us both a lot of pain. Had one of us broached the topic, we would have had greater clarity. Don't spend a moment living from an assumption. It is not worth it, especially when there is an easy solution. Simply ask the other person what their truth is. Checking things out like this is a way to respect both yourself and them.

Be aware of your assumptions today and check them out with the others involved as soon as you can.

SEPTEMBER 27

What is a cynic? A man who knows the price of everything and the value of nothing.
—*Oscar Wilde*

Relating to the Value of Things Rather Than the Cost

How much is that class worth to you? How about that blouse or new wallet? So many of us decide worth based on outside influences. When we make spending decisions, I suggest we base them on the value we receive from that item or service. I have a massage therapist who comes to my house and gives the best massage I have ever experienced. She charges me forty-five dollars for a ninety-minute massage. I pay her sixty dollars. Not because I have to, but because I receive so much value from the massage that it doesn't meet my need for integrity to pay her forty-five dollars. Similarly, when I was starting as a trainer of Nonviolent Communication, I interned with a trainer in another city. He allowed me to go to all his trainings for free as part of my internship. Many times I paid him for the classes because I received so much value from them and because I wanted to contribute to his life. The exchange of resources, that is, exchanging money for an item or service, is enhanced and better appreciated when we are connected to its personal value. Consider shifting your focus from what something costs to the value it brings to your life.

Be aware today of a struggle you may have about
whether to buy an item or service. Consider whether
its value to you is worth the investment.

SEPTEMBER 28

To listen well is as powerful a means
of influence as to talk well.
—Chinese proverb

The Power of Being Heard

I often hear people say this in my classes, "Yeah, but don't you think if I say anything at all, it will cause the situation to escalate?" This question came up in a recent class. The person who asked it was upset with his spouse about something, so I reflected what I thought his feelings and needs were. Instantly, he started to cry because he felt so touched that someone understood what he was trying to say. He had been having the same argument with his wife for years, but in that minute of empathy, he was heard for the first time. To hear another's feelings and needs is one of the most powerful methods to defuse anger and create space for resolution that I have ever encountered. It may seem awkward at first because we are not used to talking with people in this way. It is OK to feel awkward; do it anyway. Soon it will feel as natural as breathing.

Be aware of opportunities
to empathize with someone today.

SEPTEMBER 29

Hatred does not cease by hatred,
but only by love; this is the eternal rule.
—Buddha

Peace Makes Peace

Many people think they can force others into compliance. This is often the philosophy behind one country attacking another, or one person overpowering another. We think that might is the best way to force people into submission. Conquering a person or people may lead to momentary compliance, but it never results in long-term peace. Never. Centuries of warfare have proven this. Violence does not stop violence. Hatred does not stop hatred. In fact, they are fuel for more violence and hatred. If you want peace, you must be peaceful even if others are violent. If you want love, you must be loving even when other people are hateful. It is the paradox of humankind. When people and nations understand this, we will have worldwide peace. I suggest that we start with ourselves. If you want peace in your family, live peacefully. If you want harmony at work, conduct business harmoniously. I predict that after some time, you will feel the effects of this shift in consciousness.

Make a commitment to live peacefully
today in all your actions.

SEPTEMBER 30

They have only stepped back in order to leap farther.
—Michel Eyquem de Montaigne

Continuing to Move Forward

Sometimes it looks like we're not making progress, or even that we're moving backward. It's all in the perspective. At these times, consider where you were last month or last year, and the length of the leap that brought you to where you are. Give yourself a break. Emotional growth isn't linear, and we can't always see our progress.

Years ago, I decided not to be intimate with people who had poor follow-through. They didn't meet my needs for respect, trust, and fun. Still, I kept finding myself in situations with people whose follow-through habits didn't meet my needs. I spent years in utter frustration about this issue. I had such powerfully negative judgments about these people, yet I was attracted to them as lovers, friends, and business colleagues. Then one day I felt something shift inside me. I literally felt it. For the first time in all those years, I realized that there was nothing wrong with other people's follow-through, and there was nothing wrong with my ability to get things done. In fact, we wanted the same things—trust, success, and fun. The issue was that we *chose different strategies* to meet those needs, *and* I also had a strong need for predictability that they didn't share. In that moment, I understood that the reason I was still attracting these people was because I had felt guilty about my own need for predictability. Once I was able to release my judgment of them *and myself*, I was able to acknowledge that I simply did not enjoy having people in my life whose follow-through didn't meet my needs for trust and predictability.

A short time after this revelation, someone asked me if I would work with him. The first time we did something together, he was not prepared. He had lots of reasons for this, but the fact was that he hadn't followed through on our agreement. Clearly and with love, I expressed my disappointment that my need for trust had not been met. We talked about it, and he decided that he would feel uncomfortable working in an environment that placed such high regard on follow-through because he had a stronger value for spontaneity and "going with the flow." We parted with love and compassion for each other.

Sometimes, we think we're taking two steps back and one step forward. However, each step is a move forward even if we don't recognize it. One day, we will be astounded by our lengthy leaps. Emotional growth is a process, one step and one leap at a time.

Think about one issue that you have been trying to change today. Then be aware of your progress with it.

Meditations for
OCTOBER

OCTOBER 1

Seize from every moment its unique novelty,
and do not prepare your joys.
—André Gide

Focus on Being Happy Now

You may do things you *don't enjoy* because you think they will enhance your life later. Instead, do things that you *enjoy* so that you can enjoy today! Tomorrow is only a possibility. Today is the deal. At some point in my emotional recovery I became aware of how unhappy I felt most of the time, so I started to focus on shifting my perspective. I tried to stop judging other people and stop categorizing their every flaw, foible, or misdeed, and instead look at myself. In the process, I began to take responsibility for my feelings. If I was annoyed with someone, I looked at what my underlying needs were, and I set out to meet them rather than be annoyed. Eventually, I grew to understand that I can be happy now if I choose to be. I can focus on what works rather than what doesn't. Don't decide to be happy later. Be happy now. Shift your perspective, and you will transform your experience of life.

Be aware of your perspective on life today,
and focus on enjoying your day.

OCTOBER 2

People are lonely because they build
walls instead of bridges.
—Joseph F. Newton

Changing Our Behaviors
to Shift Our Experience of Life

I spent the first several decades of my life constructing walls between myself and other people. I did this through my judgments of others, my warrior attitude which kept me from asking for help, and my incessant attempt to prove my worthiness to other people. These behaviors met my need for protection because very few people were willing to brave my gruff exterior to get to know the real me. I gained some relief, but I also experienced enormous loneliness. While I was busy protecting myself, I only met my needs for love, connection, intimacy, and acceptance in small, unpredictable spurts. I had constructed my own loneliness through my choice of strategies. I later realized that if I could build walls, I had the power to dismantle them to attain the companionship I longed for.

Sometimes we work so hard to meet one need, we forget the many others that we leave unmet. Consider all the needs you want to meet in a situation and then brainstorm strategies that will meet them. Don't be blocked by your initial fear. You don't have to settle for meeting only a few of your needs; you can live a life that meets them all.

Be aware today of times when your strategies allow you
to meet one need at the expense of others.

OCTOBER 3

The time is always right to do what is right.
—*Martin Luther King Jr.*

Integrity

What does integrity mean to you? Each person has a different definition. For me, integrity means that I live in harmony with my values. If you value freedom of expression, working for a bureaucratic organization will probably not meet your need for integrity. If you value predictability, you might not want to play the stock market. We all decide what we value. The trick is to live in integrity with those values each day of our lives. If a cashier expresses annoyance with you, or your spouse has just totaled your car, how can you respond in ways that meet *your need for integrity*? Now is the moment. Act in harmony with your values, no matter what or whom you face. When you do, you will live with integrity and feel free and at peace.

Be aware today of the values you hold dear and live in harmony with them to meet your need for integrity.

OCTOBER 4

Hate the sin and love the sinner.
—*Mahatma Gandhi*

Seeing the Needs Underlying Anger

A trainer friend of mine told me that he wants to live in a world in which we naturally move toward someone who is in emotional pain, the same way we move to help someone in physical pain. I love this idea. Consider anger, which is one way we express pain. Haven't we all said things in anger that we regretted? We tend to back away from anger in others because we are afraid of it and we want to protect ourselves. Rather than backing away, however, another strategy is to learn to deal with it by hearing the underlying feelings and needs behind it.

Imagine someone has just rear-ended your brand new car and you are furious. Instead of defending himself or hiding out in his car while he calls the police, the man who hit you might say, "You must be really furious because you have barely had a chance to enjoy your new car!" Can you imagine how that would feel? By simply guessing your feelings (furious) and need (enjoying your new car), the other driver acknowledges you and defuses your anger. It is remarkable how something so simple can cause such radical healing. Learn to see what is beneath people's behaviors. The more pain they exhibit, the more desperate they are to meet their needs.

Be aware of opportunities to connect to someone's feelings and needs when they exhibit anger today.

OCTOBER 5

In managing human affairs there is
no better rule than self-restraint.
—Lao Tzu

Avoiding "Right Fights"

When we are angry, we are at a crossroads. In that moment, we can work toward a resolution or we can work toward escalation. Say that your partner asks you to drive and then he tells you what turns to make and where to park. You may feel irritated about this and want to chew him out. Why? Because you want to prove to him that you know how to drive. Maybe you want to say something like, "You may find this amazing, but I have been driving for approximately thirty years, and I have parked all by myself probably one thousand times." Consider why you want to say this. I'd guess you want to be seen as capable of managing this situation on your own. Ultimately, this is a desire to be right. If you say this kind of thing to him, it is likely you will be entering into a "right fight;" you argue your rightness and then he argues his rightness. As tempting as right fights are, they rarely end in peaceful resolution or meet the original need, in this case, being seen as competent. A second strategy could be to express yourself honestly. "You know when you tell me how to drive and park, I feel unbelievably annoyed because I need respect. Would you be willing to sit quietly while I drive?" It's direct, honest, and more likely to meet your needs. Avoid engaging in a right fight. If that's the only strategy you can think of, don't say anything and come back to the issue when you are more calm.

Be aware of any temptation to get into a right fight. Instead, consider making a direct request to the other person that is more likely to help you meet your need.

OCTOBER 6

*The difference between a dream
and a goal is a timeline.*
—Dr. Phil McGraw

Needs Analysis—an Activity
to Uncover Your Strategies

You will experience relief and joy if you take conscious action that is in alignment with the needs you want to meet. In my first Nonviolent Communication class, the trainer led us through a process in which we each identified our greatest need. All eight participants were surprised at what they discovered about themselves. The next exercise was to identify everything we did to meet that need. Without exception, all of us did things that kept us from meeting our most important need. Mine was a need for connection, yet I actively kept people at bay. I was disheartened to realize that I had spent my life making it impossible to meet this need. Then the trainer said: "But wait. It's OK. Nonviolent Communication helps us first identify what our greatest needs are, and it then helps us create strategies to meet them." That is exactly what Nonviolent Communication has done for me: identify what I need, then choose strategies that are in alignment with it. This simple technique has profoundly changed my life.

Notice what your greatest need is today
and then take action to meet it.

OCTOBER 7

Our duty is to believe that for which we have
sufficient evidence, and to suspend our
judgment when we have not.
—John Lubbock

Transforming Your Anger

We feel anger when we judge or blame someone else. We
think the other person *should* have done or said something
differently, and in that moment, we are convinced that she
is wrong and we are right. If we continue to focus on her
foibles, we have little or no opportunity for healing. On
the other hand, if we focus on our own unmet needs, the
opportunity for healing exists.

For example, your partner has said she would arrange
for a babysitter so you two could go out on a date. You arrive
home that night and find out she forgot to call the sitter.
If you feel angry, it's probably because you are telling
yourself that she should have followed through, that she's
untrustworthy, or that she doesn't care about going out as
much as you do. If you remain focused on her, your feelings
will fester and multiply. However, if you empathize with
your unmet needs, of which there may be many, you will be
more able to feel compassion for yourself and her. In this
situation, you could say: "I am so disappointed that you

didn't call the sitter because I *really* wanted to have a night out and I would really like to trust that you'll do the things you agree to do. Would you please tell me if a night out is important to you too?" The unmet needs you expressed were a night out and being able to trust that she'll do the things she agrees to do. The request allows you to receive information about what's important to your partner, and it opens the door to resolving the issue. As a result, you will be more likely to meet your needs in a harmonious and compassionate way. This is a powerful way to heal anger.

Be aware of when you feel angry today and attempt to translate your anger into feelings and needs.

OCTOBER 8

If the only tool you have is a hammer,
you tend to see every problem as a nail.
—Abraham Maslow

Expanding Your Communication Tools

I have been creating a series of web courses lately. When I first started the project, I had never experienced a Web course, nor did I have the vaguest idea of how to create one. I had to learn a whole new set of tools, vocabulary, and materials. I could have avoided learning all this new stuff by deciding not to create the Web courses. But in order to meet my need for success, I expanded my skills and knowledge. The same is true of relationships. If you are in a relationship with someone and your limited skills don't help you meet your need for connection, intimacy, or fun, look for new skills. Expand your tool box. Different situations call for different resources. If you only have a few choices, you will shortchange yourself and your relationship. Nonviolent Communication is one tool that can help you gain relationship skills. It has transformed thousands of relationships around the world.

For today, consider whether your relationship skills are adequate to meet your needs. If they are not, consider learning something new.

OCTOBER 9

I was raised to sense what someone wanted me to be and be that kind of person. It took me a long time not to judge myself through someone else's eyes.
—Sally Field

Liberating Ourselves

Many years ago, I moved away from my hometown for the first time. It was one of the most painful, devastating, and enlightening periods of my life. I lived in a place where no one had a preconceived idea of who I was. Everyone I encountered saw me for the first time. I was both anonymous and new. I used this opportunity to discover who I really was underneath all my layers of habitual behaviors. During the first few years in my new environment, I uncovered depth, talent, and courage I never knew I had. Because I no longer had family to rely on, I learned how to be resourceful and independent. I learned that I was athletic and physically powerful. I started to see myself through my own eyes, rather than other people's. I liberated myself. If you struggle with people's preconceived notions of who you are, consider stepping out of the situation. You don't have to move to another city or state, or move at all. You could change your job or career, or go on a trip and meet new people. Look for ways to discover who you are in a new setting. Once you know who you are, you will be less likely to be defined by other people.

Be aware today of other people's ideas of who you are.
Notice if they fit your notion of who you are.

OCTOBER 10

You need only claim the events of
your life to make yourself yours.
—*Florida Scott-Maxwell*

Finding Reasons to Celebrate

I used to think that celebrations were only in order when something big occurred, such as a birthday, graduation, or wedding. Consequently, I didn't celebrate very often, and I frequently wondered if my situations warranted celebration. I often felt unworthy. Now, I see that all of life is worth celebrating. Driving through Seattle without being caught in a traffic jam is worthy of a celebration. Spending a weekend on the Washington coast with two days of clear, sunny weather is too. Writing the 333rd meditation for this book is reason to celebrate! I meet my need for celebration in a variety of ways. I might call a friend and share my happiness, or thank my higher power for creating weather that I can enjoy, or I might plan a party. The critical factor is remembering to celebrate the small things as well as the big things in life. That way we stay connected to what is working in our lives and to our gratitude.

For today, make a conscious effort to celebrate
at least one thing that works in your life.

OCTOBER 11

He who conquers others is strong;
he who conquers himself is mighty.
—Lao Tzu

Trusting Yourself

I used to close myself off from many people because I was afraid they would want something from me that I didn't want to give. I simply closed down and allowed very few people in. I was lonely, sad, and trapped when I lived from this consciousness. Can you relate? Now I know that *I* choose what I give to other people. My freedom came when I started to learn new tools for being honest, clarifying my needs, and taking care of myself in all my relationships.

Once I could trust that I wouldn't give more than I wanted, I could let all kinds of people into my world. My life became abundant, diverse, and joyful.

> Be aware of your ability to choose
> what you give in your relationships today.

OCTOBER 12

All great discoveries are made by men
whose feelings run ahead of their thinking.
—*C.H. Parkhurst*

Conflict Resolution

Anytime you're in conflict, it is likely you are arguing for a *particular strategy*, rather than connecting to *the underlying needs behind it.* This simple fact is important to recognize. The first step in conflict resolution is to remind yourself to look for needs, not strategies. Even simply recognizing this will help bring resolution. Step two is reminding yourself that you truly value everyone's needs and that you do not want to get your way at someone else's expense. Step three is looking for the underlying needs behind each request. If your partner wants to visit family for Christmas and you'd like to stay home, look at your needs. I'd guess his needs are for fun, connection with family, and contributing to their lives. Your needs might be for rest, ease, and fun. Step four, then, is brainstorming other alternatives that will value everyone's needs. Rather than focus on just two options—

spending Christmas with family or at home alone—are there other options that you could consider? It is so easy to get stuck in our strategies if we don't acknowledge the actual needs we want to meet. Once we acknowledge them, we become more open to looking at other options.

Notice today how conflicts stem from arguing a particular strategy instead of focusing on discovering and meeting everyone's needs.

OCTOBER 13

Don't compromise yourself. You are all you've got.
—*Janis Joplin*

Meeting Our Need for Respect

"You know I respect you. What's your problem?" Do you ever find yourself in an argument over whether someone respects you? This argument can be frustrating if you focus on whether the other person respects you. The real question is *whether your need for respect is being met.*

A friend of mine had a tendency to say "What a girl" to his male friends when they did things that he thought were beneath their ability, such as when they dropped the ball in a softball game. Every time I heard this, I felt annoyed because my need for respect wasn't met. When I tried to speak with him about it, he would often say: "Oh, Mary, you know I respect you. I'm not saying *you're* a girl. Only that Bob is acting like one." Then we would argue about whether he respected me or not. Neither of us was satisfied in these conversations. Then one time I said to him: "You know, every time I hear you call your friends 'girls' when you are disappointed with their behavior, I feel offended, because I value respect for all people. Would you be willing to use other means of expressing your frustration while I'm around?" He started telling me, once again, that he respected me. I responded by saying: "I hear that you feel respect for me, but when I hear you say 'What a girl,' *my need for respect as a female* is not met. So, would you be willing to choose a different way to express your disappointment to your teammates while I am present?" Once I could be clear, he agreed.

It is a waste of time to argue about whether we are respected. It is clearer and more effective to state that *our need for respect is not being met* by a particular behavior, and what we want that would satisfy our need. When we clarify this, we avoid arguments over who respects whom. I am not interested in labeling the other person as disrespectful. My goal is for the other person to exhibit a different way of showing their respect for me. Making a specific request, in this case, asking my friend to express his disappointment differently while I am present, keeps the focus on what I want.

Be aware today of times when your need
for respect is not met. Then express your feelings
and needs to the other person.

OCTOBER 14

WARNING: Statistics have shown that mortality increases perceptively in the military during wartime.
—Alphonse Allais

Are Your Behaviors Working for You?

Albert Einstein once said that the definition of insanity is doing the same thing repeatedly and expecting different results. I think this applies to our communication patterns. Many of us learn a way of being when we're young and take that information into our adulthoods without question. Eventually we notice that we're just not happy in our relationships, and in our jobs, or aspects of our lives. We may be miserable, in fact, yet we hesitate to change our behavior. Why? Because even though we're unhappy, we're on familiar ground; our lives are predictable and dependable. It may be hell, but it's our hell.

For some of us, though, we may live this way because we simply don't know another way of being. If you'd like to change the results of your life, change your behavior. First, connect with the needs you want to meet. Do you overeat to meet your needs for protection, ease, or relief? Do you yell at your children to meet your needs for ease, to be heard, and to contribute to their lives? Once you are clear on the needs, consider other strategies that might meet them and other needs you may have such as connection, harmony, or consideration. Your behavior change doesn't have to be big. Just do something different. Even changing one behavior, one attitude, or one action can alter your course.

For today, choose one behavior you would like to change. Connect to the needs you are trying to meet and change one thing that will better meet them.

OCTOBER 15

The forest will answer you in the way you call to it.
—*Finnish proverb*

Meeting Our Need for Sexual Expression

Have you ever tried to tell your partner that your sexual needs were not met? Such a conversation is bound to promote defensiveness and hurt feelings, *unless* you keep the conversation focused on your needs, not her lack of skill, *and* you make a very specific request. Telling someone that you do not enjoy making love to her anymore might not be an effective way to start the conversation. Consider saying to her: "I've noticed that the last few times we have made love, you have not seemed as present as usual. I miss the connection we have when we are both present and enjoying our lovemaking. Have you also enjoyed that connection?" This acknowledges what you have enjoyed about your love life in the past and also gives her a chance to speak to whether she enjoys that type of connection too. From there, you can explore what keeps her from being present and think of ways to rectify the situation. You will both benefit from this conversation.

Be aware today of how much you enjoy your love life and if you would like to make a request to enhance it.

OCTOBER 16

Understanding human needs is
half the job of meeting them.
—Adlai Stevenson

Control

I often hear people say that someone did something because of a need for control. Control is actually a strategy that is often confused with a need. Let's say your spouse insists on driving. You might think she needs to be in control. I suggest that her needs are more likely for safety, ease, or maybe fun. The way she satisfies that need is to control who drives. In another example, you might perceive your boss as somebody who micromanages to meet his need for control. Again, I'd guess his needs are for assurance that the job will be done well, predictability, and perhaps respect. He meets these needs by going over project details with you. Control is a strategy to meet deeper needs. This is an important distinction because it allows us to gain greater clarity about behaviors. It can also help us connect more compassionately with other people if we avoid confusing their strategies with their needs.

Notice the underlying needs behind someone's drive for control today. Does this help you feel compassion for the other person?

OCTOBER 17

*I hoped that the trip would be the best of all journeys:
a journey into ourselves.*
—Shirley MacLaine

Discovering Ourselves

I have traveled to some amazing places, and I have met passionate, worldly, intelligent, and remarkable people. I have walked on beautiful beaches, swung through the trees of the Costa Rican rain forest like Tarzan, and enjoyed ancient structures and cultures in Europe. None of these trips has been nearly as exciting, unpredictable, or rewarding as my journey to self. Once I learned to reliably connect to my feelings and needs, I could make better decisions and enjoy all parts of my life more fully. Believe me, the journey toward self is one of the most thrilling, frightening, and empowering trips we can take. It is not always easy but the rewards are plentiful.

Today, enjoy the adventure you are on as you journey toward knowing yourself better.

OCTOBER 18

Nothing in life is to be feared.
It is only to be understood.
—Marie Curie

Clarifying Feelings

When you express your feelings, try to use words that convey emotions rather than thoughts. Emotion words include sadness, happy, excitement, joy, fear, and hurt. Thought words express a judgment about someone else, such as feeling manipulated, abandoned, rejected, or abused. Each of these words expresses your opinion of the other person's actions: that she is manipulative or abusive, or that she has abandoned or rejected you. When we focus on how we actually feel about something, rather than judge the other person, we are more likely to be heard. If your wife made plans to go away for the weekend without discussing it with you first, you might feel annoyed, hurt, angry, or confused. If you tell her that you feel abandoned or rejected, she is likely to respond defensively. Express your feelings in a way that connects to others and yourself rather than mixing in your opinions and judgments, which can lead you to disconnect. Disconnecting promotes argument. Connecting promotes resolution.

Today, focus on expressing your feelings,
rather than thoughts, in an effort to connect
more deeply with yourself and others.

OCTOBER 19

Play so that you may be serious.
—*Anacharsis*

Meeting Our Need for Play

Play is the most challenging need for me to meet. I admire people who play easily. One of my brothers told me about a vacation that he, his wife, and daughter took not too long ago. They played golf and miniature golf, swam in the pool, went bowling, ate in wonderful restaurants, took tours of the local sites, and took long naps. I was astonished with how much they did in a short time and how the focus of their vacation was play. My needs for hard work and accomplishment are very well met, but I often forget to play. How about you? Is your need for play met in this moment? If not, consider a few things you can do to meet it today. For instance, how about having lunch with a friend whom you laugh with easily? Or how about going to a funny movie? Forget the drama just this once. You could also choose roller skating, ice skating, horseback riding, bowling, or golf. The activity doesn't matter as much as the joy you feel when you meet your need for play. As a friend of mine says, "Play on!"

Be aware of whether your need for play is met today.

OCTOBER 20

All serious daring starts from within.
—*Eudora Welty*

Compassionate Communication and Addictions

People often ask me how Compassionate Communication works with addictions. There are no easy answers and there are many twelve-step programs that help people overcome their addictions. Remember that everything we do is an attempt to meet needs. Compassionate Communication complements what people learn in other programs by helping them focus on finding new strategies that will better meet their needs. When looking at addictions, consider what needs the person is trying to meet. I'd guess that behind all addictions is a desire for ease, comfort, relief, and protection from painful emotions or life situations. Each person's situation is different, but the underlying needs are the same. The addictive substance, then, is the strategy people use to meet these needs. Most times there are other strategies that will meet them more effectively.

Behind every addiction is a person in pain. Empathizing, listening to someone's feelings and needs, can bring great relief to the person and to your relationship. Rather than saying, "You shouldn't smoke so much," consider empathizing and say, "Do you worry that you will be under a lot of stress if you try to quit smoking?" You might be surprised by what you will learn if you enter into a conversation about the feelings and needs of the other person. Even if she doesn't stop her addiction, you may both feel much more connected. There are no easy answers, but the more we can connect with the needs a person attempts to meet through their addiction, the greater their opportunity for recovery.

> Consider the needs people are trying
> to meet through their addictions today.

OCTOBER 21

The pain is the aversion. The healing magic
is attention. Properly attended to, pain can answer
our most crucial questions, even those
we did not consciously frame.
—Marilyn Ferguson

Choosing Whom We Empathize With

I have learned that empathizing with some people does not meet my own needs for connection, rest, or joy. This may be because my own needs are so great or because I have other, more pressing needs than I will meet through empathy. One of the basic philosophies of Nonviolent Communication is valuing everyone's needs equally. That means that I consider my needs to be equal to another person's needs. If I choose to empathize at my own expense, I am not living in a Nonviolent Communication consciousness. I can better meet my needs for integrity and caring by telling a person up front if I am unable to be present to their need for empathy.

> Be aware of your own needs today when someone asks
> you to be their emotional support.

OCTOBER 22

Never go to bed mad. Stay up and fight.
—Phyllis Diller

Committing to Full Understanding

Recently I visited my parents and I offered to take down their Christmas decorations for them. I offered because they are elderly, and I know how difficult it is for them to do certain tasks. This would meet my need to contribute to their lives. My father responded to my request by saying, in a tone I heard as impatience: "There are five big boxes that the decorations go in. Your sister is the only one who knows what goes where." I decided that he would prefer that I leave things as they were to meet his need for ease, so I said, "OK." About twenty minutes later, I realized that I had made an assumption so I checked it out with him by saying, "Pop, when you told me that there were five big boxes that hold the decorations, were you hoping it would discourage me from taking down the decorations?" "No, not at all," he said. "Oh, were you just telling me that you couldn't help me figure out how the decorations are stored?" "Yes. I don't know where anything goes." "So would you like me to take down your decorations if I figure out how to store them myself?" "Yes, I would." I almost missed an opportunity to contribute to my parents' lives because I misunderstood what my dad was trying to tell me. Part of living in a Compassionate Communication consciousness is developing a willingness to come to complete understanding before taking the next action. Don't assume anything. Check out your assumptions. Don't miss opportunities to connect with other people by ending the conversation before it's over. Everyone loses when we do this.

Be aware of times today when you assume what someone means and check it out with him.

OCTOBER 23

We lie loudest when we lie to ourselves.
—Eric Hoffer

Noticing What You Value

"Oh, I can't afford a weekly massage!" "Oh, no. I don't travel. I just can't afford it." Have you ever noticed how often people say they can't afford something? When we say this, we really mean that we choose different priorities for our money. We make choices about what is important to us. If I say I can't afford a weekly massage but I spend five hundred dollars a month on health insurance, I choose to meet my need for security over my need for nurturance. If I choose to avoid taking exotic trips but I spend thirty thousand dollars on a new car, I choose to meet my need for predictability and safety over my need for fun and adventure. If I don't go out to lunch with my friend because I want to make sure I have enough money to feed my family that night, I choose to contribute to my family's life rather than meet my need for connection with my friend. How do you spend your money? What does it tell you about what you value most? The more consciously we make choices that are in alignment with our values, the more peaceful our lives will be.

Notice how you spend your money today
and what that tells you about your priorities.

OCTOBER 24

*Do not use a hatchet to remove
a fly from your friend's forehead.*
—*Chinese proverb*

Aligning Our Strategies With Our Values

What do you value most? Do your actions match your values? I used to think that I valued integrity more than anything, yet I went to work every day for five years at a job I hated. I thought that I valued friendships, but it just didn't seem convenient to be present when friends were in dire straits. For years I maintained the illusion that I held these values, but my actions demonstrated different ones. When I noticed these inconsistencies, I was devastated. How could I have lived my life for so many years in contrast to my values? The answer came months later: that was the only way I knew to live. The truth is that I never really noticed whether my actions were in alignment with my values. I just responded to the world the way I thought I was supposed to.

Take a look at your actions and notice if they are in alignment with what you value. If they aren't, don't feel discouraged; many people develop behaviors that are counterproductive in adulthood. Take steps to create actions that are in alignment with your values and you will be able to refocus your life.

Be aware of the values that your
actions demonstrate today.

OCTOBER 25

*Running around the boat does nothing
to ensure progress through the water.*
—Anonymous

Making a Direct Request

Often it is not *what* we ask, it is *how* we ask that makes a difference. Recently, I witnessed a couple in conversation. The husband had bought his wife a water purifier. She didn't want it. He felt angry and said: "Well, I guess I should know by now that you won't like anything I buy you. I don't know why I don't give up." She said: "What do I need a water purifier for? I've been drinking our tap water for thirty years!" I felt very sad when I heard this conversation because I realized that the husband had purchased his wife a gift that he wanted. When she didn't like it, he felt angry, hurt, and hopeless. In the end, his need for clean water was not met and there was additional tension in their relationship. I honestly believe that if he had simply asked for what he wanted, he might have gotten it. "Honey, I am starting to worry about the chemicals in our water. Would you be willing to use a purifier for the water we drink?" It's direct and honest. Anytime we try to get people to do what we want without being honest about our intentions, we are drawn into a manipulative scenario that often backfires.

When this happens, it is hard for anyone to feel satisfied. When we are direct and honest about what we need, our ability to meet our needs increases.

> Notice when you attempt to meet your needs
> by manipulating another person today.
> Then stop yourself and make a direct request.

OCTOBER 26

*The efforts which we make to escape from
our destiny only serve to lead us into it.*
—*Ralph Waldo Emerson*

Our Behaviors Reflect Our Needs

Everything we do is an attempt to meet a need, no matter who you are, how you were raised, or where you live. I recently went on a trip and hired a woman to watch my cats. I gave her instructions to feed the cats dry food. She called me two days later to tell me that they had requested canned food, and since I had some she gave it to them. Would it be OK if she bought more canned food for them? I was shocked. How did my cats request this from her, I asked. "They were very clear, actually. After I fed them their dry food, they stood by the food dish and mewed and mewed. I knew they wanted something else, so I looked in your refrigerator and cupboard. Sure enough, I found the canned food and I gave it to them. Then they stopped mewing. I love how communicative they are, don't you?" I did love that. I also loved how receptive she was to figuring out their needs.

Sometimes the people who are close to us, including our animals, express themselves in ways that are difficult to decipher. When we take the time to understand them, or when we look beyond their choice of words to see the need they are trying to meet, we enhance our relationships. There is nothing more precious.

Be aware of opportunities to look beyond someone's words to understand their underlying needs today.

OCTOBER 27

Clapping with the right hand only
will not produce a noise.
—*Malay proverb*

Creating Joy in Our Lives

Compassionate Communication values the concept of only doing things that bring us joy. Sometimes when people first learn this concept, they take this literally and say things like, "I'll attend the meeting if I feel joy about it at the time." Or "I know we had plans but I just didn't feel joy about going once the time arrived." When people say things like this, or act in this manner, they are missing a key aspect of Compassionate Communication: the importance of valuing everyone's needs equally. I can feel joy if I follow through with my plans to meet my own need for fulfilling my obligations or contributing to my friend's life. If I think I'd like to change our plans, it is important for me to consider the other person's needs as well. The only effective way to do this is to ask. "Joan, I know we made plans to go to the movies tonight, but I am beat. Would it be just as fun for you to go tomorrow night?" It is important to only do things that bring us joy. It is just as important to value everyone's needs equally. The minute we value our needs more than others', we erect walls in our relationships.

> Be aware of times when you value your own needs
> more than other people's today, and choose a
> different approach that values them equally.

OCTOBER 28

*Make today something you'll
want to remember tomorrow.*
—Amity Buxton

Loving Your Body

Are you frustrated with your physical appearance, weight, or choice of foods? Rather than expend energy beating up on yourself about these things, consider looking at the needs you meet by looking and behaving this way. Remember, every action is an attempt to meet a need. If you are eating more than your body requires, what need do you think you are trying to meet? For me, overeating meets my need for predictability because it is a behavior I have had for my entire life, and relief because the focus on food keeps me from experiencing my feelings to their fullest extent. There is a part of me that thinks that overeating also meets my needs for ease and protection, but I know deep down that this is an illusion. My need for ease is met when I buy high-calorie fast foods because I spend little time preparing meals. On the other hand, it is not met when my body has to work harder to function or when I shop for clothes. Similarly, my need for protection is not met when my health is in danger. Other needs that are not met when I overeat are self-respect, love for my body, health, fun, intimacy, hope, and many others.

If you would like to change your eating habits, consider focusing on your needs. The next time you are tempted to order a burger and fries instead of a salad, consider what needs you are trying to meet with the burger and fries. Then ask yourself whether there is a healthier strategy you can use to meet that need. If you need relief, consider other ways to achieve it. Call a friend to talk about a troubling issue, take a long bath, go to the gym to work out, or take a nap. Once you trust that you have a new strategy to meet your need for relief, then consider whether you are willing to order the salad. It takes time to change a lifelong habit. Rarely does it happen overnight. If you have been struggling with your weight for a long time, one of the most loving things you can do is connect with yourself. Notice your feelings and empathize with the needs you are trying to meet, and give yourself the luxury of time.

> Be aware today of the needs you are trying
> to meet with your eating patterns.

OCTOBER 29

When Sleeping Beauty wakes up
she's almost fifty years old.
—Maxine Kumin

Staying Connected to Our Bodies

I spent much of my life disconnected from my body. This meant that I wouldn't notice that I was coming down with an illness until it hit me hard; I wouldn't have an injury checked by a doctor until it had become severe enough to cause pain. For years, I wished that I didn't have this body. I didn't like the way it looked or functioned, so I ignored its needs. Frankly, I wanted someone else to deal with it. Then I began to realize how much I neglected my physical self and in doing so, neglected *me*. No one else was going to take care of my body. It was my job.

When we don't take care of our physical selves through nurturing food, exercise, and healthcare, we do violence to ourselves and we do not live peacefully. Consider spending time each day to connect with your body. Empathize with areas of your body that feel poorly and listen to what they need to be healthy and comfortable. We can meet all our needs and still treat our bodies with loving, nurturing care.

Connect with your body's unmet needs today.

❅

OCTOBER 30

In hell, people have chopsticks a yard long so they
cannot reach their mouths. In heaven, the chopsticks
are the same length—but the people feed one another.
—*Vietnamese folk wisdom*

Nonviolent Communication and Money

In the Nonviolent Communication process, we distribute money based on need. If we had fifty dollars to distribute among five people, we wouldn't necessarily give each person ten dollars because that wouldn't meet our need for fairness. Fairness occurs when everyone's needs are equally valued. So we check in with each person to learn what his financial needs are. We may find that one person doesn't have enough money to buy milk and dinner for her family that night. Another person is flush with cash. Someone else might be a little tight for money right now, but thinks her situation will turn around in a week. Once we have connected with each person's need, we begin to make decisions about the distribution of the fifty dollars. Any scenario is possible; there are no right or wrong answers. The person who has plenty of money might opt to forgo receiving a portion to meet her need to contribute to the other group members. The person who is tight for cash might request twenty-five dollars tonight, and she will pay back twenty dollars next week when her financial situation turns around. The person who needs money for milk and dinner might request thirty dollars for her immediate use to meet her need to contribute to her family's well-being. The other two people will make their requests based on their needs. The group will continue to discuss them until they reach consensus on a final decision.

If we engage in this activity fully valuing everyone's needs and with faith in the process, everyone will end satisfied with the outcome. This is a different form of fairness than most people are used to. It is focused on individual needs, not splitting things evenly. It recognizes that people have different needs in the moment, that everyone truly wants to give and receive compassionately, and that there is no reason to hoard resources.

> Be aware of opportunities to meet your need
> for fairness by connecting and valuing
> people's needs today.

OCTOBER 31

Like begets like. We gather perfect fruit from perfect trees . . . Abused soil brings forth stunted growths.
—*Margaret Sanger*

Coming to Consensus

Some people think that reaching consensus takes too much time. On the contrary, consensus is a lovely way to go if you value your personal and professional relationships. It is a question of where you expend your energy. You may demand that a project be done your way and then expend energy afterward to soothe hurt feelings, deal with rebellious people, or supervise the project. Or from the very beginning you may take the time to consider everyone's input and come to a decision everyone agrees with. Then you will expend little energy supervising. Either way takes time. What is your priority? My highest priority is in my relationships. So the most effective use of my time is to get input from everyone and make decisions that value all their needs. Since I began living my life in this way, I have noticed that there are very few outbursts or hurt feelings in my life, either my own or others'. My life is generally more peaceful as a direct result of how I spend my time.

Be aware of opportunities today to make
decisions through consensus.

Meditations for

NOVEMBER

NOVEMBER 1

It all starts with self-reflection. Then you can know
and empathize more profoundly with someone else.
—Shirley MacLaine

Clarifying Our Needs

We often find ourselves slipping into old behaviors that we would rather change. This is because we don't have a new plan for responding to the same old situations. Let's say you work with someone who talks much more than you enjoy. You might try to listen to him politely for the first half hour, but your irritation mounts and you say something curt to him, "Bob, I need to get back to work!" You regret this every time you do it, but you can't seem to get yourself to respond differently. Rather than berate yourself or judge Bob as an incessant talker, take a moment to consider your unmet needs. They could be time, interest, or even consideration. What would it take for you to meet those needs? Would you feel better if the conversation lasted a shorter time, or if you were more prepared for a long dialogue? Once you connect to your unmet needs and have a few ideas of what it would take to meet them, make a request of the other person: "Bob, I'm feeling a little worried that this conversation may last longer than I'm comfortable with. I'm working on a deadline and I'd like to get back to it. Would it be OK with you if we set an appointment to continue this conversation when I'm not under so much pressure?" If you find that you continue to behave in ways that don't work for you, examine your unmet needs in those kinds of situations, and consider other methods for meeting them.

Notice whether you are slipping into old behaviors today. Connect to your unmet needs and then identify a new strategy for the situation.

NOVEMBER 2

You gain strength, courage, and confidence by every experience in which you really stop to look fear in the face.
—Eleanor Roosevelt

Connecting Feelings and Needs

How are you feeling right now? Do you feel happy? If so, then your needs in this moment are met. If you feel sad, tired, angry, hurt, or disappointed, they are not. Take a minute to check in with yourself. Do you need love, support, reassurance, hope, rest, safety, respect, understanding, or perhaps acknowledgment? If none of these needs is at the root of your feelings, keep searching until you find what is. Notice how you feel when you connect to this unmet need. Many people begin to feel relief just by doing this.

Now consider what you can do in this moment to help yourself meet your need. Maybe you could call a friend and make a date to discuss an issue, maybe you could take a short nap to satisfy your need for rest, or maybe you could plan to work out or to have a play date. Once you are confident in your plan, take a moment to check in with your feelings again. You may notice a deeper sense of relief. Or you may be aware that there is no easy or immediate way to meet your need. If this is the case, acknowledge how sad or overwhelmed you feel as a result, and mourn your unmet need.

We often feel relief when we can connect to the unmet needs that are the source of our feelings. We feel even deeper relief when we have a plan for meeting that need, or mourn if we realize we can't meet it. Connecting to ourselves in this way is a powerful, healing tool that is always available to us.

> Be aware of your feelings today and the unmet
> or met needs that cause them. Make plans to
> meet them or mourn them if you can't.

NOVEMBER 3

*I have to stay "turned on" all the time, to keep
my receptivity to what is around me totally open.
Preconception is fatal to this process. Vulnerability
is implicit in it; pain inevitable.*
—Anne Truitt

Getting Past Our Hurt Feelings

Are you feeling hurt, disappointed, or angry? Often these feelings signal a need for recognition or acknowledgment. When you consider your underlying needs, you may be unable to think of a way to meet them. You may instead tell yourself that you are too needy, and continue to feel uncomfortable.

Try another strategy. Rather than tell yourself that you won't be able to meet your need, simply understand it.

Just sit for a moment in your sadness and your desire to be acknowledged or recognized. It is OK to want these things, even if you can't think of how to accomplish them, and it's less likely that you will find a solution if you tell yourself there isn't one. Once you have empathized with your unmet need and the feelings associated with it, a solution often comes naturally. One possible way to meet a need for recognition and acknowledgment is to ask someone to tell you one or two reasons they enjoy working with you or enjoy you as a friend. Ask them to be specific. Ask them to tell you why they think you're fun rather than just "because you're fun." The more information you receive, the greater your sense of relief. All people need recognition and acknowledgment. Although you may feel a little embarrassed the first time you ask someone for this information, the chances are very good that the other person will enjoy this exercise as much as you do.

Ask at least one person today to tell you two reasons why they enjoy having you in their life.

NOVEMBER 4

We look out and see the goodness in other people,
but we don't see it in ourselves. The act of turning
around and catching the goodness in ourselves
is to wake up. Our consciousness, that lost,
scared soldier, finally meets itself.
—Natalie Goldberg

Understanding the Beauty Behind Your Needs

All people have the same universal needs, including love, support, caring, food, water, respect, intimacy, and joy. Everything we do or say is an attempt to meet these needs. Sometimes, when we do or say something we regret, we forget that our actions or words were an attempt to meet a beautiful universal need. The next time you feel regret about something you said or did, consider the need you were trying to meet instead of berating yourself. If you made an obscene hand gesture to the driver in front of you, is it possible that you were trying to meet a need for safety or consideration? If you snapped at the grocery clerk, could your need have been for efficiency or ease? If you told your child to shut up, did you need peace and cooperation? Once we have acknowledged the need we tried to meet, we are in a better position to consider what else we can do next time that is likelier to help us meet it. This will also help us decide whether we need to do something to rectify what we have done.

Be aware today of the needs that
drive your actions and words.

NOVEMBER 5

*Far away there in the sunshine are my highest
aspirations. I may not reach them, but I can
look up and see their beauty, believe in them,
and try to follow where they lead.*
—*Louisa May Alcott*

Connecting to Our Happiness

Are you feeling happy, content, or excited? Since all feelings are a result of needs, consider which of your needs are connected to your happiness. Are your needs for love, fun, intimacy, caring, consideration, or challenge being met? Or is a different need behind your feelings? Every time you feel happiness, excitement, or love, your needs are met. Every time you feel sad, hurt, disappointed or angry, they are not. It is important to look beyond feelings to needs. Whether we are happy or sad, this helps us connect to ourselves and how we meet or fail to meet our needs.

Be aware of the met needs behind your
feelings of pleasure or happiness today.

NOVEMBER 6

*In blocking off what hurts us, we think we are
walling ourselves off from pain. But in the long run,
the wall, which prevents growth, hurts us more than
the pain, which if we will only bear it, soon
passes over us . . . Walls remain.*
—Alice Walker

Meeting Our Needs

Discovering the unmet needs that drive our feelings is only part of the solution. The other part is to understand what it will take to meet that need and make a request that will accomplish this. Let's say your friend told a racist joke at your party last night and you are annoyed. Understanding that your needs for respect and consideration weren't met is just the starting point. The next step is to decide what could be done to meet those needs. You might consider talking to your friend about it by, saying: "When you told that racist joke last night at the party, I felt hurt and annoyed because I value respect and consideration for all people. I also felt embarrassed because I like people to feel safe in my home. Would you be willing to refrain from telling racist or sexist jokes when I'm around from now on?" Not making such a request of your friend limits your choices. You might decide not to invite him again. Or you might invite him but worry all night about what he might say. Worse yet, you could end up resenting him for years about this incident, and he would never have the opportunity to understand why your relationship has changed. When we make requests, we can resolve situations before they escalate. Everyone benefits when we are clear about what we would like.

> Notice if you have unmet needs today,
> consider what it will take to meet them,
> and make a request of someone.

NOVEMBER 7

Pay now, or pay a lot more later.
—*Mackenzie Jordan*

Deal With It Now!

I had a friend once who chewed and popped her gum with gusto. When she had gum in her mouth, I was annoyed. It didn't matter whether we were at home watching a movie, at a concert, or in church. Her gum chewing grated on me. I liked other parts of our relationship, though, so I decided not to express my feelings about her gum-chewing habits. After all, it wasn't such a big deal, right? Perhaps not at first. But I started to become obsessed with her chewing. I thought about it a lot when we were together. I wondered how strong her jaw muscles were and whether it was actually bad for her teeth, or if her habit strengthened them. Sometimes I tried to control her chewing. If I got a stick of gum for myself, I'd sneak it so she wouldn't see and ask for a piece. If she was chewing gum, I couldn't pay attention to anything. I didn't enjoy the concerts or movies we attended, and I had a hard time concentrating on our conversations. This went on for two years. I was starting to think that I simply couldn't be her friend any more. Then one evening, the two of us went to a movie with someone else. My friend popped a stick of gum into her mouth and in no time at all was ferociously chewing. Our other friend leaned over to her and said: "You know, I'm a little distracted from your gum chewing. Would you mind chewing quietly or removing the gum from your mouth?" My friend said, "Sure." I had spent two years being offended by her chewing, and I had almost ended our friendship, when all I had to do was ask her to stop! I now see how things can be simple in the beginning but become charged and painful if we don't deal with them.

Make a commitment to speak your truth
today with a loving heart.

360

NOVEMBER 8

It is astonishing how short a time it takes
for wonderful things to happen.
—*Frances Hodgson Burnett*

Joy: One Step at a Time

Many people think about a goal and feel overwhelmed and lose hope that they will ever attain it. Years ago, my goal was to learn how to be in loving relationships with people. It seemed impossible at the time, but I started to work toward it. I tried many avenues to attain it; many times I thought I would never succeed. Through Nonviolent Communication and a few other programs, I have learned that success comes closer with each step that we take toward the fulfillment of our goals. I may not need to meet my goal today, but I do want to begin the process today. It is amazing how taking that one step can shift our life and bring joy if we are present in the moment. Look around you right now and notice the beauty, love, and joy in your life. They exist here and now, but you won't feel them until you acknowledge them.

Acknowledge and enjoy three areas of your life that meet your need for joy, love, and beauty today.

NOVEMBER 9

As soon as you trust yourself,
you will know how to live.
—Goethe

Meeting Our Need for Safety

Many people misunderstand the concept of safety. They think they gain it by *protecting themselves from other people* or *choosing safe people.* Safety actually occurs when we learn to *trust our ability to take care of ourselves.* If we rely on other people to treat us in ways that we appreciate, we will always be on tenuous ground, and the people in our lives will be under tremendous pressure. The moment we begin to take responsibility for our own lives and our choices *and* begin to make decisions that better meet our needs, we are free, and so are the people around us.

In my younger years, I dated men who I thought were safe. My sense of safety depended on their good will. I tried to be what I thought they wanted me to be so they would enjoy the relationship. Sometimes this strategy worked for a while, sometimes for only ten minutes, and it always left me thinking I had been abused. When I started to recognize that it was my job to meet my need for safety, I began to enjoy relationships more, and I no longer saw others as abusers. I both empowered myself and lifted a burden from my partners.

Be aware today of any tendencies you might have
to seek safety through other people, rather than
through your own ability to take care of yourself.

NOVEMBER 10

You don't get to choose how you're going to die.
Or when. You can only decide how you're
going to live. Now.
—Joan Baez

This Is Your Life

Have you heard the saying, "Today is the first day of the rest of your life"? When I first heard it, I didn't understand what it meant. Today I know that I choose my life, every bit of it. When we start to live as the autonomous beings we are, we begin to experience life through new lenses. Our "*have tos*" become "*choose tos.*" We no longer worry about being victimized because we take responsibility for our choices, even those we regret later. We begin to create love and peace on a daily basis because that's what we want. This is your day. Right now. It may not be perfect but it is your life. How do you choose to live it? Carpe diem.

Today, be aware of the choices you have, and make decisions that will help you attain your dreams.

NOVEMBER 11

*My mind is overtaxed. Brave and courageous as I
am, I feel that creeping on of that inevitable thing,
a breakdown, if I cannot get some immediate relief.
I need somebody to come and get me.*
—Mary McLeod Bethune

Meeting Our Need for Support

We all need to reach out for support sometimes, and we
may feel embarrassed to let others know how down in the
dumps we are. We may value our image or our need for
acceptance. In these moments, we may forget that everyone
needs support. We may also forget that there may be many
options available to us. We may prefer it if our spouse or
best friend is available to support us. If they aren't, though,
we can consider other ways to meet our need for support,
such as seeing a therapist, calling another friend or family
member, or even calling a help line. If you need support
now, consider calling someone you think can help you. If
that person isn't available, take a moment to list five or more
ways that you could meet your need for support. None of
these options may feel as satisfying as calling the person you
prefer, but they could offer you immediate relief.

Be aware of the many ways that you can
meet your need for support today.

NOVEMBER 12

Don't ask the doctor; ask the patient.
—*Yiddish proverb*

Tapping Into Our Own Wisdom

One of the most exciting things I have gained from living the Compassionate Communication process is to learn to trust myself and my instincts. This started when I began to let go of my misconception that there is a *right* way or a *good* way to do things. Instead, I learned to understand my experiences based on how I felt about them or what needs I met or did not. When this happened, I began to trust myself in ways I never had before.

Recently I facilitated a private session with someone. Initially I was frightened by him and his story and questioned whether I was safe in this session. Almost as quickly as that thought entered my mind, I was able to focus on the depth of pain he experiences in his life. With that connection, I saw his beauty. I understood, once again, that as human beings we both want the same things—love, caring, understanding, and support. He was asking me to help him learn new communication tools. I knew I would be safe because I could see him for the beautiful person he was, and because I trusted my ability to take care of myself even in challenging situations. I grew to love and admire this young man and watched him take big steps to approach his life differently. Working with him met my needs for hope that people can change if they want to, love for humankind, and understanding of how some people's experiences can cause immeasurable pain in their lives. Listen to and trust yourself. There are no right answers; the best gift you can give yourself is self-trust. This gift may also change the lives of the people you encounter.

Be aware of times when you discount your instincts today and how you feel afterward.

NOVEMBER 13

*They always say time changes things,
but you actually have to change them yourself.*
—*Andy Warhol*

Consider the Full Set of Needs in a Situation

Have you ever tried to change a behavior? You see it, but you just can't seem to change it because it is a habit. An effective way to start the process of changing our behaviors is to look deeply at the needs that we meet or do not meet with the behavior. Remember, everything we do is an attempt to meet needs. Once we have connected to them, we can look at the other person's needs in the situation.

Let's imagine that you are sitting in a meeting at work. Your boss wants you to take on a new project. You're already overwhelmed and you're worried about taking on anything else, so you cross your arms, purse your lips, and respond to her with short, choppy answers. What needs do you meet with this behavior? Maybe protection. What needs do you not meet? Possibly connection, support, collaboration, respect, consideration, and understanding. What do you suppose your boss's unmet needs are? How about ease, connection, support, collaboration, respect, and consideration? Once we can connect to the full set of needs we want to meet in any situation, we are better able to choose behaviors that are more likely to meet them.

> Be aware today of the needs you want to meet
> through your behaviors. If you are dissatisfied with
> your behavior, is there another way you can
> meet all the needs in the situation?

NOVEMBER 14

Happiness is when what you think, what you say,
and what you do are in harmony.
—*Mahatma Gandhi*

Protection vs. Intimacy and Connection

When I was young, I used to put up walls between myself and other people the minute I felt hurt, angry, sad, or vulnerable. As an adult, I started to focus on the needs I was trying to meet. When I caught myself building walls to protect myself, I literally asked myself if I needed protection in the situation. I found that I was almost never in danger; protecting myself was an old outdated habit. The more I focused on the needs I wanted to meet and asked myself if I really needed protection, the more my defensive habits dwindled away.

Notice times today when you choose to meet your
need for protection and then ask yourself if there
are other needs you would prefer to focus on.

NOVEMBER 15

*A ship in the harbor is safe, but that is not
what ships are built for.*
—Proverb

Protecting Ourselves Is an Illusion

Let's say your boss offers you a raise, but you're suspicious
of his motives. You sit with your arms crossed, deliberately
showing no emotion. Or let's say that your teenage son
mows the lawn without being asked, and you say to him:
"What's that about? What's this going to cost me?" I'd guess
that you are trying to meet your need for protection in these
two scenarios. Have you ever noticed what happens when
you try to protect yourself in your relationships? My motto
used to be protect, protect, protect—at all costs, protect!
I carried it with me everywhere I went, even if I wasn't in
danger. My desire to protect myself appeared to other people
as defensiveness, anger, or a lack of caring. And because I
worked so hard to protect myself, I did not meet my needs
for intimacy, love, collaboration, fun, and many others.
Except in extreme cases of physical danger, when we protect
ourselves we also deny ourselves the opportunity to meet
our needs for connection, intimacy, love, and harmony.

Be aware of the illusion of protection in your life today.

NOVEMBER 16

Silence is one of the most effective
forms of communication.
—Proverb

Silent Empathy

You may be listening to a friend describe something that is very painful for her. You'd really like to empathize but you don't trust your skills. Consider silent empathy. It is exactly the same process as empathy—listening for the feelings and needs of the other person—except that it's done silently. When you listen for the feelings and needs of another, even if silently, you can provide profound healing and connection. Most people will know that you are connecting with them because of your facial expressions and your physical energy.

Silently empathize in at least one conversation today.

NOVEMBER 17

Each time you are honest and conduct yourself with honesty,
a success force will drive you toward greater success.
Each time you lie, even with a little white lie,
there are strong forces pushing you toward failure.
—Joseph Sugarman

Making Specific Requests

You've been in a relationship with your boyfriend for a year, and you're incredibly frustrated with your sex life. You've tried the usual vague requests, such as, "Honey, can we try expanding our lovemaking to a longer period of time?" He says, "Sure." The next time you make love, the entire encounter lasts ten minutes instead of five minutes. Do you lose hope that your needs will ever be met? There is a solution, although it's not for the fainthearted. The solution is to be *specific*. What do you want, how long do you want it, and in what order? Can you make this request without thinking that he's a rotten lover, or that he should know this already? Make your request because you want to enjoy your sex life with him, without judging him in the process. These moments can be embarrassing at first, but when handled with compassion, they can enrich and strengthen your relationship, not to mention your sex life!

Make at least one specific request of someone
today even if you feel embarrassed.

NOVEMBER 18

A man is already halfway in love
with any woman who listens to him.
—Brendan Francis

Interrupting With Love

Do you have someone in your life who talks with more words than you enjoy listening to? When this happens, do you find yourself shutting down a little (or a lot) in the conversation? Each time we do this, the other person loses the gift of our presence and connection, and we lose the opportunity to connect with ourselves and the other person. I used to think that interrupting someone was rude. Now I know that interrupting to meet our own needs for connection and integrity is an expression of love.

Here's an idea on how you can interrupt someone with compassion. Let's say you are on the phone with your elderly aunt who is talking more than you like. You start to notice that you are zoning out—thinking about other things—or maybe feeling annoyed. Consider saying the following to your aunt: "Aunt Betty, excuse me for interrupting. I'm noticing that I'm getting kind of lost in this conversation, and I really want to stay present with you. Would you mind if I took a moment to repeat back what I think you're saying? This would help me stay present." Or sometimes you disconnect not because of the number of words, but because the other person is talking about other people's lives and feelings, and you'd rather connect with her. Perhaps you could say: "Aunt Betty, I hear that your neighbor is in a lot of pain right now. How do you feel about what is going on with her?" Interrupting someone in this manner can increase your connection and deepen your relationships.

> Today interrupt at least one person
> with love to enhance your conversation.

NOVEMBER 19

The tendency of democracies is,
in all things, to mediocrity.
—James Fenimore Cooper

A New Way to Look at Fairness

I used to think that fair meant splitting things evenly. This could apply to family money, the pie we were preparing to eat for dessert, or housework, among many other things. Because I had this philosophy about fairness, I spent a great deal of time critiquing whether others were doing their share of work, eating more than their share, or spending too much of their share. I emphatically believed that fairness meant equal shares. Then I started living the Nonviolent Communication process, and my idea of fairness changed. In Nonviolent Communication, we believe that fairness is connected to people's needs. When we serve food, we might consider who is hungriest, who can best afford to buy food later, and perhaps whose schedule makes it impossible for them to eat later. In splitting housework, we might consider who enjoys doing certain jobs the most, how people contribute in other ways to the family, and whether anyone is physically incapable of contributing. In this way, we consider everyone's needs for ease, enjoyment, overall contribution to the household, and health. This process enhances the connection, joy, involvement, and investment of everyone involved.

Divide something up today by connecting to the needs of the people involved. Notice if this feels different than other times when you divided things equally.

NOVEMBER 20

Thinking based on "who deserves what"
blocks compassionate communication.
—*Marshall B. Rosenberg, PhD*

Needs-Based Negotiation

When I worked in the university system, I spent a great deal of time and energy negotiating for salary increases and position upgrades. My arguments usually focused on how I compared to other people in the industry, my years of experience, and what I thought was fair. I believed that I deserved to make more money than other people because I had more experience in our field and I had worked longer at the university. My job, I thought, was to convince my superiors that I deserved a raise. It never occurred to me to consider my superiors' needs: to manage a complicated budget, balance the needs of many people, and motivate members of a team to succeed in their jobs. It also didn't occur to me to speak openly about my needs in the situation, without placing demands and ultimatums on my bosses. Repeatedly I put both of us in a position where we could lose—if they didn't do what I wanted, I would feel angry and hurt. If they did comply with my demand, they had succumbed to the pressure I inflicted. Now I believe that the best opportunity for success when we make requests of others, including our superiors, is to speak openly and honestly, value the other person's needs, and create solutions that value both parties' needs. When we create situations that value one person's needs at the expense of another, we open the door for someone to lose. Win/win resolutions are much more satisfying to all concerned.

> Attempt to create win/win resolutions
> by valuing everyone's needs today.

NOVEMBER 21

*I believe that the most powerful and joyful intrinsic
motivation human beings have for taking any action
is the desire to meet our own and others' needs.*
—Inbal Kashtan

Asking People for Money in the
Compassionate Communication Process

The first time I requested a salary using the Compassionate Communication process, I considered my needs for financial security, both in the present and in retirement, and the organization's need for sustainability. Then I considered whether the amount of money I contemplated would also meet my needs for reciprocity and joy in doing my work. Once I worked this out, I requested a salary that was one-half what I had earned at the university. It's not that I didn't like my bigger salary; I did. However, I also knew that the Flagstaff Center for Compassionate Communication was a very new organization with a limited budget, and I valued the organization's need to sustain itself and flourish. I didn't feel any remorse or resentment. In fact, I have never felt more empowered and satisfied when requesting a salary. My needs for integrity, contribution, fairness, and compassion were fully met.

Be aware of opportunities today to value
everyone's needs in a financial exchange.

NOVEMBER 22

An eye for an eye makes the whole world blind.
—Mahatma Gandhi

Empathizing With Others to
Meet Our Need for Connection

Do I have to empathize with someone even if they have done things that stimulated hurt in me? No, I never have to empathize with anyone. Empathy is not about meeting other people's needs. It is a choice that I make because I want to meet my own need for connection. If I tell myself that I am empathizing *for the other person*, I disconnect from the needs that I want to meet. So if you feel confused or disconnected in your relationships and would like to shift your experience, try to empathize with the other person. Once his need to be heard is met, he is more likely to hear your feelings and needs. This can lead directly to meeting your needs for connection, harmony, and relief. It is amazing how healing it is when you open emotional space to hear someone else's feelings and needs. It can be profound.

Empathize with at least one person today and notice if it meets your need for connection or contribution.

NOVEMBER 23

It's kind of fun to do the impossible.
—*Walt Disney*

Engage Your Curiosity

Do the people in your life ever respond in ways that simply baffle you? In such situations, we may think: "What was he thinking? He completely reversed himself. He must have been confused, hurt, or out of his mind." We have a tendency to tell a story about what we think was behind the other person's reaction. We spend a tremendous amount of energy wondering what the other person was thinking, blaming him, and feeling, sad, hurt, angry, and resentful. I have seen people in pain for years because they never took a moment to ask for clarity.

I suggest a new process. Engage your curiosity by asking the other person what is going on. For example: "You know, when you expressed your anger just now, I felt baffled because I thought we had agreed last week to buy a Honda, so I'd like clarity. Do you have different information that has caused you to change your mind about buying one?" Notice that this statement doesn't place blame on either party. It simply expresses your confusion and your desire for more information. Usually, the minute we ask for more information, we get it. It's simple, really. We can either wonder about what's going on with the other person, create our own stories about it, or inform ourselves by asking.

Engage your curiosity today and ask at least one person what is going on with him, rather than wondering.

NOVEMBER 24

I've just got to maintain my passion for what I do.
—*Leonardo DiCaprio*

You Can Make a Difference

Lately I have been inspired by the success of grass-roots organizations in my community. Local associations and community gardens have been created. Neighborhoods that were previously viewed as low-income, dangerous places are making strides to reduce crime, clean their streets, celebrate their diversity and community, and find a shared voice that influences local politics. Small nonprofit organizations are pooling their resources, expertise, and dreams to positively affect the lives of youth and the elderly. Sometimes the violence in the world feels overwhelming, and my hope for peace in a world where all living beings are treated with compassion seems impossible. In these times, if I'm willing to remember how my own work promotes peace, and how successful many local grass-roots organizations are, I feel inspired and hopeful. Creating a peaceful world begins with me, right here and now. Living peacefully is a choice. I am so grateful that others in my own community and throughout the world share this dream.

Be aware of how your actions contribute
to world peace today. Then celebrate yourself!

NOVEMBER 25

*There is nothing like returning to a place
that remains unchanged to find the ways
in which you yourself have altered.*
—*Nelson Mandela*

Changing Ourselves Can
Profoundly Affect Our Relationships

Sometimes, people tell me that there's no hope unless someone else changes a behavior or attitude. I used to believe this was true. Now I know that if one person in a relationship changes, the relationship itself can change profoundly. I have a friend who tends to focus on what she doesn't like in her life and in other people. I used to judge her as negative, and I thought she had a relentless desire to remain a victim in her relationships. After a while I thought I had to end this friendship because I felt so depressed following conversations with her. Rather than ending the relationship, though, I started to look at my own judgments and attitudes. I empathized with my judgments about her and how I'd like her to see her life differently. It took a while, but there came a time in our relationship when I could love her for exactly who she is, and I could be present to the feelings and needs behind her view of the world. She hasn't changed, but I have transformed my own judgments and expectations. I can now feel love and joy for myself and her. We have the power to profoundly shift our relationships by simply focusing on ourselves.

For today, make a decision to focus on your own judgments and expectations of other people, rather than blaming them.

NOVEMBER 26

Change your thoughts and you change your world.
—*Norman Vincent Peale*

Developing Tolerance

I used to think that Chihuahuas were dumb dogs and bulldogs were ugly. Then one of my friends bought a longhaired Chihuahua named Tilly and another bought an

English bulldog named Emma. Once I got to know these dogs and could see how truly sweet they are, it didn't take long for me to fall in love with both of them. Once I loved them, I could see how beautiful they are. Tilly has ears that stand up comically, with long strands of hair sticking out. When she looks at you enthusiastically, her ears stand straight up and the hair makes a fan around her face. Her hair is black with caramel and white, is very soft to the touch, and shines like silk. Emma is buff. When she walks you can see her muscles move underneath her taut skin, and you get a sense of how physically powerful she is, even though her demeanor is gentle and loving. Her color is gorgeous, smooth tan and white. I am well loved by both of these dogs, and they greet me joyfully every time they see me. Tolerance and acceptance are about loving the beauty in everything. In a sense, it's about having faith that every living creature has beauty and shares space on the earth for a reason. When I release my judgments, my world is more beautiful and loving.

Make a decision today to approach your
relationships with tolerance and acceptance.

NOVEMBER 27

*It seems to me we can never give up longing
and wishing while we are alive. There are
certain things we feel to be beautiful and good,
and we must hunger for them.*
—George Eliot

Uncovering Your Greatest Need

When I was forty-one years old, I discovered that my greatest need in life was to connect deeply with other people. We can be unaware of the underlying needs that drive our behavior for years, and as a result be unable to meet them. Take a few moments to review the last three arguments you had with someone. It could be three arguments with one person, or with different people. Notice if there is an underlying theme in all three. Then review the list of needs at the front of this book and try to identify what the need is. The chances are good that all of the arguments were the result of the same need. It is likely that this is your greatest need. Pay attention to your arguments over the next few weeks and see if most of them stem from the same need. If they do, take a moment to brainstorm ways that you can meet it without creating conflict. This is the first step toward living in ways that are likely to meet your greatest need.

Take a few moments today to review your
last three arguments. Notice if they all stemmed
from the same unmet need.

NOVEMBER 28

*Your heart understands what your head
cannot yet conceive; trust your heart.*
—*Proverb*

Avoiding Compromises

Has anyone ever asked you to do something that you didn't want to do? Then did she tell you how much it would mean to her, and your feelings changed because you wanted to contribute to her life? This is what I consider a shift in needs. An example of this happened to me some time ago. A friend asked me to attend a meeting. I didn't want to go because I was not confident that my need for ease would be met, and the topic wasn't meaningful to me. Then she told me that she had a vision that this group would connect in an honest and compassionate manner, and that she hoped I would help her create that kind of energy in the group. She was very passionate about her dream. Once I connected to the need she was trying to meet and her passion, I found my own needs shifting from ease and meaning to a genuine desire to contribute to her life.

Compromise, on the other hand, happens when we decide to give up our needs for the needs of another. If I had gone to my friend's meeting just to please her, I would have given up my needs for hers. Often when we compromise, we give in to the other person's desires. This can be painful for everyone involved.

Try to avoid making compromises today. Instead, see if you can make an honest shift in needs.

NOVEMBER 29

*Man must cease attributing his problems to his
environment, and learn again to exercise his will—his
personal responsibility in the realm of faith and morals.*
—Albert Schweitzer

Denial of Responsibility

"Oh no, I can't go out tonight; my husband won't let me."
"I'm sorry, Miss, but the library closed two minutes ago;
you'll have to come back tomorrow to check out that book."
"Yes, I know you bought your plane ticket six weeks ago, but
we have too much weight on the plane, and your name is
first in the alphabet; we'll get you on a new flight first thing
tomorrow morning."

Have you heard similar statements? How did you feel
when you heard them? I tend to feel frustrated, annoyed,
angry, and sometimes confused. Any time we say something
of this nature and don't take responsibility for our actions,
we put a wall between us and other people. We can't connect
with a live human being when we blame our actions on
company policy or on somebody who is not present. If
we need to say no, acknowledging our own feelings and
needs can dramatically shift the energy of that no. The shift
occurs when you own your behavior and show the human
side of why you have decided not to comply with a request.
You might say that you prefer not to go out because your
husband won't like it and *you're worried about upsetting him.*
Similarly, you might say that the library closed two minutes
ago and *you don't want to upset your babysitter by being late.*
It may be company policy, but it is more meaningful for
another person to hear that *you'll lose your job if you comply*

with her wishes. When we own our actions, other people can connect to our humanness, which often brings agreement and relief to all parties, even if the result doesn't change.

Be aware of times today when you are tempted to avoid taking responsibility for your choices.

NOVEMBER 30

When our needs are not being fulfilled,
we follow the expression of what we are observing,
feeling, and needing with a specific request:
we ask for actions that might fulfill our needs.
—Marshall B. Rosenberg, PhD

The Difference Between Needs and Requests

In Nonviolent Communication, we see needs as universal. That means that everyone has the same needs for love, support, connection, resources, food, shelter, etc. (See the front of the book for a list of needs.) A request is a specific action we ask of another person to help us meet our needs. I may need companionship, so I ask a friend to spend time with me over the weekend. Or I may need support, so I ask my partner to help me clean the house. The need is universal; the request is a specific method by which we meet the need.

Be aware of the difference between universal needs and specific requests today.

Meditations for
DECEMBER

DECEMBER 1

*Expressing feelings is an opportunity for us and others
to connect with what is alive in us. To do this, we
need to be able to differentiate between words that
genuinely express feelings from other words that may
appear to do so, but do not.*
—Rachelle Lamb

Feelings vs. Feelings Mixed With Thought

Feelings are an expression of how something affects us. If someone yells at me, I may feel *scared or hurt.* If a friend forgets our dinner date, I may feel *worried and angry* sitting in the restaurant waiting for him. When we mix feelings with thoughts, we confuse our feelings with judgments about another person's behavior. If someone yells at you, you might say you feel that he disrespects or criticizes you. If you wait for a friend in a restaurant for a half an hour, you may say you feel that he betrayed you or he doesn't care. When you say you feel disrespected, criticized, manipulated, or betrayed, you are not really expressing what you feel. You are expressing a judgment (or thought) about the other person. Your actual feelings might be hurt, anger, sadness, or fear. It is important to learn to differentiate between your feelings and your thoughts and express your feelings clearly if you want to connect openly and honestly with other people.

Notice when you express your feelings
mixed with thoughts or judgments today
and express only the feelings.

DECEMBER 2

The deepest principle of Human Nature
is the craving to be appreciated.
—William James

Appreciation vs. Approval, Compliments, or Praise

When we express how someone's actions have positively affected our lives, we express appreciation. In contrast, when we offer approval, compliments, or praise, we label the other person as good because of what they did. We can express our appreciation using the four steps of Compassionate Communication when we say: "Wow! When you brought me chicken soup when I had the flu, I felt so grateful, because it met my needs for nurturing and care." In this example, the person is 1) expressing an observation— "When you brought me chicken soup when I had the flu," 2) expressing a feeling—"I felt so grateful," and 3) expressing a need—"because it met my needs for nurturing and care."

By comparison: "Wow! You are so great to bring me chicken soup!" labels the other person as "great" because of her action, rather than expressing how it affected our life. It may seem like a small distinction, but when we acknowledge our met needs, rather than labeling the other person as good or bad, we achieve a clarity of mind that deepens our connection to ourselves and other people.

Take at least one opportunity today to express
your appreciation of someone else by telling
him how his actions have affected you.

DECEMBER 3

Assumptions allow the best in life to pass you by.
—*John Sales*

Guessing vs. Knowing

In the Compassionate Communication process, we *guess* a person's feelings and needs and ask them if we have guessed correctly. When we tell a person what we think they feel and need, we claim to *know,* which can sound like a judgment or assumption.

When you empathize with someone and guess his feelings and needs, you might say something like, "Are you feeling scared and want some reassurance that your needs are valued?" In this example, you guess his feelings (scared) and need (reassurance that his needs are valued). If, however, you said, "You're scared and need reassurance that your needs are valued," it can sound like you are *telling* him what he feels. Often when people are told how they feel, they tend to respond with defensiveness and anger

Guesses are usually received with appreciation. If we guess wrong, the other person is likely to give us more information to help us understand his feelings and needs more clearly. This approach very often deepens our connection with others. When we tell someone what his feelings and needs are, we create distance between ourselves and the other person.

Guess the feelings and needs of at least
one person today. Notice how they respond
and how you feel about this.

388

DECEMBER 4

The leader who exercises power with honor will work
from the inside out, starting with himself.
—Blaine Lee

Respect for Authority vs. Fear of Authority

When I worked in the university setting, I had a boss who preferred to work on his own. However, he liked things to be done a certain way, so he would leave me specific, detailed instructions on how to move forward with my projects. I did what he asked because I feared the consequences if I didn't. I didn't feel much life, creativity, or fun in my work, and I rarely took the initiative to solve problems without him. This is an example of fear of authority.

In another situation, I had a boss who asked me for my opinions, openly discussed my projects, and gave me space to contribute my own ideas on how to proceed. He also gave me advice when I asked for it and expressed appreciation for my abilities. I followed his instructions because I respected his position and trusted his expertise. I saw him as my partner. I took responsibility for my actions and decisions. I enjoyed my work with this boss. When we respect authority, we value the person's position and expertise. When we fear it, we are afraid of their position and the consequences if we don't do as they say.

Notice today whether your tendency
is to respect or fear authority.

389

DECEMBER 5

You will find as you look back upon your life that the moments when you have truly lived are the moments when you have done things in the spirit of love.
—Henry Drummond

Life-Connected vs. Life-Alienated

We are life-connected when we do things that will enhance our connection to and compassion for other people. We are life-alienated when we do things that bring distance between ourselves and others. Life-connecting activities might be empathizing, being honest, and valuing everyone's needs as much as our own. Life-alienating activities might include labeling someone good or bad, gossiping, comparing ourselves to other people, and not taking responsibility for our actions.

For example, let's say you come home an hour later than usual, and your partner says in an angry voice, "Where have you been?" Your life-alienating response could be: "What's your problem? You're always late yourself!" A life-connected response would either focus on his needs or your own: "Were you worried because you wanted to be sure I was safe?" or "Gee, when I walk in the door and hear you say that before I even have a chance to take off my coat, I feel shocked and annoyed, because I need consideration and caring. Would you be willing to tell me what you heard me say?"

The more you choose life-connected activities, the deeper your connections with others will be.

Notice when you do things today that enhance your connection with other people.

390

DECEMBER 6

We are what we repeatedly do. Excellence,
then, is not an act, but a habit.
—Aristotle

Nonviolent Communication as a Way of Life

People often ask me how to handle unexpected emotional outbursts, such as a spouse coming home angry, an irritable cashier, or any situation where we're surprised by the kind of response we receive. In these situations, I rely on my Nonviolent Communication habits. I practice this consciousness in easy situations so I can practice it in challenging ones. If a friend calls me to share exciting news, I empathize by listening to her feelings and needs, to help meet both our needs for celebration. If someone calls me to express sadness, I empathize to meet my needs for connection and compassion. If I find myself judging another person, I translate the judgmental thoughts to my feelings and needs, such as "When I see large SUVs, I feel worried about our ability to sustain ourselves and our resources," instead of "Oh I hate SUVs. Doesn't that person know how much precious gas that vehicle is using?" If I feel sad, I empathize with myself or ask someone else to empathize with me. If I feel happy, I express my celebration. I have made living Nonviolent Communication a habit. If I only practiced this consciousness when times were challenging, I would not have the skills to handle such situations. However, through continuous practice, I can rely on well-established habits of connection, compassion, and communication to help me resolve even the most challenging situations in ways that meet my need for integrity.

Begin to make the Nonviolent Communication process a habit today by empathizing with one person.

DECEMBER 7

*Sometimes I've believed as many as
six impossible things before breakfast.*
—Lewis Carroll

Living Abundantly

How many times in a day do we stop ourselves from asking for what we want because we are sure it is impossible? Think about times when you wanted something but were afraid to ask for it. Maybe you wanted a friendship to evolve into a partnership, or you were sick and wanted someone to bring you food, or maybe you wanted your boss to consider you for a promotion. Now think of a few times when you wanted something that you thought was impossible, but you asked for it anyway and got it! Those moments bring such joy, don't they?

We need to know what we want before we can ask for it and then receive it. I suggest we start an abundance movement, where we all know in our hearts that there is enough love, support, acknowledgment, and resources for everyone to meet their needs. If we meet someone who doesn't want to help us meet our needs, then we find other creative ways to meet them. In this abundance movement, we concentrate on meeting our needs, and we don't get stuck on particular strategies. If one person doesn't want to date us, we know we will find someone who will. If one person doesn't have the time or desire to deliver soup when we're sick, we'll find another way to feed ourselves. If we want more responsibility at work, we will find a way to expand our career. We don't stop there, though. In our new abundant world, we value everyone's needs as much as our own. We no longer try to meet our needs at another's expense. Doesn't this sound exciting? This movement already exists. It is called Compassionate Communication!

Make an effort today to value everyone's needs and notice the abundance in your world.

DECEMBER 8

The first point of courtesy must always be truth.
—*Ralph Waldo Emerson*

Authenticity

Is it sometimes hard for you to be honest about who you are? Do you ever censor yourself to meet your needs for acceptance or community? It can be challenging to be the only one on the bus who wants to go to the mountains, when everyone else wants to go to the beach! The truth is, if you say that you would prefer to go to the mountains, that doesn't mean that you are asking everyone else to change their plans. You are only expressing your preference and opening the dialogue for discussion. Is it possible that you have assumed that the others prefer the beach? Maybe some people would enjoy the mountains just as much or more. Or maybe you were right that everybody except you wants to go to the beach. What now? Consider how important this issue is to you and the needs of the group. Having considered everyone's needs, what is your solution? Can you go to the mountains alone? Is there something you could ask of the group that would make a beach trip seem more fun for you, such as stopping to buy sunscreen, or visiting an old church along the way? Perhaps once you have heard how much everyone else wants to see this particular beach, you feel more joy about contributing to their needs. When we are authentic about who we are, we give everyone and ourselves a better opportunity to meet needs. We simply express our truth, and in that way value our own needs as much as those of others.

Make a commitment today to be authentic even if you are worried your need for acceptance won't be met.

DECEMBER 9

Let not a man guard his dignity,
but let his dignity guard him.
—Ralph Waldo Emerson

Ethics

Some time ago, one of my clients ran into me in a restaurant. She still owed me some money from an earlier session, so she handed me the money in cash. I ordered my food and then paid with the money my client had given me. Afterward, I noticed that I felt uncomfortable about this transaction. The money actually belonged to the Flagstaff Center for Compassionate Communication, which is a nonprofit organization. It was not my money because the Center pays me a salary. I pondered this for a couple of days, wondering what the ethical course would be. Then I started to doubt my knowledge of ethics, and I wondered if I should take a class at the local university on this topic. Fortunately, it didn't take long for me to notice that I was looking to other people to determine my ethics. I heard this voice inside me saying: "How does it feel to *you*, Mary? If it feels good, it meets your need for integrity. If it doesn't feel good, it doesn't. What other information do you need?" So many times I have turned to other people to tell me what is ethical and what isn't. Now, I simply look inside myself for the answers. In this case, I returned the cash to the center's account.

If you are grappling with a question of integrity today, notice how you feel about the situation and what your needs are. Then make a decision that is in alignment with your values.

DECEMBER 10

It's simple really, if you are feeling happy, joyful,
or content, your needs are being met.
If you are feeling sad, lonely, or depressed,
your needs are not being met.
—Mary Mackenzie

The Connection Between Feelings and Needs

Our feelings are a direct result of whether our needs are met or not. Other people's behaviors are often the stimulus for our feelings, but they are not the cause. For example, consider a time when it took you ten minutes to get to the front of a grocery store line and you felt content, relaxed, and cheerful. I'd guess your need for efficiency was met because you had plenty of time to get to your next destination. On another day, you may have been pressed for time and when it took you ten minutes to get to the front of the line, you felt annoyed, exasperated, and angry because your need for efficiency was not met. The stimulus was the same; you were in line for ten minutes. However, your feelings were quite different depending on whether you had a need for efficiency at the time. The clarity that comes with understanding this dynamic can help us identify our unmet need, to either empathize with ourselves or choose other strategies that will better support us in meeting that need, such as going to a different line or coming back later to buy our groceries. Recognizing the difference between the stimulus and our feelings frees us to take action to meet our needs.

Be aware today of how your feelings are an
indication of your met or unmet needs.

DECEMBER 11

*Look everywhere with your eyes; but with your soul
never look at many things, but at one.*
—V. V. Rozanov

Seeing the Beauty in Others

Don't we all have moments when we express ourselves in
ways that we don't value? In Compassionate Communication, we look for the needs people try to meet with their
actions, rather than focusing on their behavior. That doesn't
mean that we enjoy the behavior, only that we acknowledge
that it is an attempt to meet a specific need. Focus less on
what you don't like in people and more on their needs. You
may not enjoy the method a person uses, but when you
recognize the need behind it, you can see the beauty in them.

Be aware today of how people try to meet
their needs using behaviors you don't enjoy.

DECEMBER 12

The ancestor of every action is a thought.
—Ralph Waldo Emerson

The Unmet Needs Behind Our Anger

When we feel anger, we judge ourselves or someone else. We may think that the other person *should* do something they aren't doing, or that they *shouldn't* do what they are doing. Judgments are thoughts. When we can look beneath them to uncover our unmet needs, such as support, love, connection, understanding, or consideration, we have a better chance to transform our anger into positive action. What if you are angry with your mother because she doesn't stick up for you when your uncle is critical of you? Your judgment is that your mother *should* say something to your uncle in your defense, or that she *shouldn't* be such a wimp. But she has never stood up to her brother—either in her own defense or anyone else's. The chances are good that she won't start now. You can either stay angry or choose a different approach. What do you think your underlying needs are? I'd guess they are support, understanding, compassion, and love. Are there other ways you could meet those needs besides expecting your mother to stick up for you? Consider her needs as well and try to come up with a request. You could say to her: "Mom, when Uncle Bob tells me I'm lazy and you don't say anything, I feel really hurt because I'd like your support. Would you be willing to tell me how you feel when Uncle Bob tells me I'm lazy?" Such a simple request can help you connect with your mother in ways that are not possible when you judge her, and it can relieve your anger.

Notice if you have a tendency to blame other people
when you are angry today. Then try to connect
to your unmet needs instead.

DECEMBER 13

*This is my simple religion. There is no need for
temples; no need for complicated philosophy. Our
own brain, our own heart is our temple.*
—Dalai Lama

Living in Harmony With Our Values

When I learned that U.S. troops had abused prisoners of
war, I felt heartbroken. Then when I heard reporters and
U.S. leaders saying things like, "It's not half as bad as what
they have done," I felt downright discouraged. The fact
that our behavior isn't as bad as the behavior of people in a
different country is not the least bit consoling to me. I had
hoped we Americans held ourselves to a different standard.
That's also how I feel in my personal life. I want my actions
to reflect *my* values. I meet my needs for integrity when I
succeed in this. I don't accept the abuse of others or myself,
even though some people do. I follow my own heart. This is
living peacefully.

Spend the day making decisions that are
based on your values, not those of others.

DECEMBER 14

Man is the only creature that refuses to be what he is.
—*Albert Camus*

Natural vs. Habitual Ways of Being

Natural ways of being include the attitudes that we are born with. Habitual ways of being reflect the attitudes that we learn from our surroundings, such as family, schools, or society. This is an important distinction. I often hear people say that Nonviolent Communication is "unnatural" because it feels awkward when they first learn the process. On the contrary, I think we were all born with an innate desire to give and receive compassionately. It is the natural state of being. If you doubt this, notice a very young child who gives his last piece of candy or his favorite toy to his brother. Then notice this same child a few years later. He has probably learned to hang on to his things, and he may be reluctant to share. At some point, he learned how not to live compassionately. For many of us, by the time we become adults, we have forgotten how to live from our true compassionate nature. This is tragic and prevalent in our society. Living the Nonviolent Communication process actually helps us return to our natural way of being.

Be aware of the difference between your habits and
your natural way of being today.

※

DECEMBER 15

To different minds, the same world is hell,
and a heaven.
—Ralph Waldo Emerson

Value Judgment vs. Moral Judgment

Value judgments are judgments based on our own experience and values. We make moral judgments when we judge someone as good or bad. Let's say that I'm spending time with my Aunt Betty, who tells me all the reasons she doesn't like her neighbor. My value judgment could be that I feel drained and annoyed when Aunt Betty speaks about others in this way *because I value respect and consideration.* My moral judgment might be that *Aunt Betty is negative or intolerant.* I judge that there is something wrong with Aunt Betty that causes her to speak about her neighbors in this manner. When we focus on our value judgments, we are less likely to be critical of other people.

Notice how your feelings change when you focus on value judgments as opposed to moral judgments.

DECEMBER 16

Those who speak most of progress measure it
by quantity and not by quality.
—George Santayana

Noticing Progress

Change is an amazing thing. Sometimes we spend months or even years trying to shift a behavior or an attitude. Often because we are in the middle of practicing the process, it is difficult to see our progress. Then, one day, without expecting it, we've changed our behaviors or our attitudes. It can feel like magic.

If you'd like a reality check about your progress, visit long-time friends or family whom you haven't seen in a while. Notice if you feel differently when you're with them, or how you feel about spending time with them. With this awareness, give yourself credit for every moment of your personal growth. You might even ask your friends and family if they experience you differently.

Years ago, after I'd lived in Flagstaff for a short time, one of my sisters said to me: "You know, Mary, I think we're all trying to find a way to see the old you in your new self. But I'm starting to understand that you have changed so much, the old description doesn't fit at all. You've truly remade yourself." When I heard this, I felt deeply touched because I had recently been telling myself that I hadn't made enough progress. Today I know that every time I try to change a behavior, even if I'm not successful, I contribute to my ultimate change. It is an ongoing moment-by-moment process.

Touch base with a long-time friend or family member today and notice how much progress you have made.

DECEMBER 17

I was shipwrecked until I got aboard.
—*Seneca*

Mediating Conflict With Other People

What do you do when you see two colleagues arguing about something? Fortunately, you're not part of the argument but you'd like to contribute to their ability to resolve the situation amicably. Here is a method that often works. Step in and express this desire: "I guess that this is very difficult for both of you. I'd like to support you both by assisting in this. Is that OK with you?" If both agree, remain neutral. To be effective as a mediator, one must not choose sides. Both parties must trust that you have everyone's best interests at heart. Help both people identify the underlying needs in their disagreement. Remember, if there is conflict, it is likely that people are arguing strategies rather than needs. Strategies can include a course of action, timing, or thinking there is only one right way.

Try to reflect their needs. "Albert, it sounds like you want the project to be done by next week because you think the return will be greater before the holidays. And Jean, you want another month because it will give you more time to work out the kinks, and you think that will affect the return. So actually, you both want to get the most effectiveness out of this mailing. Is this true?" Acknowledging both people's needs helps them understand that they want the same thing. The next step is to see if there's room to brainstorm solutions that will meet both their needs.

Sometimes the real struggle in mediation is to determine the underlying needs of each person. This can be time consuming. However, don't worry about the time involved because while you are uncovering their needs, you are building trust and helping both parties gain clarity as well. It is time well spent. Also, both people may have different needs. That's OK too; simply identify them, acknowledge them, and seek solutions that value them. Mediation takes time and effort, but helping people come to mutually satisfying solutions is a joyful experience.

If you witness a conflict between two people today, offer to help them resolve the situation by focusing on their needs.

DECEMBER 18

Looking back, I have this to regret,
that too often when I loved, I did not say so.
—David Grayson

Finding Out How We Contribute
to Other People's Lives

Do you ever wonder why people ask you to participate in certain projects? Or, do you ever think that you're not doing enough? Several years ago, I was asked to chair a committee. This group was working on an issue that I knew very little about and that I had little passion for. After three meetings, I started to feel uncomfortable because I didn't think I had anything to offer the group. In fact, I began to wonder if my lack of experience was a drag on their progress. I almost resigned as the committee chair, but I decided to talk to one of the committee members. I told him my dilemma and then I asked him: "What needs of yours are met by me chairing this committee? If it doesn't meet your needs, I will happily step out so that the committee can flourish." His response shocked me. He told me that I met his needs for trust and respect. He trusted that I would value hearing everyone, that I would help people speak up, that I would strive for full consensus, and that I would handle conflict respectfully. "Oh," I said, "you're looking for a mediator, not a leader in this field." Once I understood his intention, I understood why I was asked to chair. At the next meeting, I expressed my dilemma with the rest of the group; I asked them if they also wanted me to act as a mediator, and if they were disturbed that I didn't have experience in their field. Every one of them had seen me as a mediator from the start.

Sometimes we find ourselves in situations that we don't understand. Rather than run, consider asking the other people involved which of their needs are met by your participation. The answer may surprise you. You may learn something about yourself that you hadn't recognized before, and your heart may be warmed through and through!

Ask at least one person today to tell you three specific reasons why their life is enhanced by your presence.

405

DECEMBER 19

Our grand business in life is not to see what lies
dimly at a distance, but to do what lies
clearly at hand.
—*Thomas Carlyle*

Connecting to Your Needs

All people have the same basic needs no matter where they live, how much money they make, what language they speak, or what their gender is. This is a universal law. Here is a list of needs: autonomy, choice, love, shelter, food, water, friendship, support, caring, passion, compassion, play, joy, humor, rest, safety, sexual expression, touch, inspiration, ease, beauty, and equality. This is not an exhaustive list. If you are trying to decide whether a need is universal, ask yourself if everyone in the world has this need in one form or another. If your answer is yes, it is probably a universal need. If you think that most people, but not everyone, would need it, the chances are good that it is a strategy. If you feel sad, depressed, angry or hurt, your needs are not being met in the moment. If you feel happy, joyful, excited, love, or fun, your needs are being met. When you take the time to connect to your needs in the moment, you have the opportunity to change your experience.

See if you can tell the difference today between your
strategies and the universal needs that they meet.

DECEMBER 20

Reexamine all that you have been told . . .
dismiss that which insults your soul.
Whatever satisfies your soul is the truth.
—Walt Whitman

Honoring Our Feelings

Do you ever feel ashamed to admit how you feel about something? Do you ever say to yourself, "I shouldn't feel that way"? Here's the thing. Feelings aren't good or bad, positive or negative, or even big or little. They are simply how you feel. If someone accidentally elbows you, you might feel pain. You might recognize and appreciate that the person didn't intend to stick his elbow in your side, but it still hurts. How you express the pain could differ. Some of us would yell at the top of our lungs. Others might simply say "ouch" and ask the person to remove their elbow. No matter how we express it, though, the feeling of pain stays the same.

Emotions operate similarly. You don't feel too much or have feelings that are too big. Maybe the way you express them is bigger than you enjoy, but the feelings themselves aren't too big. I used to think I was too passionate because I saw that my passion turned people off. Yet a friend told me that if I were to diminish my passion, I would lose one of the most positive aspects of my personality. Years later, I began to understand that it wasn't my passion that turned people off; it was the way I expressed it. As a result, I changed my behaviors, not my feelings of passion. The next time you notice yourself discounting your feelings or feel embarrassed about them, try to remember that your feelings "just are."

Then determine whether you'd like to change the way you express them.

Notice how you express your feelings today
and whether you'd like to develop new skills
that may be more effective for you.

DECEMBER 21

The art of love . . . is largely the art of persistence.
—*Albert Ellis*

Persisting vs. Demanding

Persisting is the active attempt to meet our needs by continuing to connect with another. Demanding is the insistence that someone do something to avoid negative repercussions. Let's imagine that you want to go on vacation with a friend. She says she doesn't have enough money. A demand would sound something like this: "You never have enough money. This time you just have to go. It's an opportunity of a lifetime and I don't want to miss it!" Persistence may involve empathizing with her. "You're really worried about money, aren't you? You just don't want to do anything that will hinder your ability to pay your bills?" "No, I don't, and you always plan extravagant trips and I'm scared to spend that much money!" "So, you're worried that I'll plan the trip outside your comfort level?" "Yeah, I'm worried about that." "Wow. I'm glad to hear this because I wouldn't want you to be worried about money on trips with me. How would you feel if we created a budget and I planned the trip around the budget?" In this example, you persisted by listening to the needs of your friend and continued to look for a solution that would meet both of your needs. When we persist and consider all needs, we are more likely to meet all of them. Many times this results in a win-win solution.

Notice whether you are making demands today.

DECEMBER 22

The cure for all ills and wrongs, the cares, the sorrows and the crimes of humanity, all lie in the one word "love." It is the divine vitality that everywhere produces and restores life.
—Lydia Maria Child

Speaking Up for Our Needs in a Group

Sometimes, when a person first realizes that her needs are important, she becomes over-zealous in trying to meet them. For example, she may interrupt a group process because she just realized that her need for being heard or understood wasn't met. In her urgency to meet a need to be heard, she can lose perspective on the bigger picture—what the group is trying to accomplish. Or she may forget that there are many ways to meet her need. It's tricky, because in my own experience, every single person in a group process makes a valuable contribution to the whole. Any person who is not fully present can hinder the group's ability to succeed. On the other hand, if someone interrupts the group process to take time to meet a personal need, it can be a distraction. What can she do instead? She can consider empathizing with herself for a moment, silently connecting with her unmet needs and feelings. Then she can ponder whether it is worth it to her *and the group* to interrupt it for more empathy, or if she can meet her need in other ways that do not hinder the group's progress. Remember, it's about valuing everyone's needs, not just her own. If you find yourself in such a situation, consider what would meet everyone's needs. And remember that there are unlimited ways to meet every need. Often our first knee-jerk solution does not fully value everyone's needs.

Notice how you participate in groups today. Are you fully present and participating? What could you do to meet your own and the group's needs?

DECEMBER 23

Do all things with love.
—Og Mandino

Focusing on Needs Instead of Strategies

In Compassionate Communication, we strive to value everyone's needs equally. For some of us, that means that we learn to value our own needs. We may have spent so much of our lives focusing on the needs of others that we forgot our own. Or it might mean learning to open emotional space to help other people meet their needs. Wherever you find yourself on this spectrum, shifting this basic attitude can be a painful process because it forces you to look at yourself and your world differently. What if you value environmental sustainability so you prefer a small car, but your six-foot-seven-inch spouse values ease and comfort and wants to buy an SUV? Do you try to meet both of your needs, or simply insist that he buy a smaller car? I'm not suggesting that we condone actions that are contrary to our own values. I'm suggesting that we value everyone's needs equally even if we don't enjoy the specific ways people attempt to meet them. Just opening our hearts to fully value everyone's needs can bring about a powerful shift in consciousness.

Be aware of opportunities today
to value everyone's needs equally.

DECEMBER 24

Men's natures are alike; it is their
habits that carry them far apart.
—Confucius

Needs Are Universal

All of us, everyone in the world, have the same needs. Consider love, shelter, nurturing, support, caring, and joy. Each one of these is a universal need. So if we all have the same needs, how is it that there is so much conflict in the world? Because we differ in the methods we choose to meet them. Most people argue for their methods, not their needs. Consider Al Qaeda's bombing of the World Trade Center in 2001. Can you imagine that this action was an effort to meet needs for autonomy, solidarity, and to be heard? Isn't it likely that all world leaders have the same needs for their countries? Consider the conflict between the Palestinians and Israelis. Can you imagine that both sides have similar needs for peace, respect, understanding, freedom, safety, and land to call their own? When parents argue about what school their child will attend, is it possible that they are both trying to meet their needs for financial security as well as their child's safety, learning, and fun? Very often, all parties are trying to meet the same needs, but their strategies differ. Once we understand this, we can start to focus on the needs rather than the strategies when negotiating with others, and in this way increase everyone's opportunity for peaceful, mutually satisfying resolutions.

Today, be aware of opportunities to shift
a conversation from strategies to needs.

DECEMBER 25

Parents can tell but never teach,
unless they practice what they preach.
—*Proverb*

Meeting Your Need for Respect
by Acting Respectful to Others

Not long ago a mother and her fifteen-year-old daughter came to a Sunday night training I offered. The daughter sat by the door, physically distant from the rest of the group. The mother sighed and said, "She won't come over." I asked the daughter if she would join us and express her discontent to the whole group. She said: "I don't know why I'm here. This is stupid. My mom and I communicate fine." After empathizing with the daughter, I learned that Sunday night was the one evening a week that she had to herself. She spent this time doing her homework and laundry, talking to friends on the phone, and enjoying her solitude. On this Sunday evening, her mother told her that they *were* going to a Compassionate Communication training and that the daughter had no choice in the matter. I further discovered that the mother frequently asked the daughter to do things that she didn't like to do, such as hiking, camping, and fishing. If she told her mom she didn't like these things, her mother got angry with her. After empathizing with the mother, I discovered that she missed her daughter terribly. The daughter was at the stage where she focused more on her friends than family. Although the mother understood that this was normal, she still missed her. So she kept coming up with ideas for how they could spend time together. After about ten minutes of empathy with mom and daughter, each had greater clarity about the other's needs, and how their own strategies exacerbated the situation. With this understanding, they could come to agreements. They decided that the daughter would spend one weekend day a week with the mom and they would create activities that they both enjoyed. They came up with a few ideas they could start with. They also decided that they both would like to work on their communication with each other, but they wouldn't take classes Sunday evenings so the daughter could keep that night to herself. The whole process took about twenty minutes.

It is difficult, maybe impossible, to meet our need for respect when we don't offer it to others. If you'd like your children to value your needs and meet your need for respect, offer them the same gift.

Consider what you value most in your relationship.
Then be that for the other people in your life today.

DECEMBER 26

Your best is going to change from moment to
moment; it will be different when you are healthy
as opposed to sick. Under any circumstance,
simply do your best, and you will avoid
self-judgment, self-abuse, and regret.
—Don Miguel Ruiz

Just Do Your Best

Have you ever noticed that the minute you tell yourself that you should know something, your skill in that area diminishes? When I first started teaching people the Nonviolent Communication process, I thought I should be "a good model of compassion." As soon as I told myself that,

I felt pressure, and my ability to be compassionate crumbled. True authenticity is about striving to live in harmony with our values, noticing when we don't hit the mark as well as we would like, owning and loving our foibles, and then trying again. We're not perfect, so let's release the pressure of thinking we should be. Instead, let's just do our very best to live within our values. It's a much more humbling, peaceful, and joyful place to reside. Don't you agree?

> Commit to living your values today.
> Then celebrate your success.

DECEMBER 27

A man is but the product of his thoughts.
What he thinks, he becomes.
—*Mahatma Gandhi*

Loving Ourselves

It is very painful to think we're unlovable and unworthy. Many of us received this message as children, and when we bring it into our adult lives, it can color our every thought and action. For me, this belief affected my relationship with myself and other people. When I thought I was unworthy, I felt angry, hostile, hurt, and hopeless. When I told myself I was unlovable, I felt panicked, sad, hurt, and hopeless. I would do almost anything to meet my need for love, even date people who didn't meet my other needs for trust, respect, or consideration. I convinced myself that if I was more lovable, these people would love me, and that it was my job to convince them to. I focused on other people's feelings. I wondered if they enjoyed being with me, if they would show up when they said they would, or if they thought I was OK. Through many years of personal work, including living the Compassionate Communication process, I have come to understand that people do things to meet their own needs. If someone calls me a name, they are trying to meet a need, possibly for acceptance. Their actions are not a reflection of my worth. Today, I notice how I feel and which of my needs are met when I'm with other people, and I spend time with those who meet my needs for respect, consideration, fun, and trust. When someone who doesn't meet these needs crosses my path, I let them go, with love and without judgment. I don't have to tell myself that there is something wrong with them, nor do I have to prove my lovability to them or myself. I know I am valuable, as all people are. I know I am lovable, as all people are. And I know that my need for love will not be met by everyone. My job is to find the people who love me and to cherish their presence in my life.

Notice how you feel and what needs of yours
are met or unmet when you spend time with
different people today. What does this tell you?

DECEMBER 28

Where there is love there is life.
—*Mahatma Gandhi*

Love Is the Answer

Several years ago, my sister was with a dear friend when she died. She called that evening to tell me about the experience. I was so struck by the change in her. She was soft and full of love and hope. She told me that this friend and she had had a falling out a few years before, but they came together again when the friend was diagnosed with a fast-progressing cancer. Then, as her friend took her last breath, my sister looked into her eyes and was overcome with love and compassion. She knew in that moment that all had been forgiven.

The only important thing is to love each other. If you have moments when you are a bit more gruff than you had hoped, or you struggle with valuing everyone's needs, or you are judgmental, forgive yourself, move on, and try to do it differently next time. Love yourself and other people as best you can. Love is the one truly important thing we can do to resolve our conflicts, bring peace to the world, and heal our inner pain.

Make a conscious effort to make love the primary focus of all your interactions today.

DECEMBER 29

There is more to life than increasing its speed.
—Mahatma Gandhi

Deciding Where to Use Our Time

I often hear people say things like: "We can't use this process in our business. It will take too much time!" Or: "We'll just tell them how they have to do it. We don't have time to discuss it." Every time I hear comments like these, I feel both sad and amused. When we try to meet our need for speed and efficiency, we very often operate under an illusion. We think that telling someone that they have to do something we want will actually save time. In reality, though, we can spend endless hours, days, weeks, months, or years clearing up the hurt feelings, rebellious attitudes, and anger that are stimulated when we make demands of others. On the other hand, if we take the time up front to build consensus and come to agreements, our projects will likely run themselves because everyone is invested in the outcome. Consider what happens when you tell your teenage daughter that she cannot get her nose pierced. Or when you tell your employees that the company is undergoing a restructuring and they will be notified about their new roles. In both of these situations, the possibility exists that through connection, empathy, and valuing everyone's needs, an agreement can be reached that is satisfying to all concerned. It may be time-consuming to come to consensus, but in the end there's agreement, and the next step is implementation. Rarely is there negative backlash when people willingly come to agreement. It's a choice, really. Where do you want to put your effort and time—coming to mutually satisfying agreements that value everyone's needs, or trying to force people to do it your way?

Notice where you decide to use your time today.
Does this meet your needs?

418

DECEMBER 30

Insanity: Doing the same thing over and over again
and expecting different results.
—*Albert Einstein*

Changing Our Behaviors to Meet Our Needs

Have you ever found yourself responding to similar situations the same way and then being frustrated with the results every single time? I spent most of my life wanting deeper connection with people and then constructing emotional walls between myself and them. Whenever I felt hurt, scared, or vulnerable, I would either shut down emotionally or lash out in some way. For example, one time a group of friends and I joined a race to benefit a local nonprofit organization. I was the slowest one in our group so two friends went ahead and one friend stayed with me. From the moment the two friends went ahead until the end of this two-mile race, I felt insecure, embarrassed, and hurt. I told myself that I was boring, too slow, and too out of shape. The judgments were especially cruel because every one of these women was at least thirteen years older than I was. The more painful my thoughts, the deeper my feelings of despair grew and the deeper inside myself I went. It became difficult for me to even participate in conversation. Two days later, I realized what I had done. The minute I felt insecure and vulnerable, I went inside and locked myself up tight. My true needs were acceptance, connection, and understanding. The likelihood that I could meet them when I shut down emotionally was slim to none. Once I realized this, I called each of my friends who had participated in that run with me. We talked about what happened and how I felt about it. Those conversations helped me meet the needs I was unable to meet the day of the race. Sometimes, it is very painful to change our behavior patterns, but if we look closely we may find that some of them have not helped us meet our needs. They will continue to produce the same results: sadness, despair, loneliness, and shame.

Notice what needs you meet through your defensive behaviors today. If you are not happy with the result, consider another way you could handle a similar situation in the future.

DECEMBER 31

Laugh and Be Well.
—*Matthew Green*

Humor, the Great Healer

Doesn't it just feel good to laugh fully and loudly? Sometimes I get so wrapped up in life, I lose perspective. If I'm working hard to accomplish something, I'm not present to the moment, and I'm certainly not enjoying it. In Compassionate Communication, we teach mindfulness— to be present at each moment to our choices and to the abundance of the Universe. If I acknowledge that the Universe provides enough of everything I need, I can relax and enjoy life. Rather than feel embarrassed when I back my car into a tree after doing a training, I can feel amused at the look on people's faces when I tell them I just drove into a tree. My need is to enjoy life. That doesn't mean I want to stuff my feelings or ignore my other needs. It only means that I want to focus attention on the areas that will best serve my enjoyment of life wherever possible. I want to focus on the abundance of humor available to me each day.

Take the opportunity to let out one
huge belly laugh today.

Index

consensus process, 299,
350–51, 418
consequences of actions, 10,
12–13, 293–94
contributing to the life of others,
as human need, 60–61,
80–81, 124–25, 404–05
control, as strategy, 334–35
cost vs. value, 311–12
creativity, as need, 123
criticism, 175–76, 401
curiosity, cultivating, 168–69,
376–77

D

dead conversations,
resuscitating, 40–41,
371–72
demanding vs. persisting,
408–09
demands
rebellion or submission, as
response to, 116–17
vs. requests, 21–22, 96,
135–36
dependence/independence
paradigms, 86
directness, 130–31
dishonesty, 35–36
disorganization, 132
divine energy, in others,
249–50
doability of requests, 106–07,
217–18, 266–67

E

eating patterns, 346–47
Einstein, Albert, 332
emotional bank account,
115–16

emotional liberation, 32–33,
216, 326–27
empathy for others
acknowledging reality of
others, 112–13, 205–06
vs. agreement, 13–14, 23
balancing with other needs,
339–40
in conflict situations, 49–50,
160–61, 240–42, 264–65,
403–04
converting judgments into,
162–63, 165, 168–70,
224–25
healing power of, 16–17, 93,
177, 226–27, 375–76
modeling with children,
13–14, 36–37, 203–04
practicing, 103–04, 126, 255,
312–13, 391–92
responding in silence, 369
responding to silence, 231
as response to message of
others, 89–90
vs. sympathy, 93, 294–95.
See also conflict resolution
with NVC process;
connection with others;
needs; self-empathy
empathy from others, 115–16,
128–29, 364
enemy images, 18–19
"enjoying the jackal show," 78,
82–83
"enough," defining, 74–75,
117–18, 185–86, 266–67
enriching life, as motivator, 8,
198–99
equality vs. fairness, 372–73

Clearly expressing
how **I am**
without blaming
or criticizing

Empathically receiving
how **you are**
without hearing
blame or criticism

OBSERVATIONS

1. What I observe *(see, hear, remember, imagine, free from my evaluations)* that does or does not contribute to my well-being:

   "When I (see, hear) . . . "

1. What you observe *(see, hear, remember, imagine, free from your evaluations)* that does or does not contribute to your well-being:

   "When you see/hear . . . "
   (Sometimes unspoken when offering empathy)

FEELINGS

2. How I feel *(emotion or sensation rather than thought)* in relation to what I observe:

   "I feel . . . "

2. How you feel *(emotion or sensation rather than thought)* in relation to what you observe:

   "You feel . . ."

NEEDS

3. What I need or value *(rather than a preference, or a specific action)* that causes my feelings:

   " . . . because I need/value . . . "

3. What you need or value *(rather than a preference, or a specific action)* that causes your feelings:

   " . . . because you need/value . . ."

Clearly requesting that
which would enrich **my**
life without demanding

Empathically receiving that
which would enrich **your** life
without hearing any demand

REQUESTS

4. The concrete actions I would like taken:

   "Would you be willing to . . . ?"

4. The concrete actions you would like taken:

   "Would you like . . . ?"
   (Sometimes unspoken when offering empathy)

About the Center for Nonviolent Communication

The Center for Nonviolent Communication (CNVC) is an international nonprofit peacemaking organization whose vision is a world where everyone's needs are met peacefully. CNVC is devoted to supporting the spread of Nonviolent Communication (NVC) around the world.

Founded in 1984 by Dr. Marshall B. Rosenberg, CNVC has been contributing to a vast social transformation in thinking, speaking and acting—showing people how to connect in ways that inspire compassionate results. NVC is now being taught around the globe in communities, schools, prisons, mediation centers, churches, businesses, professional conferences, and more. Hundreds of certified trainers and hundreds more supporters teach NVC to tens of thousands of people each year in more than 60 countries.

CNVC believes that NVC training is a crucial step to continue building a compassionate, peaceful society. Your tax-deductible donation will help CNVC continue to provide training in some of the most impoverished, violent corners of the world. It will also support the development and continuation of organized projects aimed at bringing NVC training to high-need geographic regions and populations.

To make a tax-deductible donation or to learn more about the valuable resources described below, visit the CNVC website at www.CNVC.org:

- **Training and Certification**—Find local, national, and international training opportunities, access trainer certification information, connect to local NVC communities, trainers, and more.

- **CNVC Bookstore**—Find mail or phone order information for a complete selection of NVC books, booklets, audio, and video materials at the CNVC website.

- **CNVC Projects**—Participate in one of the several regional and theme-based projects that provide focus and leadership for teaching NVC in a particular application or geographic region.

- **E-Groups and List Servs**—Join one of several moderated, topic-based NVC e-groups and list servs developed to support individual learning and the continued growth of NVC worldwide.

For more information, please contact CNVC at:

9301 Indian School Rd., NE, Suite 204, Albuquerque, NM 87112-2861
Ph: 505-244-4041 • US Only: 800-255-7696 • Fax: 505-247-0414
Email: cnvc@CNVC.org • Website: www.CNVC.org

About PuddleDancer Press

PuddleDancer Press (PDP) is the main publisher of Nonviolent Communication™ related works. Its mission is to provide high-quality materials to help people create a world in which all needs are met compassionately. By working in partnership with the Center for Nonviolent Communication and NVC trainers, teams, and local supporters, PDP has created a comprehensive promotion effort that has helped bring NVC to thousands of new people each year.

Since 1998 PDP has donated more than 60,000 NVC books to organizations, decision-makers, and individuals in need around the world.

Visit the PDP website at www.NonviolentCommunication.com to find the following resources:

- **Shop NVC**—Continue your learning. Purchase our NVC titles online safely, affordably, and conveniently. Find everyday discounts on individual titles, multiple-copies, and book packages. Learn more about our authors and read endorsements of NVC from world-renowned communication experts and peacemakers. www.NonviolentCommunication.com/store/

- **NVC Quick Connect e-Newsletter**—Sign up today to receive our monthly e-Newsletter, filled with expert articles, upcoming training opportunities with our authors, and exclusive specials on NVC learning materials. Archived e-Newsletters are also available

- **About NVC**—Learn more about these life-changing communication and conflict resolution skills including an overview of the NVC process, key facts about NVC, and more.

- **About Marshall Rosenberg**—Access press materials, biography, and more about this world-renowned peacemaker, educator, bestselling author, and founder of the Center for Nonviolent Communication.

- **Free Resources for Learning NVC**—Find free weekly tips series, NVC article archive, and other great resources to make learning these vital communication skills just a little easier.

 *PuddleDancer* P R E S S

For more information, please contact PuddleDancer Press at:

2240 Encinitas Blvd., Ste. D-911 • Encinitas, CA 92024
Phone: 760-652-5754 • Fax: 760-274-6400
Email: email@puddledancer.com • www.NonviolentCommunication.com

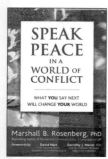

Speak Peace in a World of Conflict
What You Say Next Will Change Your World

By Marshall B. Rosenberg, PhD

$15.95 — Trade Paper 5-3/8x8-3/8, 208pp
ISBN: 978-1-892005-17-5

International peacemaker, mediator, and healer, Marshall Rosenberg shows you how the language you use is the key to enriching life. *Speak Peace* is filled with inspiring stories, lessons, and ideas drawn from more than forty years of mediating conflicts and healing relationships in some of the most war-torn, impoverished, and violent corners of the world. Find insight, practical skills, and powerful tools that will profoundly change your relationships and the course of your life for the better.

Discover how you can create an internal consciousness of peace as the first step toward effective personal, professional, and social change. Find complete chapters on the mechanics of Speaking Peace, conflict resolution, transforming business culture, transforming enemy images, addressing terrorism, transforming authoritarian structures, expressing and receiving gratitude, and social change.

Nonviolent Communication: A Language of Life, 3rd Edition
Life-Changing Tools for Healthy Relationships

By Marshall B. Rosenberg, PhD

$19.95 — Trade Paper 6x9, 264pp
ISBN: 978-1-892005-28-1

What is "Violent" Communication?

If "violent" means acting in ways that result in hurt or harm, then much of how we communicate—judging others, bullying, having racial bias, blaming, finger pointing, discriminating, speaking without listening, criticizing others or ourselves, name-calling, reacting when angry, using political rhetoric, being defensive or judging who's "good/bad" or what's "right/wrong" with people—could indeed be called "violent communication."

What is "Nonviolent" Communication?

Nonviolent Communication is the integration of 4 things:

Consciousness: a set of principles that support living a life of compassion, collaboration, courage, and authenticity

Language: understanding how words contribute to connection or distance

Communication: knowing how to ask for what we want, how to hear others even in disagreement, and how to move toward solutions that work for all

Means of influence: sharing "power with others" rather than using "power over others"

Available from PuddleDancer Press, the Center for Nonviolent Communication, all major bookstores, and Amazon.com. Distributed by Independent Publisher's Group: 800-888-4741.

Being Genuine

Stop Being Nice, Start Being Real

By Thomas d'Ansembourg

$17.95 — Trade Paper 5-3/8x8-3/8, 280pp
ISBN: 978-1-892005-21-2

Being Genuine brings Thomas d'Ansembourg's blockbuster French title to the English market. His work offers you a fresh new perspective on the proven skills offered in the bestselling book, *Nonviolent Communication: A Language of Life*. Drawing on his own real-life examples and stories, Thomas d'Ansembourg provides practical skills and concrete steps that allow us to safely remove the masks we wear, which prevent the intimacy and satisfaction we desire with our intimate partners, children, parents, friends, family, and colleagues.

"Through this book, we can feel Nonviolent Communication not as a formula but as a rich, meaningful way of life, both intellectually and emotionally."

—Vicki Robin, co-founder, Conversation Cafes, coauthor, *Your Money or Your Life*

Based on Marshall Rosenberg's Nonviolent Communication process

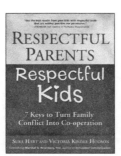

Respectful Parents, Respectful Kids

7 Keys to Turn Family Conflict Into Co-operation

By Sura Hart and Victoria Kindle Hodson

$17.95 — Trade Paper 7.5x9.25, 256pp
ISBN: 978-1-892005-22-9

Stop the Struggle—Find the Co-operation and Mutual Respect You Want!

Do more than simply correct bad behavior—finally unlock your parenting potential. Use this handbook to move beyond typical discipline techniques and begin creating an environment based on mutual respect, emotional safety, and positive, open communication. *Respectful Parents, Respectful Kids* offers *7 Simple Keys* to discover the mutual respect and nurturing relationships you've been looking for.

Use these 7 Keys to:

- Set firm limits without using demands or coercion
- Achieve mutual respect without being submissive
- Successfully prevent, reduce, and resolve conflicts
- Empower your kids to open up, co-operate, and realize their full potential
- Make your home a *No-Fault Zone* where trust thrives

Available from PuddleDancer Press, the Center for Nonviolent Communication, all major bookstores, and Amazon.com. Distributed by Independent Publisher's Group: 800-888-4741.

438

ABOUT THE AUTHOR

MARY MACKENZIE, MA, is the co-founder of the NVC Academy, an online school for learning Nonviolent Communication; executive director of Peace Workshop, International, a nonprofit organization dedicated to supporting practical methods for living nonviolently; certified trainer of Nonviolent Communication for the Center for Nonviolent Communication and mediator.

Mary brings extensive experience in creating and maintaining collaborative organizations and partnerships in the business world and within families, in finding a way forward that values all needs even in challenging decision-making processes, and how to balance efficiency and authenticity in all interactions.

She is a deeply spiritual person with a keen sense of humor, inner clarity, and insight. Mary's guiding vision is to help people learn concrete, practical tools for living peacefully day-to-day. She believes that if each of us steps up to the plate to transform our own negative behaviors and thought patterns we can create world peace, one heart at a time. Her individual coaching sessions with people who want to fully integrate Nonviolent Communication into their daily lives, workshops, retreats, organizational development, group facilitation, public speaking engagements, and personal daily life reflect this passion.

Mary lives in Long Beach, California, with her wife, Kimberly Fox.